UNCERTAIN IDENTITY

CONTEMPORARY WORLDS explores the present and recent past. Books in the series take a distinctive theme, geo-political entity or cultural group and explore their developments over a period ranging usually over the last fifty years. The impact of current events and developments are accounted for by rapid but clear interpretation in order to unveil the cultural, political, religious and technological forces that are reshaping today's worlds.

SERIES EDITOR
Jeremy Black

In the same series

Britain since the Seventies
Jeremy Black

Sky Wars: A History of Military Aerospace Power
David Gates

War since 1945
Jeremy Black

The Global Economic System since 1945
Larry Allen

A Region in Turmoil:
South Asian Conflicts since 1947
Rob Johnson

Altered States:
America since the Sixties
Jeremy Black

The Contemporary Caribbean
Olwyn M. Blouet

Oil, Islam and Conflict
Rob Johnson

The Road to Independence?
Scotland since the Sixties
Murray Pittock

UNCERTAIN IDENTITY

International Migration since 1945

W. M. SPELLMAN

REAKTION BOOKS

In Memory of Mary, Dan, Mol and Jack.

Published by Reaktion Books Ltd
33 Great Sutton Street
London EC1V 0DX
www.reaktionbooks.co.uk

First published 2008

Copyright © W. M. Spellman 2008

Printed and bound in Great Britain
by CPI Antony Rowe, Chippenham, Wiltshire

British Library Cataloguing in Publication Data
Spellman, W. M.
    Uncertain identity : international migration since 1945. – (Contemporary worlds)
    1. Emigration and immigration – History – 20th century
    2. Emigration and immigration   3. Globalization – Social aspects
    I. Title
    304.8'2'09045

ISBN-13: 978 1 86189 364 2

Contents

Introduction: Dimensions of Recent International Migration

Why a book about international migration during the late twentieth and early twenty-first centuries? After all, even with the rapid development of commercial air travel following World War II and the doubling of world population from 3 billion in 1960 to 6 billion in 2000, and despite the ever-present language of globalization and internationalization, ours remains a largely sedentary global community. Certainly tourism, student exchanges and overseas business postings are more common now than at any previous time. But if we consider today's international migrants as a proportion of overall world population, we are struck by the propensity of humans *not* to relocate. Most people, for good or ill, remain throughout their lives firmly attached to their immediate locale, to the known and familiar – even in the most difficult of times.[1] Only about 3 per cent of the world's current population of just over 6.3 billion find themselves residing outside the country of their birth. The proportions certainly were much greater at the start of the last century, when millions of people departed Europe on large steamships for a new life in the Americas and Oceania, while hundreds of thousands more – poverty-stricken and with no property – exited South Asia, Japan and China as indentured servants, destined for tedious and exhausting work in Europe's far-flung colonial empires. Most of the latter would remain poverty-stricken and without property throughout the experience, but the prospect of material betterment, however slim, was deeply compelling.[2]

One century ago, destination countries were generally underpopulated and eager to recruit free labour, while the indenture system was revived as a solution to acute labour shortages after the demise of slavery. These flows were encouraged by the leading world powers since they complemented the emerging transnational economy. During the first wave of transoceanic migration from Europe, a convergence of labour conditions occurred as real wages improved both for migrants who left and for those who remained behind.[3] Unskilled workers in particular found that their wage levels increased as competition for jobs in Europe lessened with an upsurge in emigration before 1914. The great age of oceanic human migration reshaped the demographic profile of two continents, transforming the United States into a richly multicultural society, and giving Europeans cultural, political and numerical predominance in Oceania. For many historians, the half-century before the outbreak of World War I remains the quintessential age of mass migration across international frontiers.

The difference today involves two pre-eminent factors: a sharp increase in absolute numbers of migrants from multiple destinations worldwide (this despite the emergence of state-sponsored immigration restrictions); and the perceived vulnerability of both source and destination states to the disruptive forces of globalization, ethno-nationalism and international terror. Approximately 175 million people, representing every continent, now reside in countries other than the land of their birth. To place that number into better perspective, the United Nations' Population Division estimates that the total was only 75 million in 1965 and 105 million in 1985. The overwhelming majority of these transnational migrants have relocated for simple economic reasons, for a better life. Such people normally respond to 'pull' factors, the potential opportunities for economic betterment in another country. Very often these new migrants are catalysts in the phenomenon known as chain migration, where spouses, children, siblings, parents and in-laws eventually follow the primary economic migrant to the new host country. Recognizing the unity of the family as a fundamental human right, the United States and European Union member states maintain generous policies in this area. Almost 80 per cent of all recent US immigration is family-related, while the figure for the EU is closer to 60 per cent.[4] If migrants arrive with specialized skills, they typically reside in the new 'global cities' and assume well-paid jobs in select industries such as engineering, medicine and, more recently, computer services. If the migrants are unskilled, they serve an important – if under-appreciated – function in low-wage labour markets that are, by and large, eschewed by native workers. The construction trades, agriculture, domestic service and assembly-line (normally textile) work constitute the major forms of unskilled employment in developed states.

The second category of international migrants consists of those who are 'pushed' to depart their home country in the wake of natural disaster, civil conflict or out of fear of persecution due to their ethnic, political or religious identity. Because they are more numerous, individuals in the first category have traditionally received the greatest media attention, but in the post-Cold War era involuntary or refugee migration has become both more recognizable and more controversial. It is more recognizable because so many of the approximately 12 million migrants have suffered greatly at the hands of brutal regimes or intolerant neighbours, and more controversial because many states, having embraced the UN's Universal Declaration of Human Rights and committed themselves to accept political refugees as a humanitarian duty, now balk at sustaining a generous admissions policy. Almost 150 UN member states have signed the Convention Relating to the Status of Refugees, obliging them not to penalize refugees who have entered illegally, and to refrain from repatriating refugees if they have a legitimate fear of persecution at home. Requests for asylum have risen sharply in recent years, most notably in Western Europe, to the point where there is now a significant public backlash against the phenomenon due to suspicion that many applicants are in fact economic migrants seeking to expedite their relocation to the affluent countries of the northern hemisphere and Australasia.

Anxiety in the receiving countries is heightened by the fact that they are now demographically stagnant, with birth rates at or below replacement level, while most sending countries are facing acute social and economic problems related to overpopulation. In 2000 the United Nations Population Division produced a report that set out to establish the levels of migration that would be needed to offset population decline in developed states and concluded that maintaining current levels of immigration would be essential to the overall well-being of these states. While one might assume that developed countries with low birth rates would welcome energetic newcomers as important economic assets who help maintain the economic productivity levels of the host country, fund pension and social security systems and provide caregiver services to an ageing population, the opposite has been the case in most states of the affluent North.

Modern states exist primarily to defend the security of their citizens, and security typically encompasses both physical and economic well-being. Emerging out of the cauldron of religious warfare in the seventeenth century, centralized political units with sovereignty over a fixed territory and population gradually took the place of personal kingdoms where loyalty to a hereditary dynastic elite was normative. Modern states emphasized autonomy and freedom from external interference in domestic affairs, and by 1800 – in the wake of the American and French Revolutions – the appeal was infectious. Yet even with the growth of international cooperation under the aegis of the UN since 1945, and despite the interdependence of national economies after the Cold War, there remains widespread consensus among political leaders that mutually exclusive sovereign states, not international organizations, provide the strongest foundation for human flourishing as defined by education, health, employment, participatory politics and the rule of law. And while the perceived vulnerability of states can take the form of overt threats involving violence and terror, it can also manifest itself as concern over the state's ability to provide essential social services to large numbers of new arrivals, especially if they are poor and in need of public assistance.

In addition, large-scale immigration often prompts a more diffuse fear that the predominant culture is under siege by groups who know little about the destination country's history and traditions, who (allegedly) refuse to adapt to receiving societies and who thus represent a threat to social cohesion and public order. Immigrants who fail to learn the language of the host country, who are unemployed and dependent upon the host country's welfare system, and who are unfamiliar with the social and cultural traditions of the majority population become the particular targets of anti-immigration sentiment. Hostility is sometimes fed by the local and national mass media's focus on the negative aspects of new immigration. And it is at this juncture that the nation comes to be distinguished from the state. The former is associated with a shared history, common language and culture, and a corporate sense of community. Indeed, national consciousness can exist even where the territorial state is absent, and this consciousness can sometimes drive movements for political independence. Modern states that contain more than one national group often struggle to maintain cultural cohesion. In more recent decades, so-called identity politics, centred on ethnicity, language or religion, posed a challenge to states that seek to homogenize their populations around a set of unifying symbols. Many of the world's approximately 200 sovereign countries contain within them ethnic minorities who are ever more resistant to the assimilative project. Primordial identities consisting of shared historical memories, language, belief systems and social customs resist the homogenizing tendencies of modern nation building.

States have always claimed authority over national borders, reserving for themselves the right to set immigration policy and, by implication, to preserve and protect a particular national identity. When the aggregate number of immigrants rises within the context of heightened security concerns, anti-immigrant political movements gain momentum, as they did in Western Europe during the 1980s and 1990s, and as they have in the United States since the terror attacks of 9/11. The result has been an intensification of efforts to restrict the flow of migration, especially refugee migration, in the interest of national security. Total expenditures on migration management in developed states are today 'close to official development aid flows of about $50 billion a year'.[5]

Thus at the very moment when ideas, money, business, manufacturing and products move ever more easily across international borders, restrictions on the movement of humans across those same borders have become more rigorous. International corporations produce and sell in a transnational market where one of the few constants is the rivalry between poorer states that seek to attract businesses and generate employment opportunities at home. Not infrequently, developing states find themselves bidding against each other to attract international corporations and their nomadic top executives. The mobility inherent in economic globalization means that employees of transnational firms are afforded opportunities for cross-border residence that are not available to most prospective migrants. The result has been a distinct, if unintended, privileging of the wealthy: those who make their living by investing their capital may do so across international borders, while those who support themselves by selling their labour can only do so in their natal land. Adam Smith's assertion that 'man is of all sorts of luggage the most difficult to be transported' seems especially true in today's security-conscious world. And with global population projections indicating that the most dramatic growth over the next fifty years will occur in the poorest countries, immigration policy in each of the world's nation states, and particularly in the most affluent states, is poised to become a central topic in international politics.

In the end, the phenomenon of international migration since 1945 is largely a function of a widening North–South divide. It is largely about wealthy destination states whose population levels are either stagnant or shrinking, as in Europe and North America, and poorer sending states whose populations are growing, but whose economies are inadequate to the task of providing for their citizens, and – in some cases – whose national identities are rent by ethnic conflict, authoritarian rulers and/or widespread human rights violations. A mere 15 per cent of the world's population lives in 25 highly developed countries where women average 1.5 children each.[6] Speaking in very general terms, nineteenth-century migrants moved from densely settled and industrialized areas of Europe to sparsely settled and underdeveloped regions. Migrants after 1945 originated in densely populated and poor countries and sought material improvement in densely settled post-industrial states.[7]

The recent flows are also very much about economic divergence. In 1960 per capita Gross Domestic Product (GDP) in the richest twenty countries was eighteen times that in the twenty poorest countries, but by 1995 the gap had widened to 37 times.[8] By 2005 approximately 60 per cent of all recorded migrants were to be found in the world's more prosperous countries.[9] As the North–South divide intensifies – despite the sanguine forecasts of those who champion economic globalization and the virtues of the market as key to economic convergence – the pressure on the poor and oppressed to relocate will intensify, and the prerogatives of sovereign states will collide more frequently and more directly with international standards of justice, equality and human rights. In its 2005 report to the UN, the Global Commission on International Migration recommended that greater efforts be undertaken to support economic development in poor countries so that the citizens of such states do not feel compelled to migrate. A similar conclusion was reached the following year by researchers and policy makers who were involved in the 'Cooperative Efforts to Manage Emigration' (CEME) project funded by a number of private agencies and foundations. The participants called for greater development and democratization in source countries with significant aid from destinations countries, together with increased dialogue between sending and receiving states.[10] It is a very tall order indeed, one that is too often trumped by the provincial interests of affluent sovereign states in the developed North.

Since the end of the Cold War, and especially with the collapse of the Soviet Union, points of departure have proliferated and the number of poor and unskilled migrants seeking to improve their standard of living has grown. Thanks to the spread of electronic communications technologies (cinema, television and, most recently, the Internet), the material attractions of the developed world are now widely disseminated. The persistence of sovereign nation immigration controls, irrespective of the rapid expansion of globalization in the areas of economics and communications, threatens to further aggravate disparities between the developing and the developed world. Without the option of emigration to more affluent states (an option that was available to Europeans from the seventeenth to the early twentieth century), the challenges facing the world's poorest nations will only intensify, with obvious implications for the well-being of the entire global community.

Approaching the phenomenon of post-1945 international migration and migration policy from the context of this larger North–South divide, the chapters that follow are organized into key geographical regions. Chapter One concentrates on two opposing trends in recent European history: the effort to transcend national distinctions within the European Community, thereby facilitating the movement of humans (as well as capital, goods and ideas) across national borders, and the countervailing move to restrict the entry of unskilled non-European migrants. Europe was a massive refugee zone in the aftermath of World War II, and post-war efforts at reconstruction depended in part on the success of guest worker programmes and the enhancement of cross-border cooperation. The move toward European integration began in the 1950s and accelerated during the 1960s, as citizens secured rights to live and work in other member states, and as monetary union and a single market was agreed in an effort to further economic development. Political union has remained an elusive goal but the end of the Cold War energized the Western democracies to take further steps towards integration, especially in light of general economic prosperity during the 1990s.

Despite the excitement over economic union, however, a more troubling trend has emerged in some political quarters. Europe has moved away from its post-World War II acceptance of temporary guest workers and residents of former colonies. While labour migration has become easier for citizens of EU countries, immigration into Europe from former colonies is now tightly regulated. And resentment against descendants of 1950s and 1960s guest workers (especially during downturns in the economy) continues to cloud the domestic horizon in some countries, prompting charges of racism and discrimination by the children and grandchildren of immigrants. Living in substandard housing, experiencing high levels of unemployment and lacking access to political power, second- and third-generation citizens have called into question the democratic heritage of receiving states. Some critics allege that a 'fortress Europe' mentality has arisen over the past decade, further undermining the ability of the international community to find common solutions to this pressing public policy issue.

The second chapter focuses on the strained relationship between the United States and its southern neighbours in general, and with Mexico in particular. The US was the largest receiving nation throughout the twentieth century and during the final two decades of the century the influx of legal and illegal immigrants from Central and South America accelerated dramatically. Current projections indicate that, by the middle of the current century, a significant 'browning' of the population will occur, with Hispanics constituting the fastest growing segment of the total. Responses to this influx have varied widely. Large parts of the North American business community, especially in the agricultural and construction sectors, find themselves in an unlikely alliance with proponents of diversity in calling for an open immigration process. Seasonal agriculture, building and service industries now rely heavily on temporary, low-wage Latino workers. Many business owners echo the mantra of nineteenth-century political economists who maintained that a healthy economy is every bit as dependent upon the free movement of peoples as it is upon the free movement of goods. For their part, diversity advocates argue that new peoples bring to destination countries fresh ideas, a strong work ethic and a set of cultural resources that enrich the quality of life for all citizens.

Opponents, on the other hand, contend that the new immigrants place a disproportionate strain on the receiving nation's social services infrastructure. These new immigrants allegedly refuse to learn the majority language and fail to assimilate into the majority culture, thereby undermining national unity and threatening social cohesion. Finally, unskilled immigrants undercut the bargaining power of American workers, forcing down wages and fracturing workplace morale. Interestingly, each of these claims was made against Irish, German, Italian and Jewish immigrants after their arrival in the early twentieth century. This chapter will separate myth from reality in this highly charged debate, placing special emphasis on the years since the adoption of the North American Free Trade Agreement.

Chapter Three explores transnational migration in post-colonial Africa, where since 1945 voluntary relocation has been the exception rather than the rule. Most African migration takes place overland, both internally and between countries sharing a common border. As a rule, most borders are porous, and since so many of the borders were established by Europeans during the era of imperialism, ethnic groups sometimes find themselves separated from their kin by artificial national distinctions. Forty years after the end of direct control, African immigration patterns continue to be influenced by the colonial experience. Today nearly half of the world's estimated 12 million refugees live in Africa. Fleeing famine, civil war, ethnic violence and military dictatorship, the promise of prosperity that accompanied so many African independence movements during the 1960s has been shattered. By the early 1990s, more than seventy military coups had occurred in Africa, most in the name of restoring social and economic order, but invariably the successful coup plotters have only made conditions worse.

In many African states, population growth continues to outstrip the ability of governments to provide basic services like health care and education. As foreign investment in Africa shrank during the 1980s in response to the emergence of state-controlled economies, material conditions plummeted. More recently, the spread of AIDS has been added to the list of crises facing a continent already struggling with low life expectancy and widespread civil unrest. Since the end of the Cold War, the African continent has lost much of its strategic value to the developed North, and immigrants are no longer welcome within the borders of former European colonial powers. This chapter will examine the problem of modern refugee migration from the vantage point of international complicity in the disasters that have befallen those states in Africa where the refugee question is paramount.

Our attention turns to the Islamic world in chapter Four, and more particularly to the temporary guest worker programmes in the major oil-producing states. In general, the sparsely populated Arab states have been reluctant to accept migrants – even fellow Arabs – on anything other than a temporary basis. This is especially the case in the oil-rich kingdoms of the Persian Gulf region, where conservative monarchies fear the potentially destabilizing effects of mass immigration. Sweeping and fast-paced modernization projects in these kingdoms, all made possible by booming oil revenues after 1973, necessitated the recruitment of skilled and unskilled guest workers. The restrictions placed on these temporary residents, the vast majority of whom were Muslim, far exceeded anything practised in Western Europe in the 1960s and 1970s. Non-resident workers in the Gulf States were prohibited from remaining beyond the term set by their labour contracts, and their legal standing was always precarious.

Political upheaval and war in the Islamic world also created huge refugee crises. The formation of Pakistan in 1947 triggered a massive exodus of Muslims from India (and Hindus from Pakistan), while in the Middle East a traumatic Palestinian diaspora occurred in the wake of a series of Arab–Israeli wars. In the mid-1990s, Afghans earned the unhappy distinction of being the world's biggest refugee population due to a series of body blows, including a brutal Soviet invasion during the 1980s and the rise of an intolerant Islamist regime in the 1990s. After the events of 9/11, Muslim migrants living in the Western democracies found themselves under greater scrutiny, as governments moved to identify and detain potential terrorists whose historical consciousness reaches back to the era of Saladin and the epic struggle against the infidel.

Finally in chapter Five we examine the impact of economic globalization on the emerging powers in South and East Asia. Optimists in the neo-liberal tradition believe that the solution to current global economic disparities (and increasing levels of international migration) rests with the extension of market forces to regions of the world long harried by burdensome, highly regulatory governments and command-style economies. Foster economic growth through market mechanisms, these analysts say, create a truly integrated world economy, and the root cause of transnational migration will be removed. Until the setbacks of the late 1990s, the 'Economic Tigers' of East Asia (Hong Kong, South Korea, Singapore and Taiwan) served as the test cases for this theory.

Unfortunately, most of the focus has been on the professional elite in these countries who benefited from the emergence of the global economy, while less attention is paid to the labouring poor. This chapter will address recent migration patterns among the educated and highly skilled elite of South and East Asia. As winners in the emerging global economy with prized professional skills, the departure of these migrants for developed states (often after costly state-sponsored education in their natal land) further disadvantages Third World economies. The relocation of First World manufacturing facilities in developing countries boosted job prospects for a few, but the generally low-paying '3-D' jobs (dirty, dangerous and difficult) have not led to the sort of educational and career opportunities that would lift most participants out of endemic poverty. Thus unskilled workers from South and East Asia have migrated both regionally and more widely in search of a better quality of life for themselves and for loved ones left behind.

The book will conclude with a consideration of how immigration policy continues to function as the principal tool in the creation and clarification of national identity while simultaneously fuelling the envy and resentment of people in the developing world. In microcosm, the State of Israel's 'Right of Return' policy serves as a poignant example of how immigration can both foster national sentiment for one people while simultaneously frustrating the nationalist ambitions of another (3.3 million Palestinians living in Israel and in the occupied territories). At the global level, we will review the ever-widening wealth and resource gap between rich and poor states, demographic projections and the acceleration of a North–South divide that begs for creative solutions in a new century. One of the solutions may involve the adoption of more generous, and truly international, standards governing the peregrination of peoples around the world. After all, while nations have always claimed the right to set migration policies, prior to World War I few states intervened in the decisions of people to relocate across frontiers. Immigration regimes are, after all, a very recent phenomenon in global history. In our current fixation on national security and collective identity formation, it is too easy to forget the many benefits that immigrants have historically brought to both sending countries (in the form of remittances) and to the intellectual, cultural and economic life of receiving countries.

In its landmark 1948 Universal Declaration of Human Rights, the United Nations adopted a non-binding resolution that enumerated 'a common standard of achievement for all peoples and all nations'. Among the rights outlined in the Declaration, three involve human migration. Article 13, section 2 claims that every person 'has the right to leave any country, including his own, and to return to his country'. Article 14 provides for a right 'to seek and to enjoy in other countries asylum from persecution' while Article 15, section 2 mandates that no one 'shall be arbitrarily deprived of his nationality nor denied the right to change his nationality'. In essence, the UN was asking member states to reconsider the moral implications of a global system where the accident of birth is the most significant determinant of human potential. It was asking whether the notion of sovereign states as congeries of special ethnic, religious and ancestral attributes could ever be reconciled with the Enlightenment values of neutrality, equality and universal human rights. The question remains unanswered in our own time, even as the debate intensifies within the larger context of economic globalization.

Chapter 1

The Changing Face of Europe

Beginning in the early sixteenth century and continuing until the second decade of the twentieth, Europe was the world's pre-eminent sending continent. The first overseas migrants during an era of mercantile capitalism were few in number and consisted mainly of soldiers, administrators and planters from Spain and Portugal. Claiming large sweeps of territory in Central and South America for their respective monarchs, the early conquistadors hoped to exploit native peoples as a source of cheap agricultural labour. But when European diseases like smallpox and malaria began decimating the indigenous population almost from the moment of first contact in the 1490s, the planters turned to black African bondsmen for labour, inaugurating three centuries of plantation slavery in the Americas. Throughout the colonial period, the Spanish and Portuguese settlements attracted few immigrants from Europe; many of those who did arrive eventually intermarried with indigenous peoples, creating a new mestizo population that was excluded from access to crown-dominated political office.

The Spanish and Portuguese were followed in the seventeenth century by the representatives of English, Dutch and French joint stock-trading companies, together with various religious dissenters who wished to practise their particular versions of Christianity without hindrance from crown authorities. By the middle of the eighteenth century approximately 1.5 million Britons had made the dangerous

Atlantic passage under sail to North America. Modest numbers of additional newcomers arrived during and after the Napoleonic era, but it was a series of political upheavals and poor harvests during the 1840s that triggered a period of unprecedented mass migration lasting just over half a century. A quarter of a million emigrants per year on average left Europe during the 1840s, and as the era of industrial capitalism evolved, the annual total continued to grow, until the outbreak of World War I in the late summer of 1914.[1]

Over the course of the nineteenth century, government involvement in human migration was fitful and unsystematic. If anything, state support for the building of roads, canals and rail systems facilitated both internal and cross-border movement. Before the 1870s most of this movement involved the transfer of rural inhabitants to emerging industrial cities, but at the very time when the major European powers were carving out empires in Africa and Asia, millions of Europe's inhabitants elected to begin their lives anew in North America. Steamship technology lowered costs and accelerated the Atlantic passage, while prospects for economic betterment in a rapidly developing but still underpopulated region of the world were strong. Approximately 13 million Europeans, mostly Irish, British and Germans, disembarked for ports in the Americas between 1840 and 1880, and that figure was easily matched during each of the following two decades. By the 1890s new immigrant groups joined the exodus: Italians, Poles, Russian Jews and smaller groups from the Scandinavian countries completed the Atlantic passage and initiated a process of further chain migration.[2]

Most of the late nineteenth-century migrants were from economically depressed and overpopulated rural regions of their respective countries, men and women who had not relocated to the burgeoning industrial cities. Of a total transatlantic migrant population of 52 to 55 million between 1860 and 1914, almost three-quarters settled in the United States and Canada, while the remainder found new homes in the emerging nation states of South America, especially Argentina. In addition to the Atlantic passage, another 3.5 million Europeans – mostly British – settled in Australia and New Zealand during the same half-century. This relative freedom of movement into sparsely populated regions of the globe accounted for nearly one-quarter of Europe's dramatic population growth in the nineteenth century, serving as an important safety valve in the aftermath of poor harvests, famines and severe slumps in the rural economy. In other words, just as Western Europe was reaching industrial maturity and imperial mastery, and as its population was approaching record highs, potential sources of political and social unrest in the countryside were deflected by the ready option of inexpensive migration overseas. The disgruntled and dispossessed now had the ability to escape their dire circumstances. It was a remarkable confluence of favourable conditions for Europe at a time when rapid demographic and economic change was upsetting centuries-old patterns of rural life. Unhappily, the developing post-colonial states of the mid-twentieth century would enjoy no such advantages in their efforts to modernize. For the disgruntled and dispossessed of these new states, the migration option was complicated by protocols that restricted the flow of humans across international borders.

EUROPE AS A RECEIVING ZONE, 1945–73

Two horrific world wars, separated by a prolonged global economic depression, brought voluntary international migration to a standstill after 1914. Developed states adopted restrictive immigration systems during the 1920s, and anti-immigration political sentiment gained ground in the United States, the world's largest destination country. Job losses occasioned by the Great Depression of the 1930s exacerbated anti-immigrant sentiment in all receiving countries. The demand for domestic labour, male and female, was at a premium during World War II, making voluntary international migration almost impossible as governments struggled to retain an adequate workforce. After the defeat of Nazism in 1945, however, war-ravaged Western Europe underwent a dramatic transformation, becoming for the first time since the late Middle Ages a net receiving zone. The social, cultural and political consequences of this demographic shift were enormous, with the decisions made by post-war governments inaugurating fierce debates over the meaning of national identity and the obligation of states to accommodate victims of persecution worldwide.

The demographic scene in May 1945 was unprecedented. Approximately 60 million combatants and civilians had been killed during the conflict, important European cities had been levelled in massive air raids, and the productive capacity of farms and factories was at one-fifth of pre-war levels. Suddenly and shockingly, a once-proud Europe had become a migrant and refugee continent. During the war years, millions of people had been forcibly removed from their homes by the Nazi terror state; by 1944 one worker in five was either foreign-born or a prisoner of war.[3] When the war ended in 1945, there were 30 million displaced persons in the Soviet and Allied zones of occupation, and few of them had the personal resources to rebuild their shattered lives. Hitler's Germany stands as a harrowing example of how states, not impersonal economic forces, are often responsible for involuntary migration flows, how political ideology, not material conditions, compels the movement of peoples across international borders.

Relief agencies struggled greatly to assist the dispossessed after May 1945 and, remarkably, most of those who had been uprooted by the Nazi regime were able to make their way home by the end of the calendar year. The task of rebuilding a war-torn landscape was daunting, however, and as the political relationship between the United States and the Soviet Union deteriorated in the immediate post-war period, it became clear that reconstruction efforts in Western Europe would not succeed without considerable financial aid and additional sources of labour. In 1947 the first need was addressed by the American-sponsored Marshall Plan, a package of recovery funds administered by the Organization for European Economic Cooperation and accepted by sixteen countries in Western Europe. When the Marshall Plan concluded in 1952, over $13 billion in direct grants and credits had been awarded, and participating countries were experiencing strong economic growth. Labour shortages in these revived economies, on the other hand, were acute and threatened to undermine the recovery. A combination of low birth rates during the economically depressed 1930s and high mortality during the war left the countries of north-western Europe in dire need of additional able-bodied workers.

The short-term solution to Western Europe's labour shortage involved the recruitment of men and women across international borders. It featured a South–North intra-continental movement during the late 1940s and '50s, with Italy, Spain, Portugal and Greece exporting workers, while Britain, France, the Netherlands, Switzerland, West Germany and Belgium served as the main receiving states. Total immigration from southern to northern European countries between 1955 and 1973 reached about 5 million people.[4] During the 1960s the circle of sending countries widened to include a larger Mediterranean context, with Turks, North Africans and people from former colonial holdings arriving in Western Europe by the hundreds of thousands. Virtually all of the migrants came by invitation, under host government auspices or as a result of bilateral agreements between source and destination countries. For the labour-needy economies of Western Europe, the new recruits were to serve in a stopgap capacity and were expected to return home after a limited period of residency, skills training and gainful employment. This was acceptable to the newcomers, most of whom were young, single, poorly educated males motivated solely by a desire to save enough money to purchase land and livestock back in their home countries.

Europe's so-called guest worker systems of the 1960s adopted a core principle of classical economics: labour was a commodity to be bought and sold like any other commodity in the marketplace. By denying foreign workers permanent residency or citizenship rights, employers were free to treat people as flexible economic units, not as rights-bearing members of a commonwealth or national polity. They were, in short, easier to hire and fire than native stock workers. Or at least this was the operating assumption. None of the receiving states was prepared for the possibility that the guest workers might overstay their conditional welcome and encourage family members to join them.[5]

Foreign labour recruitment remained strong into the early 1970s, when a major economic downturn, triggered by the global oil crisis of 1973, led most European countries to suspend their guest worker programmes. But while the formal recruitment schemes ended, many foreign workers whose economic prospects at home remained dim elected to remain in Western Europe, and family reunification provisions in existing immigration laws permitted spouses and children to relocate. Rather than visit their families and risk being denied re-entry into Europe, guest workers encouraged family dependants to join them. By the mid 1970s the countries of north-western Europe had become home to approximately 10 million migrants from Eastern Europe, North Africa, sub-Saharan Africa, South and East Asia. One in seven manual labourers in Germany and Britain, and one in four of all industrial workers in France, Switzerland and Belgium, was an immigrant.[6] Overnight, it seemed, the nineteenth century's great sending continent had become a centre of ethnic, racial and religious diversity. The majority of the migrants who were admitted as temporary workers in the 1950s and '60s had become permanent residents of their host countries and as such aspired to citizenship rights and the full range of social and economic opportunities that were available in the West.

Unhappily, the new reality of a multicultural Europe was not always embraced by the indigenous culture, and governments gave little thought to how these immigrant communities might be integrated into the mainstream. The combination of job losses and inflation that followed the jump in oil prices on world markets in 1973 exacerbated the tension in the already tense relations between immigrants and native majorities. Ethnic minorities became scapegoats during periods of economic contraction, unfairly blamed for structural problems within market economies that transcended national frontiers. Normally concentrated in the poorer neighbourhoods of major cities, migrant communities were often stigmatized as havens for criminals, welfare cheats and dangerous subversives who refused to embrace the dominant culture. As immigration requirements were tightened during the 1970s and '80s, tensions over the role of religion in secular societies, over language as a marker of national identity and over access to jobs, housing, education and political power, all intensified. In addition, more recently 'terrorism and crime, identified in the public mind with particular nationalities, have become continent-wide obsessions'.[7]

FRANCE TAKES THE LEAD

Prior to World War I, foreigners were allowed to enter and exit the French Republic without hindrance. The age of passports, visas and border checkpoints lay in the future. Unlike most of its European neighbours, France's birth rate had begun to decline as early as the mid-eighteenth century, prompting some officials to view migrants as both an economic opportunity and a long-term demographic necessity.[8] Indeed, prior to the twentieth century the presence of foreign migrants and refugees rarely troubled the political establishment. There were approximately 381,000 foreign-born persons in France in 1857 and, by the early 1880s, as the industrial revolution gained momentum, the total passed a million.[9] There was never an exodus from the countryside to the cities in France as there had been in Germany and Britain during the early stages of the industrial revolution, thus foreign labour made up an important part of the emerging urban working class, especially in the coal and steel industries. Private firms took the lead in recruiting workers from neighbouring Belgium and Italy, and most of the newcomers quickly learned the French language and assimilated into mainstream culture.

Concern over the country's population decline continued during the early years of the twentieth century, but the government failed to develop a consistent immigration policy. During World War I, as the death toll mounted on the Western Front, the Ministry of Armaments began actively recruiting new workers from France's colonies. Almost a quarter of a million non-Europeans entered the country during the course of the war, and by 1917 the government was insisting that the newcomers carry official identity cards. Still, even with the loss of nearly 1.5 million men during the conflict and the immediate need for additional sources of labour, a policy of repatriation was adopted at the end of the war in 1918, and by 1920 only 6,000 of the wartime foreign workforce remained in the country. By the mid 1920s a commercial recruitment agency called the *Société générale d'immigration* was permitted to assist domestic employers in the agricultural and coal industries, and some 50,000 workers were allowed to enter the country for specific jobs in these sectors. But during the Great Depression of the 1930s, the central government's Ministry of Labour moved to suspend all immigration and even established a programme of assisted repatriation.[10] World War II and German occupation interrupted virtually all voluntary migration flows, so that by 1946 there were fewer than 1.7 million foreign-born residents in France.

Shortly after the end of the war, the government of Charles de Gaulle and the successor Fourth Republic, prompted mainly by employers in agriculture and industry who were unable to fill vacancies with native workers, inaugurated Western Europe's first formal programme of foreign labour recruitment. Supporting the employer lobby was a strong pro-natalist movement that championed additional immigration as a solution to a century and a half of steady population decline. Led by academics and civil servants in the Ministry of Population, the *populationnistes*, as they were called, enjoyed considerable influence and pushed primarily for the recruitment and assimilation of Italian workers, on the assumption that as fellow Catholics they would be culturally and ethnically compatible with the French population.[11] The aim was to encourage permanent settlement and to create new French men and women. The powerful national trade unions, however, wary lest employers recruit cheap foreign labour to undercut wages for French workers, called for the creation of a neutral state agency to regulate the process. The result was the establishment of the Ministry of Population and the National Immigration Office in 1946. Partnering with domestic employers and prospective sending countries in Southern Europe, National Immigration Office officials sought to regulate the travel and entry of documented workers into the country.

According to official records, about 2 million migrants from other European countries, together with almost 700,000 dependants, entered France as registered workers between 1945 and 1974. But the National Immigration Office's monopoly over recruitment activities was challenged repeatedly – and successfully – by employers who bristled at the cumbersome procedures and fees required by the agency, and by the difficulty of attracting Italian migrants who were lured by better opportunities in Switzerland and the United States. Hundreds of thousands of economic migrants flowed into the country on tourist visas, secured low-paying jobs and remained in France without official sanction. Others crossed the border clandestinely and were hired into temporary unskilled jobs. By 1968 more than 80 per cent of migrant workers in France had entered the country without proper documentation, and once the new arrivals had taken up employment, lethargic

French authorities were prone to grant them proper work and residence permits.[12] As long as the economy continued to expand, and until the impact of new arrivals on existing social services became a political issue, those who circumvented the official rules of entry were forgiven their transgressions.

Recruitment from neighbouring states that shared a common border with France continued throughout this period, but a robust economy and a seemingly insatiable demand for labour in the late 1950s prompted the government to conclude treaties further afield. Morocco, Tunisia and Portugal concluded worker transfer agreements with France in 1963, while Yugoslavia and Turkey did the same in 1965. The period of decolonization from 1958 to 1962, and especially the relinquishment of Algeria in the latter year, led to a sharp spike in immigration activity. Algerians who had sided with the French during the struggle for independence and who, as a result, were now very much unwelcome in their own country, were given full nationality rights. Average annual figures of immigrants from Algeria rose from 66,400 in the period 1946–1955 to almost 250,000 in the decade after 1956.[13] For citizens who lived in any of the French colonies or former colonies, immigration with minimal restrictions was the norm until 1974. By 1973 there were almost 800,000 Algerians, 200,000 Moroccans and 120,000 Tunisians living in the country, together with 740,000 Portuguese, 573,000 Spaniards and 571,000 Italians.[14] Almost without forethought, France was becoming a diverse ethno-racial state as its temporary workers were granted contract renewals and former colonial subjects exercised their right to settle in the country.

In theory, at least, the transformation should have been painless. The French republican ideal always refused to recognize ethnic or religious differences, stressing instead the secular values of liberty, fraternity and equality for all. Only by establishing such a transcendent French identity, it was thought, would the country avoid the social stratification that was so common before 1789, and the cultural fragmentation and divisiveness that was identified with multi-ethnic states like the US. In reality, however, the post-war political establishment was slow to acknowledge the emergence of a multi-ethnic society, or to use ethnicity or religion as legitimate categories when tracking inequality. The arrival of significant numbers of black migrants from former colonies in West Africa and the French West Indies resulted in heightened racial tensions in the early 1960s, particularly in France's urban areas where migrants lived in substandard housing and experienced high rates of unemployment. Since a significant percentage of the migrants were Muslim, serious questions were raised and debated regarding the place of religion in a secular republic. Suddenly there was renewed interest in empowering the National Immigration Office to regulate and perhaps reduce the number of migrants from non-European sending countries. Racially motivated attacks against black settlers led to the passage of national anti-discrimination legislation in 1972 but enforcement was lax in many areas. Goods and ideas continued to flow between the post-colonial periphery and the metropole, but the enlargement of the migrant population was having a troubling impact on domestic attitudes – and actions.

EARLY IMITATORS

The French decision to recruit workers from states in Southern Europe and beyond was quickly adopted by nearby countries facing similar labour shortages after World War II. Belgian authorities negotiated a series of bilateral agreements with countries in Southern Europe to support the country's labour-intensive iron and steel industries. Thanks to liberal family reunification laws, the foreign-born population of Belgium grew to 716,000 in 1970 and reached 851,000 seven years later.[15] A similar programme was undertaken by the Netherlands, where labour shortages in the 1960s led to competition with France for newcomers from Spain, Portugal, Greece, Morocco, Yugoslavia and Tunisia.[16] Black workers from Surinam in the Caribbean began arriving after 1965. By the time of independence in 1975, an estimated 150,000 Surinamese had made their home in the Netherlands. This small country also absorbed 300,000 Eurasian political refugees from Indonesia, formerly the Dutch East Indies, during the 1950s. Many of the immigrants were of mixed Dutch and Indonesian parentage, but held Dutch citizenship. After repatriation, the government's Ministry of Social

Work set up a 'Special Care Commission' whose charge was 'to prevent social degradation as much as possible, and if possible to cure it'. The new arrivals were instructed in everything from the Dutch style of housekeeping to budgeting and child rearing. Turks and Moroccans represented by far the largest percentage of Mediterranean immigrants in the Netherlands, totalling over 350,000 by the early 1990s.[17]

Switzerland, a self-declared non-immigration country despite the fact that over 15 per cent of its population in 1914 was foreign-born, accepted guest workers from a host of nearby nations, even encouraging frontier workers who crossed the border each day to work for Swiss companies. The post-war Swiss economy grew at an unprecedented rate, and the boom continued until 1974. As a result, the number of foreign workers in Switzerland increased from 90,000 in 1950 to just over a million in 1974. By the latter date almost half of all factory workers, and a third of Switzerland's total labour force, was foreign-born. Following a common strategy, the Swiss government did not extend civil and political rights to migrants, and even children of migrants who were born in Switzerland were denied citizenship. Even with these restrictions in place, however, opposition to uncontrolled migration began to emerge in the 1960s, and in 1970 a plebiscite was held on the issue of restricting the overall foreign population to 10 per cent of the whole. Although narrowly defeated, the initiative led to the formation of a quota system for permits of abode, limiting the number of permits to 10,000 annually.[18]

Sweden, which had been a net emigration country throughout the nineteenth century, began to welcome immigrants during the economic depression of the 1930s. Approximately one-fifth of the population had emigrated to North America by the start of the twentieth century, leaving a total of 5 million Swedes in the Baltic country. There was an inflow of refugees from neighbouring countries during World War II, and when a common labour market was established by the Nordic countries in 1954, the pace of immigration accelerated. Gross National Product increased by an average of 4 per cent each year between 1946 and the early 1970s, with the manufacturing sector growing at a rate of 7 per cent. Gradually visa requirements for non-Nordic citizens were dropped, and additional newcomers were admitted from as far away as

Greece and Turkey. The majority of these labour migrants found little difficulty securing employment and adequate housing, and residence permits were rarely denied. During the 1960s, however, the powerful Swedish labour unions, seeking to reduce wage competition, began to call for restrictions on immigrants from non-Nordic countries. Their efforts were successful, but during the following decade family reunion migration continued to grow, just as the industrial sector declined and the oil-related shocks set in. Suddenly non-Nordic residents, together with a growing number of refugees, were viewed with suspicion as threats to national identity and economic well-being.[19]

THE GERMAN FEDERAL REPUBLIC

It was only with the creation of a pan-German state in 1870–71 that a precise definition of German citizenship first emerged. The unified Reich that was established in the aftermath of the Franco-Prussian war built upon an already strong sense of national consciousness, one that had first taken root during the long conflict with Napoleon Bonaparte in the early nineteenth century. Thus the social, political and economic institutions of a modern centralized state were superimposed on an already developed sense of national identity, even though some German-speaking lands, especially Austria, were left outside the new Reich.

An emphasis on cultural nationalism gave German citizenship a distinctive ethnic character, perhaps best illustrated in the foundational law of 1870 that defined Germans as a community united through blood instead of place.[20] One result of such thinking was the exclusion of non-ethnic Germans from any right to citizenship through permanent residency and assimilation. In the late nineteenth century, for example, landowners in the rural eastern part of the country faced a shortage of agricultural labour due to high levels of rural–urban migration. In response, the German government instituted a worker programme that allowed Polish agricultural labourers and migrants from the Habsburg lands temporary, not permanent, entry. There was to be no right of settlement for these unskilled, low-wage workers, and state power was employed regularly in setting the terms of temporary work contracts.

Most of the foreign workers were obliged to return home during the winter months.[21] 'Germany for the Germans' was a common refrain of militant nationalists who feared the 'Pole-ization' of the eastern frontier, an attitude that put foreign workers on notice that they could be expelled at any time.

The identification of German citizenship with an advanced or unique culture reached its destructive nadir with the coming to power of the Nazi dictatorship. Severe wartime labour shortages were addressed by the mass conscription and resettlement of foreign workers. For Slavs and Jews, resettlement and slave labour was but a prelude to extermination, but for millions of others the war years were dedicated to propping up the Nazi war effort. Dutch, French and Belgian workers took the place of native Germans who had been drafted into the military, carrying out essential 'home front' duties for the regime. The Ministry of Labour even envisioned a post-war role for conscripted labour in a triumphant Germany. Ironically, the Nazi vision of a pure national community, the *Gemeinschaft*, could not be pursued without the vital contributions of allegedly inferior peoples from occupied territories. By the end of the war, foreigners made up a remarkable quarter of the overall German workforce, reaching as high as one-third of the total in the areas of agriculture and arms production.[22]

With its ability to absorb fellow ethnic Germans from regions under Soviet domination, the post-war German Federal Republic was the last of the major countries in Western Europe to recruit foreign labour.[23] In particular, the forced removal of long-established German communities in Central and Eastern Europe at the end of the conflict led to the relocation of some 8 million refugees. Most of the newcomers were welcomed and quickly assimilated, receiving citizenship and entering the job market in positions previously occupied by conscripts. They were joined by a steady influx of disillusioned and disaffected people from Soviet-controlled East Germany. During the 1950s approximately 3.5 million East Germans (20 per cent of Communist East Germany's population) fled to the Federal Republic. The political and economic exodus continued until the summer of 1961, when an embarrassed Soviet premier, Nikita Khrushchev, ordered the construction of the Berlin Wall to prevent further East–West relocation.

Even with the addition of East Germans after the war, labour short-ages in the Federal Republic continued into the 1950s as the economy grew at a rapid pace. An 11 per cent unemployment rate in 1950 plummeted to 1.3 per cent ten years later, and the demand for additional sources of labour, especially for unskilled workers who would accept low-paying jobs, intensified. Germany's brief colonial experience during the late nineteenth century precluded a reliance on that particular source of labour.[24] Building on the experience of neighbouring countries that had begun the process of labour recruitment earlier, West Germany created Europe's most regimented and highly organized system of state-sponsored migration. Even before the flow of ethnic Germans was brought to a halt by the escalating Cold War, the Bonn government had concluded modest bilateral agreements with Greece and Italy. A Federal Labour Office opened recruitment stations in these sending countries, selected suitable applicants and transported them in groups to West Germany, where they were housed in employer-provided accommodation close to their work sites. New arrivals were issued temporary residency and work permits, with the latter often valid for only specific types of employment. Dependants were discouraged from accompanying migrant workers, virtually all of whom arrived in the country under temporary guest worker status. The goal was to create a flexible labour force that could be sent away at the first sign of an economic downturn, thereby avoiding the considerable social costs associated with permanent housing and welfare benefit.

With the erection of the Berlin Wall, the Federal Labour Office undertook an intensive effort to expand state-to-state recruiting pacts. In the 1960s, additional nations entered into guest worker – or *Gastarbeiter* – agreements with West Germany, including Yugoslavia, Tunisia, Morocco, Spain and Portugal. By far the most important relationship was that concluded in 1961 with the government of Turkey, where population pressures, urban unemployment and widespread rural poverty prompted the authorities in Ankara to outsource its considerable human capital. Under the initial agreement, 650,000 Turks, the majority of whom were Muslim males and 25 per cent of whom were members of Turkey's Kurdish minority population, entered the Federal Republic under *Gastarbeiter* status. Most found themselves employed in the low-skill service sector, or in the mining, metal processing and construction-related trades. In 1969 the one-millionth Turkish guest worker stepped off a train in Munich; he was met there by the president of the Federal Labour Office in a ceremony that celebrated the contributions of Turkish nationals to the German economy.[25] Their numbers increased sharply after a military junta took control of Turkey in 1980; by autumn 1982 over 1.5 million Turks were legally resident in West Germany.[26] Another half million were resident in other European countries.

From the very beginning of the guest worker schemes, the assumption was that non-ethnic Germans were to be allowed into the country on a temporary basis, a flexible reserve force that assisted in discreet sectors of the economy until such time as native labour resources could meet the demand. As temporary workers, the first generation of arrivals made little effort to learn the German language, and as late as 1980 almost 30 per cent of Turks living in Germany had no knowledge of the majority language.[27] Continued economic growth and the resulting intense competition for workers during the 1960s, however, together with employers' calls for a reduction in labour turnover and costs associated with retraining, led to a momentous decision. The German government, always loath to admit that the Federal Republic was a country of immigration, began to ease restrictions against family reunification. The proportion of women in the foreign population grew from 31 per cent in 1961 to 41 per cent two decades later, while the percentage of foreign-born children also rose dramatically.

Once in the country, spouses and children became part of West Germany's temporary labour force, taking up less desirable positions that were eschewed by native-born workers. In 1956 there were only 95,000 foreign workers in West Germany, but a decade later the total reached 1.3 million. When the global economy faltered in 1973, an estimated 2.6 million workers, or just below 12 per cent of the entire workforce, was foreign-born.[28] The West German economic miracle had been built upon the shoulders of its temporary workers, most of whom were now committed to permanent residency in a nation that was deeply ambivalent about their presence. That ambivalence was manifested in the state's denial of citizenship rights to non-ethnic Germans irrespective of their length of legal residency in the country.

The British Isles have played host to many newcomers over the centuries, highlighted by the Roman occupation that began in the first century of the common era. Pushing the Celtic population (themselves descendants of even earlier immigrants) into the west and north, Britain's Roman inhabitants were in turn replaced by Angles and Saxons during the fifth and sixth centuries. Danish and Norse invaders made their mark upon the islands during the eighth and ninth centuries, and the descendants of all of these groups failed in their efforts to repulse powerful and well-organized Norman invaders in the late eleventh century. It was the Norman presence that had the most profound impact on the political and legal culture of Britain, and as the institutions of royal authority developed, Norman power expanded into the so-called Celtic fringe areas of Wales, Scotland and Ireland. Throughout the medieval and early modern periods, Britain became increasingly mono-ethnic. The kingdom's small Jewish community was expelled in 1290, while only a small number of merchants from northern Italy and the German Hanseatic League were permitted to take up residence in the cities. During the seventeenth and eighteenth centuries, Britain became home to French Huguenot refugees, German merchants, Irish labourers, black African slaves and (after the ban was lifted by Oliver Cromwell in the 1650s) Jewish traders, clothiers and bankers. But while economically important, none of these groups was very large in terms of the country's total population.[29]

That population was growing at an unprecedented pace during the nineteenth and early twentieth centuries. In 1850 there were approximately 20 million Britons; one century later the number approached 50 million, and this did not take into account the 11 million who had emigrated to North America and Oceania. In the years between the defeat of Napoleon and the end of World War II, between 1.5 and 2 million people entered the country, and half of these came from Ireland, officially part of Britain since 1800. Throughout the nineteenth century, there was nothing to resemble an immigration authority in Britain; as in the rest of Europe one simply entered the kingdom and took up residence. The great 'pull' factor was employment related to the country's industrial revolution, which meant that most immigrant communities were located in or near the factory towns and cities of the Midlands and the North. Conditions in these industrial centres have been well documented; in the 1840s, for example, Friedrich Engels chronicled the plight of the Irish in the city of Manchester. The vast majority of newcomers worked at low-wage, low-skill jobs in the service and manufacturing sectors. Huddled into ethnic enclaves, poor migrants were subject to varying degrees of resentment and hostility, especially during periods of economic hardship. By the start of World War II, British experience with colonial peoples worldwide had done little to advance inclusiveness at home. Instead, the war years seemed to solidify a rather narrow definition of national identity, one that left many Britons ill-prepared for the accelerated pace of post-war migration.[30]

In the immediate aftermath of the war, the majority of migrants to Britain were refugees from the Continent. Members of the Polish government and armed forces in exile, together with Balts, Ukranians and Sudeten Germans who had been displaced by the conflict, began new lives and found employment in understaffed industries. In 1945 the British government set up the European voluntary worker scheme and recruited approximately 90,000 workers from refugee camps on the Continent. All jobs were assigned by the Ministry of Labour, and participation in the programme was limited to single men and women who were not allowed, as a rule, to bring dependants with them. British labour unions did not favour the scheme and, in 1951, it was abandoned.[31] A further 250,000 migrants arrived from Europe between 1946 and 1951, and for the most part the newcomers were able to rebuild their lives without complication. But when the Labour government passed the British Nationality Act of 1948, ensuring the right of all colonists and Commonwealth citizens to enter the United Kingdom without restriction, a new and more controversial period began.

In June 1948, a ship carrying 500 passport holders from the West Indies island of Jamaica docked in London. The passengers were black males who were about to test their de-territorialized British identity, and their arrival marked the symbolic beginning of multiracial Britain.[32] Two-thirds of the men had been in Britain during the war and found themselves unemployed when they returned home in 1945. Most of them arrived back in Britain under a formal recruitment scheme. Attracted by the strength of Britain's post-war economy, which grew at an annual average rate of 2.7 per cent during the 1950s, these non-white migrants had been contracted for jobs in sectors that were previously occupied by the Irish – public transport, sanitation and manual tasks in the National Health Service. During the 1950s they were joined by immigrants from other so-called 'New Commonwealth' countries in Africa and on the Indian subcontinent. Once settled and employed, a pattern of chain migration developed, with workers sending remittances back to their country of origin in order to pay for the transportation costs of family and friends. There were 218,000 persons of New Commonwealth origin in Britain by 1951. The total grew to half a million over the next decade, and doubled again by the late 1960s.

Poorly educated and lacking fiscal resources, Britain's 'coloured' immigrants worked almost exclusively in unskilled and semi-skilled positions. As a result, they tended to live in ghetto areas of major cities like London, Bristol, Leeds, Bradford and Manchester. Incidents of discrimination were reported but rarely investigated, and when serious race riots took place in Nottingham and in London's Notting Hill area in the late summer of 1958, MPs from both major parties and the media took up the issue of unregulated migration from the New Commonwealth.[33] It seemed unimportant that only 92 per cent of the population of England and Wales had been born in England and Wales, or that there were twice as many Irish in the country as there had been thirty years earlier. The only relevant fact was the more visible presence of 'dark strangers' with their peculiar religious traditions, social customs, dress codes and cuisine.[34] Negative stereotyping was not uncommon in the popular tabloid press, and anti-immigrant organizations, from the fascist Oswald Mosley's Union Movement, founded in 1948, to the Birmingham Immigration Control Association, established in 1960, constantly pressured the political establishment to take action against the perceived floodtide of 'coloured' immigration.

The first restrictive legislation, the Commonwealth Immigrants Act, was passed in 1962, over the opposition of the minority Labour Party. The new law limited entry into Britain to those with demonstrated skills in occupations where labour was needed. Just under 78,000 vouchers were issued during the period 1962 to 1968, but almost 260,000 dependants were allowed to enter under existing law. It was this much larger dependent population that gave rise to the most virulent anti-immigration rhetoric of the 1960s. In 1968 the Conservative MP Enoch Powell, in an address before a Tory Party audience in Birmingham, intoned that:

> We must be mad, literally mad, as a nation to be permitting the annual inflow of some 50,000 dependants, who are for the most part the material of the future growth of the immigrant-descended population. It is like watching a nation busily engaged in heaping up its own funeral pyre.[35]

In the wake of these remarks Powell was expelled from the Conservative shadow cabinet, but his views were endorsed by a wide cross section of the British public. The Labour government, generally less paranoid although sensitive to the concerns of union workers, attempted to address the problem of widespread discrimination against those who were already settled in Britain with the passage of the 1965 Race Relations Act. The new law forbade discrimination in public places and incitement to racial hatred either verbally or in writing. A Race Relations Board was established to enforce the new legislation, and in 1968 a new law extended the anti-discrimination provisions of the Race Relations Act to cover housing and employment.[36]

In that same year, however, Harold Wilson's Labour Party passed a new law that denied right of entry to British passport holders unless they, or a parent or grandparent, had been born, adopted or naturalized in Britain. Despite the protestations of Home Secretary James Callaghan, the law clearly favoured white people from the 'Old Commonwealth' countries (Canada, Australia and New Zealand) and was disadvantageous to Africans, West Indians and South Asians. The Immigration Act of 1971 further tightened controls on New Commonwealth immigrants, reflecting the deep-seated fear that too much mixing of non-white peoples would adversely impact the British way of life. It was a view made infamous by Margaret Thatcher in 1978 when she observed that, 'People are really rather afraid that this country might be swamped by people with a different culture.'[37]

EUROPE'S IMMIGRANT 'PROBLEM', 1974–2005

Western Europe's post-war period of rapid growth and underemployment ended in the wake of the oil shocks of 1973 and the fears of recession that followed. As a result the flexible and cost-effective labourers from poor and overpopulated states, or from the post-colonial periphery, were no longer welcome. Since their inception, the guest worker programmes represented an extreme example of the commodification of labour. Unskilled migrants would enter a country on a short-term contract, working long hours for low wages under poor conditions at tasks that were generally avoided by the nation's citizens. The migrant's temporary status reinforced work discipline, for dismissal by an employer carried with it the very real threat of deportation. Employers were relieved of long-term commitments, thereby bolstering profits while allowing for maximum business flexibility. In terms of the advantages that accrued to receiving states, guest workers did not make any claims on social benefits or citizenship rights. In principle, the guest worker systems as originally conceived by post-war governments in Western Europe would jump-start capitalist economies that had been severely damaged during a combined two decades of depression and global warfare. The programmes allowed states to maintain control over access to citizenship, the essential badge of independent statehood, by reducing a significant percentage of the unskilled labour force to the level of material factors in the productive process.[38]

This vision for Western Europe's guest worker programmes began to fray almost immediately after the first cohort of migrants arrived. Rather than send workers home after the conclusion of their initial contracts, employers lobbied for the extension of temporary residence permits. During the 1960s, the demand for labour continued to rise, and as guest workers acquired experience and skills appropriate to their jobs, their status began to take on a level of permanency that was largely unanticipated at the outset. In order to keep these workers and recruit new ones, employers and host governments began to allow for family reunification and in some cases provided resettlement assistance. Workers began to establish residential communities and social organizations. Many joined trade unions, while some intermarried with citizens of the host country. Young couples started families and worked to become better integrated into the dominant culture, although efforts in this area were often rebuffed by racist elements within the majority population.

Since the elimination of the temporary worker programmes on the Continent, and with Britain's more restrictive posture towards members of the Commonwealth, immigration has been treated by most native politicians as a problem rather than an opportunity, as a threat to the receiving state instead of a benefit. In demographic terms, this attitude is puzzling, and speaks to the continuing strength of xenophobic and neo-racist tendencies. Although the world's population has grown at an unprecedented pace since the end of World War II, Europe has not mirrored the global trend. In fact, during the final quarter of the twentieth century, Europe's developed states experienced a sharp decline in birth rates. In Spain and Italy, sending states in the early post-war period but net receiving areas by the 1990s, the drop-off was most pronounced, with an average birth rate of 1.1 children per woman in the late twentieth century. A number of factors account for the anomaly. The widespread availability of modern birth-control technology, better education and a growing awareness of the resource and lifestyle implications of overpopulation had a pronounced effect on the thinking of Europeans at child-bearing age. The desire to enjoy more of the material goods available in the expanding capitalist economies of the West prompted many young couples to engage in family planning. In the area of population management, then, Western Europeans had become the world's model citizens.

But as couples elected to have fewer offspring, politicians and policy planners began to worry about the potential economic impact of demographic free fall. Would a greying European workforce remain competitive in an increasingly global business environment? How could states continue to provide generous retirement and health benefits if the number of younger workers continued to decline?

Would the benefits-rich welfare state, the centrepiece of post-war social policy in most European states, need to be scaled back? Increased immigration offered a compelling solution to the dilemma. In the 1990s, for example, Europe's modest population increase was attributable in large measure to immigration from non-EU countries. By 1993, children born to Europe's 18 million legally resident aliens represented a significant percentage of total births in many European countries: 8.5 per cent in Belgium, 11.7 per cent in England, 10.8 per cent in France, and 14 per cent in Germany. Still, at the end of the century only 5.3 per cent of EU residents were foreign-born, compared to 11 per cent in the US and 25 per cent in Australia.[39] Thus fears of Europe being inundated by foreigners, a common refrain of strident nationalists, were grounded in emotions and prejudices that took little or no account of data from other major receiving areas.

Greater openness in immigration policy seemed to offer tangible benefits over the long term, but most of the EU states, and in particular those that had been at the forefront of the guest worker programmes of the 1960s, remained adamantly opposed to accepting more immigrants from the non-Western world. An indispensable factor in the continent's prospects for twenty-first century economic well-being – a strong pool of working-age adult taxpayers – clashed with a set of deep-seated misconceptions about the impact of people from poor countries on social order, security and national (or European) identity. The misconceptions, fears really, were shared by government officials, the media, educators and the wider public. The erosion of territorial boundaries that marked the process of globalization was, on balance, welcomed by Western Europeans, but the inclusion of people into the process of global exchange, especially people from the Muslim world, represented an untenable disordering of collective identity as embodied in the sovereign territorial state. With between 11 and 13 million non-EU citizens living in the fifteen-member EU at the end of the century, and with asylum claims and illegal entries on the rise, the 'outsider' had replaced the spectre of communism as the greatest threat to the integrity of Western Europe.[40] The question 'who belongs?' took on greater meaning in the representative democracies of the West. And given the secularist political traditions of the leading states within the EU, the religious diversity of immigrant populations further complicated the issue of core national – and European – identity.

Islam and Europe

At the start of the 1970s, Muslims had become the most numerous of the new immigrant populations in Europe. Whereas most other non-Christian groups – Hindus and Sikhs in Britain, Vietnamese in France – were largely restricted to one country, Muslims of various nationalities fanned out across the receiving states of Western Europe. The Turks, Algerians, Moroccans, Surinamese, Indonesians, Indians and Pakistanis who took up jobs as guest workers or as Commonwealth citizens were but the latest representatives of a civilization that had, over many centuries, an enormous impact on life in Europe. From the Arab occupiers of Spain, to the Mongol invaders in Russia, to the Turkish overlords of the Balkans, the armies of an expansive Islamic empire had repeatedly put a less advanced Europe on the defensive.

But the interaction was not limited to the clash of arms. Medieval Muslim scholars like Avicenna, Averros, Ibn Khaldun and many others communicated the culture of Greece and Rome to the Christian West at a time when the European intellectual life was in dire need of assistance. Muslims introduced the West to Indian numbers, where they became known as Arabic numerals, and to new techniques in medicine and the treatment of disease. They also expanded and enriched the diet of medieval Westerners, introducing them to a wide variety of nutritious foods including oranges and lemons, spinach, asparagus and aubergines.[41] Western kingdoms enjoyed a brisk trade with the world of Islam, which under Ottoman direction served a crucial middleman role in the movement of goods from Asia westwards to Europe.

The power relationship between Islam and the West changed dramatically after 1500, and in succeeding centuries the disparity in wealth and influence had become more pronounced in Europe's favour. Europe's imperial age found no parallel among Muslim powers in the nineteenth century, and the collapse of the once feared Ottoman Empire in 1918, together with its replacement by the Western-orientated Republic of Turkey, served to further undermine the prestige of Islamic kingdoms. The Muslim migrants to Western Europe in the post-war period came not as conquerors nor as educators, but as impecunious and unskilled representatives of overpopulated and underdeveloped states.

But even in this modest context they were, each of them, symbols of a longer history of interaction between two related, but often hostile, religious traditions. For if there was a post-war European culture, its main basis was religious, and more specifically Christian. Even if the horrors of war and the inhumanity of the Holocaust had shaken the foundations of religious belief; even if regular church attendance dropped to historic lows during the second half of the century; the one thing that most inhabitants of the north-west corner of the Eurasian land mass shared was their Christian heritage. And that heritage was in large measure shaped by centuries-long conflict with Islam. From the northern flank, where Russian armies battled Mongols and Tartars, to the south-east, where the Holy Roman emperors engaged Turkish and Arab forces, to the Iberian peninsula, where Spanish Christians under Ferdinand and Isabella put an end to a flourishing Islamic civilization, Muslims (along with Jews within Europe) were the quintessential 'other'. That status had briefly been appropriated by communists during the forty-year Cold War, but towards the close of the century it was reassigned, almost instinctively, to the Prophet's followers now resident in Europe. It seemed unlikely that this rich and distinct culture would be easily assimilated or absorbed but, in light of earlier encounters, the question of integration and the limits of multiculturalism were really matters for the majority culture to address.

France, Islam and National Identity

At the start of the twenty-first century France was home to the largest non-European immigrant population in Europe, including over 5 million Muslims, or 10 per cent of its total population. Under the country's liberal nationality laws, children of foreign-born parents were awarded nationality automatically on reaching the age of majority. In addition, the children of naturalized foreigners (those who married a French person or who applied for and secured citizenship) also become citizens. Muslim communities grew rapidly in the decades after the formal end of labour immigration. The 300,000 Algerian Muslims who had settled in France in 1962, for example, had grown into a community of 800,000 by the early 1980s. The result was the gradual formation of a new, racially and religiously diverse French citizenry. But many of these citizens, including the children and grandchildren of post-war migrants who were born and educated in France, did not feel French and believed that their own circumstances made a mockery of the revolutionary ideal of national identity anchored in a commitment to a set of political principles. The question of national identity has been an especially difficult one for France, with its long tradition of secular democracy dating back to the great revolution of 1789. With a colonial experience that assumed the pre-eminent value of French language, cultural forms and political values, the growth of a significant non-European, non-Christian population over the past quarter century challenged the assimilationist tradition. And the challenge centred most directly on France's Muslim minority.

In 1974, following a precedent set by West Germany, the French government instituted a ban on further labour migration involving anyone from outside the European Community and created the first centralized immigration agency, the Secretary of State for Immigration. By this date there were an estimated 3.5 million foreign residents in France, representing almost 6 per cent of the nation's population, a vulnerable cohort whose status as unskilled and semi-skilled workers placed them at a severe disadvantage once recession hit in 1973. Initially the government tried to include family reunification in the ban, but it subsequently retreated from this extreme position, with the result that overall migrant figures continued to grow during the 1970s and '80s.

In 1977, however, the government stepped up the process of deporting undocumented residents, and a plan was introduced to pay foreigners 10,000 francs to leave the country voluntarily. Around 100,000 people took advantage of the offer, but most of these were Portuguese and Spanish, fellow Europeans whom the government was desirous of keeping.[42] The majority of those deported for immigration violations during the late 1970s and early 1980s were North Africans and blacks, since residents of EEC countries were protected under Community agreements. Despite these measures, and the reduction of undocumented entries from a high of 82 per cent in 1968 to a low of 28 per cent in 1983, family reunification insured that the migrant population continued its upward trajectory. By the end of the 1970s there were just over 5 million people of migrant origin living in France, and family members of foreign residents legally living in the country were now afforded the opportunity to work. On the demographic front, migration contributed 15 per cent to overall population growth during the period 1975–86.[43]

During the 1960s the French government had erected numerous urban high-rises that were designed to accommodate residents of old tenements in the cities and poor people from the provinces. The goal was to create vibrant communities in proximity to city centres at reasonable cost. Non-European immigrants began moving into this housing stock in the late 1960s and, for the most part, the facilities were well maintained by the working-class and immigrant tenants. By the 1980s, however, the majority of the native French inhabitants had moved out of the estates as part of a government initiative to bolster home ownership. Most immigrant families, however, were left behind, their efforts to secure better-paying jobs frustrated by a majority culture that engaged in widespread discrimination, some of which was rooted in majority resentment over the fall of empire.

Immigrants – especially Muslim immigrants – stood as a daily reminder of French colonialism, and of the rejection of French authority by colonial elites during the 1960s. Levels of unemployment among France's Tunisian, Moroccan and Algerian population escalated, reaching as high as 40 per cent for young people, and the sprawling housing estates gradually became centres of crime, drug dealing and disillusionment. A police crackdown in 1983 prompted a summer of sporadic rioting in the ghettos and a march for equal rights that began in Lyon and concluded in Paris. President François Mitterrand received a delegation of the marchers in the capital, but few substantive improvements were made in the aftermath of the disturbances.

Instead, the presence of millions of economically and socially marginalized Muslims, the children and grandchildren of guest workers from the 1960s, fuelled new and disturbing demands to link French identity with race and culture. Mitterrand resisted calls from the political right to end the automatic naturalization of children born in France to foreign nationals, but efforts to amend the 'nationality through place of birth' laws continued. Former French president Valéry Giscard d'Estaing was not alone when, in 1991, he called for the abandonment of the revolutionary heritage that identified people with their commitment to a set of common principles. According to d'Estaing, the 'right of blood' should be the sole determinant of citizenship.[44] By the late 1990s the far right in France, led by the xenophobic politician Jean Marie Le Pen, commanded the support of more than a third of the electorate. The leader of the National Front Party, Le Pen denounced what he saw as the 'Islamization' of France resulting from official immigration policies. Increased popular support for stridently anti-immigrant parties led the government to institute a crackdown on illegal immigration in 1993. The so-called 'Pasqua Laws', named after Charles Pasqua, the interior minister, prohibited foreign university students from accepting employment offers upon graduation, increased the waiting period for those pursuing family reunification and limited appeals for refugees who had been denied entry. The new regulations continued in place until 1997, when the Socialists regained control of the National Assembly.

France's strong tradition of secular democracy, and the country's long-standing emphasis on the importance of assimilation and cultural cohesion, led to a series of controversial and highly publicized clashes with Muslim citizens at the opening of the twenty-first century. In February 2004 the government banned the wearing of religious symbols in state schools, including traditional headscarves worn by Muslim women. The following year, as employment prospects for Muslim youth dimmed, levels of frustration with the police, who were assigned to patrol housing estates in the major cities, and with the government's refusal to address the problem of widespread discrimination, escalated into a wave of violence. In October and November of 2005 youths in urban ghettos across the county severely tested an understanding of national identity that was forged during the French Revolution. As thousands of cars were set alight and businesses vandalized by youths from the economically depressed suburbs of major cities, the government seemed unwilling to acknowledge the deeper roots of immigrant fury. Instead, the interior minister, Nicolas Sarkozy, referred to the vandals as 'scum' and President Jacques Chirac's government declared a state of emergency, imposed a curfew in major cities and revived a law to stem civil unrest that was first used during the Algerian war for independence. The riots heightened fear that the growing alienation felt by youth of immigrant parentage would provide an opening for Islamic extremists. Although the majority of young people who lived in the ghettos were non-practising Muslims, the search for identity and meaning in a society that appeared unwilling to accept them only advantaged the proponents of anti-Western extremism.

Germany Reunited: Citizens and Residents

Between the end of the war in 1945 and the fall of the Berlin Wall in 1989, the Federal Republic of Germany became Western Europe's leading receiving country. Eighteen million people had relocated to the Western portion of divided Germany by the end of the Cold War, a figure that was larger than total immigration to the United States over the same period. By 1988, almost half of Germany's foreign-born population – many of them Muslim – had been living in the country for fifteen years or longer.[45] Easing the rules on family reunification, and higher birth rates among immigrant families, had momentous long-term implications for the cherished belief that ethnicity alone defined German citizenship.

Despite the fact that by the end of the century one-tenth of the country's population was foreign-born, most native Germans continued to dismiss the notion that theirs was an immigrant nation. From the very beginning of the guest worker programme, reservations and misgivings were expressed by political figures on both the right and left. In 1964, the Christian Democratic Union chancellor Ludwig Erhard called upon German workers to increase their level of productivity in an effort to ease the country's reliance on foreign workers. A 'foreigners' law' of 1965 stated that a residence permit may be granted 'if it does not hurt the interests of the German Federal Republic'. The vagueness of the law allowed for broad police discretion over the guest worker population. Levels of xenophobia intensified during a brief economic downturn in the late 1960s and again after a wave of strike activity by foreign-born workers at the end of decade. After Chancellor Willy Brandt banned further recruitment of guest workers in November 1973, West Germany's foreign-born inhabitants were increasingly scapegoated and described as a 'problem' population that placed undue strain on the country's social service infrastructure – schools, health services, housing. Polls conducted in the 1980s revealed widespread resentment of the Muslim Turkish population, with two-thirds of Germans supporting repatriation for Turkish immigrants. Financial incentives were offered to encourage return migration in 1983, but very few foreign-born residents accepted the invitation to depart.

After the fall of the Berlin Wall in 1989, official policy towards ethnic Germans from Eastern Europe, and towards inhabitants of the former East Germany, continued the racialized ideology that lay at the core of Germany's understanding of citizenship. The 1949 Constitution of the Federal Republic included an article that afforded citizenship to all ethnic Germans who relocated to the West, and with the collapse of Soviet control hundreds of thousands exercised this option. Some 377,000 migrants arrived during 1989, followed by another 400,000 in 1990. The newcomers, few of whom spoke German, hailed from Romania, Poland, Czechoslovakia, Yugoslavia and Hungary. The host government immediately stepped in to assist with housing accommodation, job training and language classes.[46] Similarly, the 538,000 East Germans who moved into the West during 1989–90 were immediately assisted as fellow citizens.

But long-term foreign residents who were not ethnic Germans, including some 2 million Muslim Turks, continued to struggle to secure comparable privileges. German labourers from the former German Democratic Republic, facing widespread unemployment at home, began to compete with Turks and Slavs who were already established in the

West, although many of the latter had yet to win citizenship rights. 'Germany for Germans' re-emerged as a troubling refrain while elements on the far right invoked the mantra of blood and race as the only legitimate criteria for citizenship claims. Most disturbing of all was the emergence of neo-Nazi groups, some of whose younger adherents engaged in indiscriminate acts of violence against Muslim residents.

Finally, beginning in 1990, a centre-right coalition government introduced a new 'Foreign Law' that enabled second- and third-generation residents to begin the process of naturalization. And in 1999 the socialist government of Gerhard Schröder amended the law to allow for dual citizenship and the automatic granting of German citizenship to third-generation residents. Children of foreign-national parents who had been resident in Germany for at least eight years were awarded temporary dual citizenship and at the age of 23 they were required to choose between German citizenship and that of their parents. These political moves to broaden the definition of German citizenship did not serve to lessen the incidence of racial attacks against non-native residents by extreme right groups, nor did it fully dispel the myth of Germany as a 'non-immigration' state.[47] But the concessions to long-term residents, the majority of whom were Muslim, represented an important commitment on the part of the German government to end decades of denial regarding the practical consequences of the guest worker programme. Non-European men and women who for years had supported the state pension fund, paid local and federal taxes and played a pivotal role in the nation's service and trades sectors were at last included in a more expansive understanding of German nationhood.

ILLEGALS, REFUGEES AND THE EUROPEAN UNION

During the 1980s, as the bulk of legal immigration focused on family reunification, the attention of European states – and the European Community – shifted to the control of illegal immigration and the adjudication and management of refugee cases. In the early 1970s, illegal immigrants were estimated to make up approximately 10 per cent of the total foreign population in Western Europe, and the number continued to rise as the century closed.[48] The emergence of sophisticated smuggling networks made the work of border officials more difficult while endangering the lives of those who paid high fees to criminals who organized the illicit transport. Appeals from displaced refugees also increased. All of Europe's industrialized democracies were signatories of the 1951 Geneva Convention, which guaranteed asylum for those persons with a 'well founded fear of persecution on the basis of race, religion, political opinion, or belonging to a particular social group'. And most Western European states had observed their obligations during the Cold War, accepting refugees from the Communist bloc as a matter of course.

The situation changed dramatically in the 1990s, however, as post-Cold War regional conflicts and civil strife around the globe generated a sharp increase in the number of asylum applications. In Germany, for example, there were 200,000 claims in 1991 alone. Mindful of the horrible persecution carried out under the Nazi regime, German policy allowed anyone claiming asylum as a political refugee the right of entry while the case was examined – a process that could take years. The number of people seeking asylum in the EU during the 1990s grew to almost half a million, or approximately one-third of the total number of migrants, each year. This compared unfavourably with the United States during the same period, where fewer than 10 per cent of migrants gained entry under the refugee heading. Of this total, 43 per cent were from other European countries, 19 per cent were from African nations, and 35 per cent were from Asia.[49] In general the non-European asylum seekers were victims of ethnic civil conflict in places like the former Yugoslavia, Afghanistan, Iraq and Somalia. Their appeals were made more poignant due to the fact that regional conflicts were broadcast on television news throughout the developed world.

Sorting through the claims and distinguishing the legitimate political refugees from economic migrants intent on abusing the system was a difficult and time-consuming process. During the 1990s the term 'asylum seeker' was increasingly employed to denote someone whose bona fides as a refugee had yet to be proven. Public upset over rising numbers of asylum claims (and suspicion that many asylum seekers were really economic migrants) complicated efforts to develop uniform and enforceable policies regarding the rules for reception, examination and adjudication. EU countries tried, with varying levels of success, to persuade sending countries to accept the return of asylum seekers who had been denied admission. States like Italy, Germany and Austria, where the number of asylum claims and illegal residents was high during the 1990s, proposed a burden-sharing system within the EU, but this was rejected by other member states. Since national sovereignty had always been closely associated with control over borders, there remained strong reluctance on the part of many EU states to surrender final jurisdiction in this area to a supranational authority.[50]

Not surprisingly, the presence of large numbers of 'illegals' and the surge in asylum applications contributed to a further politicization of European migration policy. Economic migrants who represented themselves as refugees had the effect of alienating public opinion from migrants. Resurgent nationalism, ethnocentrism, xenophobia and outright racism, quiescent for much of the post-war period, strengthened under the guise of an imagined core identity now under siege, the notion that the peoples of Europe constituted distinct, stable and immutable social and cultural units. Questions of national identity remained at the foreground of public debate during the 1990s and early 2000s, with critics bemoaning the 'failure' of refugees to assimilate and alleging that the rhetoric of multiculturalism was a one-way street obliging the majority population to accept all levels of cultural separateness – and all applicants for asylum.

One of the more controversial figures in this debate was the writer, politician and successful entrepreneur, Pim Fortuyn. An openly gay figure known as a reformer in his hometown of Rotterdam, Fortuyn questioned the compatibility of Islam with Western secular values after two imams called for the death penalty for homosexuals. In 2002 Fortuyn's political movement, called Liveable Rotterdam, captured sixteen city council seats (36 per cent) on a platform that included a 'zero Muslim immigration' policy. Although he was assassinated later that same year, when like-minded politicians won 26 of the 150 seats in the lower house of the Dutch parliament, mainstream parties began to oppose further Muslim immigration.[51]

At the level of the European Community, officials failed repeatedly to reach agreement on a comprehensive plan for the control of illegal migration or for the admission of legitimate refugees. It was not for lack of trying. As early as the mid 1970s, justice and interior ministers from leading EC states had formed the so-called Trevi group to formulate and advance consensus solutions on issues ranging from cross-border crime to grants of permanent asylum. And in 1985, in an effort to open up inner-EC frontiers, France, Germany and the Benelux countries, at a meeting in the tiny Luxemburg town of Schengen, agreed to end all border post formalities for their respective citizens. In subsequent years the initial signatories were joined by Greece, Italy, Spain and Portugal. But Britain, Ireland and Denmark, citing ongoing security concerns, declined to join the supranational 'Schengen Group'.

The real trigger to coordinated action was the 1989 collapse of Communism in Eastern Europe. Fearful that the implosion would lead to a massive East–West exodus, the twelve EC member states met in December and declared their 'right and duty to combat illegal migration'.[52] The 1990 Dublin Convention, whose provisions became effective in 1997, established rules to prevent migrants from 'asylum shopping', the practice of submitting multiple applications in different European Union countries, and for determining which EU state had jurisdiction in an asylum case. EU member states also participated in a number of international conferences on migration during the 1990s, including those sponsored by the UN's High Commissioner for Human Rights, the International Organization for Migration, and the Organization for Economic Cooperation and Development. At a meeting in Paris in 1991, delegates signed the European Convention on Security and Cooperation in Europe, whose goal was to create a wider European space where essential human rights were respected. The Convention put an end to asylum applications from Eastern European states like Poland and Hungary. Later in the decade, the newly liberated states of Eastern Europe agreed to begin receiving some asylum seekers of their own on terms similar to those established by countries in Western Europe. But the break-up of Yugoslavia in the early 1990s and the terrible refugee crisis that ensued as successor states descended into ethnic civil war pointed up the still considerable limits of emerging transnational policy.[53]

Balkan Refugees

Religious and ethnic chauvinism was by no means the monopoly of Western Europeans. With the collapse of Communism and the implosion of the Soviet Empire, issues surrounding minority rights, religious differences and ethnic nationalism precipitated bloody civil conflicts from the Balkans eastward to Russian-controlled Chechnya. Demands for political autonomy based on ethnic identity replaced the solidarity of peoples in the former Soviet sphere of influence, leading to the 'othering' of long-established minority peoples, acts of discrimination, racist assaults and the resort to arms. In the Balkans, it was the opportunistic Serb leader Slobodan Milosevic who first fanned the flames of ethnic nationalism and helped to destroy whatever opportunity remained in the post-Tito era for a democratic Yugoslavia. The upsurge in Serbian nationalism was matched in neighbouring Croatia where Franjo Tudjman demanded an independent Croatian state whose boundaries would include a significant Serb minority. Considerable financial support for the independence drive came from Croatian emigrant communities in Canada, the United States and Europe. Declaring independence in June 1991, Croatia subsequently joined with Serbia in the partition of Bosnia-Herzegovina, where restive Croat and Serbian minorities chafed under a largely Muslim government located in Sarajevo.

Fighting erupted in Bosnia in 1992 as the minority populations declared their own break-away republics. The Serbian siege of the Bosnian capital of Sarajevo in 1994, where the deaths of innocent civilians filled the evening television news programmes with brutal regularity, and Serbia's savage 'ethnic cleansing' that forever marked this conflict, failed to prompt a coordinated EU response. Member states disagreed over how best to intervene in the spreading conflict, and when a joint UN–EU peace plan for Bosnia was rejected by the warring parties in 1993, the Community was reduced to providing humanitarian assistance, while individual member states contributed soldiers to the UN peacekeeping force. Only US leadership and heavy NATO air attacks in 1995 brought the Serbian atrocities in Bosnia to an end. The Dayton Accords of 1995, although signed in Paris, emphasized the predominant role of the United States in the region. The EU's attempt to create a formidable defence and security apparatus was a shambles.[54]

Confusion and disagreement also marked the EU response to the refugee crisis that was created by the conflict. Bosnians began fleeing to neighbouring states and the EU as early as 1992 and, given the widespread occurrence of 'ethnic cleansing', the migrants clearly qualified as refugees under the terms of the 1951 Geneva Convention. By 1995 there were just under 350,000 Bosnian refugees in Germany and half that number again in the other EU states combined. The process of repatriation was slow after the fighting ended in 1995, however, even though the host countries had insisted all along that they were providing only temporary residence until peace and stability returned.

When a second refugee crisis erupted in 1998 after Serbia unleashed its military against Albanians in the southern province of Kosovo, EU countries refused to accept additional victims of repression. Instead, a pledge of assistance was made to refugees living in neighbouring states, ostensibly on the grounds that by accepting additional refugees in Western Europe the EU was playing into the hands of Milosevic, who would welcome the permanent removal of the majority Albanian population. When it became apparent that the aid was inadequate to the task in a war zone, EU member states reluctantly agreed to offer temporary protection to Kosovo refugees. A total of 85,000 places were assigned, and approximately 50,000 had been evacuated before Serb forces were forced to withdraw in the wake of NATO air attacks on Belgrade. But very public bickering within the EU over burden sharing and the pace of evacuation to certain host countries pointed up the still fragile nature of EU coordination efforts.[55]

As support for asylum seekers waned during the final decade of the twentieth century, populist anti-immigration parties gained broad electoral support. These parties achieved significant advances in Austria, Denmark, Belgium and France, demonstrating the power of xenophobic politics at the very moment when the EU was expanding into Central and Eastern Europe. The most surprising advance for the far right occurred in France in 2002, when Jean Marie Le Pen, candidate for the anti-immigration National Front Party, defeated the mainstream Socialist Party candidate in the first round of the presidential elections, sending shockwaves through the political establishment. Eventually defeated by incumbent President Jacques Chirac, the results alarmed EU leaders who had long been supportive of a common immigration policy. In response to the popular backlash, however, the EU withheld from new member states in Eastern Europe the right to the free movement of peoples across borders for a period of seven years, thus striking at one of the four main elements of the Single European Act of 1987.[56] While extremist anti-immigrant parties were not able to triumph in national elections, they were able to drive mainstream parties to adopt some elements of anti-immigrant rhetoric.

Indeed, immigration policy became the source of more than a little ideological discomfort for both the political right and left in Europe. Conservative politicians, strong supporters of market-based approaches to economic development, found themselves defending labour migration on economic grounds, while simultaneously expressing concern that large numbers of foreign migrants weakened civic culture, diluted national identity and, in an age of global terror, occasionally provided a security risk. Political liberals, on the other hand, generally supported the principle of freedom of movement across international borders as a fundamental human right, but also felt obliged to defend the position of domestic unions and labour organizations that viewed new arrivals as a threat to jobs and a living wage. In 2005, second- and third-generation descendants of Europe's guest worker population continued to find themselves treated as the outsiders within, disadvantaged in terms of economic opportunity, resented because of their unwillingness to fully assimilate and the subject of intense debate over the contours of national – and European – identity. Their contested status in the new Europe was very different from the experience of Europeans who in early centuries had themselves sought a better life in new lands overseas. Sadly, the idea of Europe involved by definition an idea of that which is not Europe.

IMAGINED COMMUNITIES

In many respects, post-war Europe was ideally situated to realize the promise of integration and to set a new precedent of liberal inclusion with respect to the movement of peoples. With the need for additional workers paramount, we have seen how Western European countries hosted a variety of ambitious and creative newcomers, both from former colonies and from poorer states around the Mediterranean basin. Arriving initially as temporary labourers but eventually securing permanent residency for themselves and their families, these non-European immigrants were essential to Western Europe's economic recovery after World War II. Just as economic globalization anticipated a 'world without borders' with respect to the movement of goods, services and finance, post-war Western Europe's status as an immigration zone signalled new possibilities for the supranational integration of peoples. After centuries of exporting human resources, Europe was now in a position to rebuild with the assistance of talent from a variety of sending zones, including Muslim-majority ones.

Few of these possibilities have been realized, however, and more recently a mood of disquiet about further immigration (especially Muslim immigration) has gripped the member states of the EU. It is a mood rooted partly in the history of modern nationalism. Most contemporary opponents of immigration to Europe subscribe to a conception of the nation state that was invented during the nineteenth century by intellectuals and politicians for the purpose of cultivating a shared identity across what for centuries had been loosely autonomous regions.[57] Fastening on a mythical 'moment of birth' in the early Middle Ages, modern nationalists maintained that a people's identity was somehow fixed during the first millennium and that newcomers always pose a threat to the integrity of an otherwise immutable and homogeneous culture. The constituent elements of that essential culture were sometimes in debate, but that there existed a metaphysical core that *could* be identified was never in doubt.

It is all too easy to forget that Europe's present nation states are the result of multiple waves of migrations over the centuries, reaching as far back as the speakers of Indo-European languages who overspread and absorbed what may have been the indigenous populations of south-eastern Europe. Similarly, Celtic, Roman, Germanic, Slavic, Magyar, Scandinavian and Turkic peoples all underwent periods of migration into European lands that were already occupied.[58]

Contemporary French and German nationalists will allow for, even celebrate, the arrival of Francs and Saxons into lands formally controlled by the Romans but apparently no parallel allowance can be made for modern-day Algerians or Turks. In the aftermath of the formation of modern nation states, it seems, opportunities for the future unfolding of national identities, the enrichment of culture through the infusion of new ideas and traditions, is precluded. The fact that intra-European migration continued during the modern period – Italians, Portuguese and Spaniards to France, for example – seems unimportant.[59] The imagined communities of the modern world, polemical inventions of nascent nationalists in the nineteenth century, have effectively undermined the possibility of cultural evolution.

And yet the idea of European Union posits the existence of a shared cultural and historical legacy, and the potential for common policies in light of this bond. The process of deconstructing centuries-old intra-European borders, and the extreme nationalist ideology that fuelled two world wars, had begun modestly with the creation of the European Coal and Steel Community in 1952, involving six nations in a project to eliminate tariffs and promote economic recovery. By 1958 this free trade zone had expanded to include all industrial and agricultural goods, capital and services. France and West Germany led the effort, but early members of what became the European Economic Community (EEC) included Belgium, the Netherlands and tiny Luxembourg.

The success of this Common Market was immediate, and by the early 1970s and '80s additional states were acquired, including Britain, Ireland, Spain, Denmark and Greece. Even Muslim-majority Turkey was extended associate status in 1963. The full potential of a free trade bloc of over 300 million people was outlined with the creation of the twelve-state European Union (EU) in 1994, the adoption of a single currency in 1999 and the expansion of the Union into Eastern Europe in 2004. Under the EU, insular nationalism began to give way to genuine economic integration (symbolized by the euro) and the drawing down of borders between member states. The Single European Act, signed in Luxemburg in 1986 and re-affirmed by the 1997 Treaty of Amsterdam, embraced the earlier EEC commitment to open borders within the Community.

The 25 nations of the EU have committed, however haltingly, to the prospect of a transnational identity, of fluid and permeable borders where the acceptance of difference is allowed. In certain respects, EU 'nationalism' has recaptured the values of the nation state as they first took form during the period of the American and French Revolutions, and before the parochialisms of the nineteenth century intruded into the equation. The European idea is in part guided by the Enlightenment's emphasis on humanity's capacity for action informed by reason. With sovereignty anchored in the actions of an enlightened citizenry, the nation state was conceived as a mechanism for protecting and advancing universal human rights. State sovereignty and jurisdiction was limited to discreet territorial boundaries, but state influence was transnational insofar as each nation upheld the values of human equality, personal freedom and religious inclusion. When Jefferson wrote in the Declaration of Independence that certain truths were 'self evident' and that 'the laws of nature and nature's God' were of universal application, he was making epistemological and moral claims that transcended national frontiers. The United States deserved independence from Britain, Jefferson held, but the formation of a new nation could only be legitimized insofar as the citizens and their elected leaders upheld the principles of universal human rights. The German philosopher Immanuel Kant, in his 1795 defence of 'hospitality' for aliens, directly applied these universal principles to migrants, insisting upon 'the right of a stranger not to be treated with hostility when he arrives on someone else's territory'.[60]

The growing importance of understanding politics in terms of individual rights that take no account of cultural difference has been of special significance to migrants. Only recently have European governments come to acknowledge the importance of better integrating their minority populations into mainstream national life. To not do so, to continue to host a significant population of resident aliens who are denied citizenship and opportunities for material improvement, is to deny the equalitarian vision of the Enlightenment.

The rise of anti-immigrant political parties, acts of discrimination and violence against foreign-born residents, increasing levels of anger amongst urban dwellers who feel trapped in decaying ghettos and the potential appeal of radical Islam for marginalized youth all contribute to the heightened level of awareness of immigrant aspirations. Only now are European states recognizing that they are, in fact, zones of immigration. There were over 13 million non-resident foreign nationals living in the EU in 2003, or around 4 per cent of the total population. In global context, of course, these numbers are really quite modest, making the widespread perception of a 'migration crisis' in Europe rather ironic. Despite the fact that as recently as the early 1970s more people left the continent than arrived in it, and even though migration to Europe remains small when compared with current outflows to other countries around the world, perception continues to shape popular opinion and government action.[61]

Unfortunately, aside from ad hoc intergovernmental agreements, there was no EU-wide strategy for addressing migration from non-EU countries. And there was certainly no consensus on how to address the increasing alienation felt by young Muslim residents. The euphoria surrounding the end of the Cold War and the integration of European peoples in the early 1990s had given way by the second year of the twenty-first century to a heightened sense of distrust and suspicion on the part of Europe's native stock. Unassimilated immigrants, especially unemployed and disaffected Muslim youth, posed a new challenge to the democratic West.

In autumn 2004, the Dutch film-maker Theo van Gogh, having recently completed a controversial film titled *Submission*, was gunned down and stabbed to death on an Amsterdam street by a 26 year-old Dutch-born Muslim named Mohammed Bouyeri. The film involved the alleged harsh and unequal treatment of women in Islamic countries. At his sentencing for murder, Bouyeri declared that 'the law compels me to chop off the head of anyone who insults Allah and the Prophet'. In the aftermath of the brutal killing, anti-Muslim violence affected schools, shops and mosques across the Netherlands. And the dangerous trends continued. In summer 2005, British-born Muslim suicide bombers attacked London's underground system, alienated Muslim youth rioted in cities across France and, a few months later, anti-Muslim cartoons in a Danish newspaper prompted widespread condemnation across the Muslim world. With some estimates projecting that Muslims will become a majority in some German, French and

Dutch cities within a generation, a chasm of distrust, bred by decades of social and economic marginalization, was threatening the very fabric of Europe's open, liberal and secular societies.[62]

With increasing migration flows around the world, the priority of the EU in the early 2000s became internal security and the integrity of Union frontiers, not the promotion of greater freedom and equality for non-European residents and citizens. The increasingly restrictionist immigration posture does not bode well for the future of the Union in terms of global political influence and economic prowess. 'Fortress Europe' will be an ageing and underproductive collection of developed states whose existing health and pension systems will be funded by a shrinking workforce. With net migration contributing up to 70 per cent of the EU's total population growth in 1997, the policy of exclusion appears, from a purely economic standpoint, increasingly untenable. From the vantage point of universal human rights and democratic participation, exclusion appears morally problematic. As two observers noted in the mid 1990s, 'Europe's problems of a declining and ageing population with high material demands and expectation have to be faced in the context of a still rapidly growing world population that looks to Europe and elsewhere in the developed world for its expectations of what can be achieved in material progress.'[63] 'Looking to Europe' continues ten years later and, as we will see in succeeding chapters, the 'New Europe' is not alone in its ambivalence over the emergence of poly-ethnic societies. But within the context of current demographic trends, Europe's ability to embrace a wider definition of community will be key to its status in the emerging global century.

Chapter 2

North–South Divide in the Americas

It is one of the larger ironies of the modern era that North and South America, both settled and developed by Europeans after a terrible epidemiological disaster shattered native populations in the sixteenth and seventeenth centuries, remain continents at odds. It is as though the old rivalry between the Spanish Habsburg and English Tudor dynasties, a chasm borne of religious division in the mid sixteenth century, still overshadows every element of commonality that exists across artificial and arbitrary borders. Spanish and English, poverty and plenty, Catholic and Protestant, agriculture and industry – the antinomies are as deep as they are wide. And behind each of them lie a priori assumptions about culture, economic initiative and capacity for self-government that always reflect poorly on the Hispanic South. By the year 2000 Latin America had become an unflattering anomaly within the spectrum of sending and receiving zones. A European destination area for over 400 years, Central and South America devolved into a net emigration region during the post-war decades. Burgeoning populations, troubled democracies, recurring debt crises, high unemployment and chronic poverty had combined to drive increasing numbers of people to the jobs and material opportunities associated with life in North America.[1]

And it was not merely the unskilled who ventured or fled to *El norte*, although it was most often the image of the poor day labourer or undocumented domestic that framed media stereotypes. In reality the movement also involved the departure of educated men and women from a number of countries. For example, just over half of the Latino immigrants in the US in 2000 were high school graduates, while only a fifth of the total population of Latin America held a degree. Eighty-five per cent of South Americans living in the US had a secondary education or better, and in the case of the Caribbean islands of Jamaica and Haiti, two-thirds of their college-educated citizens were resident in the US.

Of course human capital has long been considered an essential resource for developing countries seeking to join the ranks of the industrial North. Even if educated expatriates remitted large sums to families in their native country – and in the case of Latin America recent figures of $32 billion in remittances outstripped all direct foreign investment – the talent pool was being employed most directly to advance the interests of the destination country.[2] The multi-year investment in education made by the sending country – often at public expense – furthered the new global economy in stable democracies that already enjoyed a significant advantage over neighbours in Latin America. There remains much debate within scholarly circles over the net impact of so-called 'brain drain' on sending countries, but whatever the economic consequences, the loss of talented and dynamic individuals from emerging cultures is always to be lamented.

Post-war migration out of Latin America and between states in the region had the unhappy result of perpetuating an image of the people of the resource-rich continent as feckless and incapable of effective self-government. Refugees fled before the depredations of dictators who assumed the mantle of populist saviours; landless labourers from a variety of countries were smuggled across Mexico's extensive border with Texas, California, Arizona and New Mexico as source countries lurched from crisis to crisis; and Cuban political exiles in South Florida excoriated the failed socialist experiment in their homeland and looked with longing to the death of Castro. What is often overlooked in such critiques is the century-long unequal relationship between Latin America and the superpower to the north. US interference in the affairs of Latin America can be traced back from mid nineteenth-century military conflict with Mexico, to 'big stick' diplomacy carried out by President Theodore Roosevelt during the early 1900s, to Cold War directives, orchestrated coups and economic interventions after 1945.

As late as the 1990s, as the majority of countries in Latin America struggled to come to grips with massive foreign debt – much of it assumed during the 1970s when Western banks, flush with deposits from Middle East oil kingdoms, giddily encouraged borrowing – the contours of economic restructuring were mandated by international institutions like the World Bank and the International Monetary Fund that were ever mindful of US preferences. Despite its long history as a European colonial sphere of influence; despite its independence struggles and embrace of Enlightenment political values in the early nineteenth century; despite its attraction as a destination continent for millions of Europeans during the great era of migration in the late nineteenth century; and despite a tapestry of cultures that included African, Amerindian, European and mestizo peoples, Latin America was viewed by many in the North as having failed, and when migrants from this troubled continent entered the North, they did so carrying this unfair burden with them.

CONFLICTED HOST: MIGRATION TO THE UNITED STATES

The United States began as the quintessential settler-state. The aboriginal population, estimated to be as high as 5 to 10 million at the start of the sixteenth century, was reduced to a fraction of that total by the inadvertent arrival of European pathogens. Deadly smallpox, measles, typhus and influenza epidemics translated into a mortality rate of 90 per cent or more in some areas, making the impact of the Columbian voyages, in the words of historian Alfred Crosby, 'the transformation of America into a charnel house'.[3] Even with this demographic catastrophe, however, migration from Europe to Britain's North American colonies was modest throughout the seventeenth and eighteenth centuries, with net immigration estimated at around 500,000. This figure included settlers from Britain, Ireland, the German principalities, Swiss cantons and Dutch cities.[4] Emigration to French-speaking

Canada was even more limited, with fewer than 50,000 settlers of European origin in the giant colony when it was surrendered to the British in 1763.

Transportation under sail was simply beyond the means of most common people who would have otherwise considered emigration to the New World. Indeed much of the white population that did travel to one of Britain's North American colonies did so under some form of indenture where the cost of passage was paid in kind through a defined term of labour. Thanks to the advent of steamship transport and an insatiable demand for unskilled labour along the country's industrial and urban eastern seaboard, the late nineteenth century was the great age of European migration to the US. By 1910 almost 15 per cent of the country's population had been born in a foreign country.

Although the early US was defined by European and West African sending zones, waves of anti-immigrant sentiment have punctuated its history. African labour was central to plantation economies, but African humanity was reduced to a property equation. In the mid eighteenth century Benjamin Franklin worried about the failure of German settlers in Pennsylvania colony to teach their children English.[5] From 'Know-Nothing' politics during the first wave of Irish Catholic migration in the 1850s, to discriminatory laws that excluded Chinese workers in the 1880s, to the race-based National Origins Act of 1924, fears that the assimilative power of the majority culture might be overwhelmed by force of numbers and diversity of sending countries has repeatedly informed public opinion to the detriment of newcomers. Yet the unprecedented success of the US economy, a jobs-creating juggernaut that with rare exceptions called for additional human resources in agriculture, industry and services, necessitated the constant influx of peoples from abroad. And at no time was this more strikingly the case than in the post-World War II environment. Relatively few immigrants were received during two decades of depression and war, but after 1945 a booming economy, combined with a slowdown in the rate of US population growth, once again made the US a prime destination – and immigrant labour essential to a growing consumer and service-orientated lifestyle.

How many immigrants would be needed, with what particular skill sets, and on what terms were questions that found no satisfactory answer in late twentieth-century America. In any case, events often outpaced reflection and deliberation on the matter. In particular, the 'Latinization' of the US took place in very rapid order, with the greatest acceleration occurring during the final decade of the century. Of special significance for Latinos was the landmark US Immigration and Nationality Act Amendments of 1965, which swept away the odious national origins quota system. In its place was erected a model whereby occupational criteria and family reunification took precedence irrespective of the source country. Before this historic shift, almost three-quarters of immigrants in the US were from source countries in Europe. At the close of the century, on the other hand, more than 75 per cent of foreign-born residents began their journeys from Asia or Latin America.

The number of foreign-born Latin Americans in the US was under 1 million in 1960, but another million arrived through official, documented channels during the 1960s. Admissions continued to grow thereafter. As civil wars plagued much of Central America, and as stringent 'neo-liberal' monetary reforms necessitated drastic cuts in social spending in most South American countries, the influx grew by 2.8 million during the 1980s. The 1986 Immigration Reform and Control Act granted amnesty to undocumented immigrants who had resided in the US for a defined period of time. Finally, in the 1990s both legal and illegal entries accelerated as the low-wage, unskilled job sector in the US expanded. Overall, more immigrants (11 million) entered the US during the 1990s than at any other ten-year period in American history. Approximately 4.6 million of the newcomers were Latinos who had entered legally, and almost certainly the number of undocumented migrants was just as large. By 2001 the overall population of foreign-born and first-generation people in the US neared one out of every five inhabitants.[6]

Much of the remarkable growth in emigration was linked to the demographic relationship between South and North America, and to the respective economic and political profiles of each continent. In 1960 Latin America's total population was in the region of 218 million.

The combined American and Canadian population that same year was 199 million. But while the North American economic powerhouses had grown to 307 million people by 2000, the total population for Latin America had surged to over 520 million. In Mexico and Brazil, the continent's two most populous countries, half the population in the year 2000 was under the age of fifteen, and neither economy could generate enough jobs to meet demand.

In addition to sheer numbers, a diversity of sending areas characterized post-war migrant flows to the US. While Mexico remained the leading source country, a greater number of Central Americans from Guatemala, Honduras, El Salvador and Nicaragua began arriving, often as exiles and refugees, beginning in the 1980s. By the end of the century these migrants numbered almost 2 million. Another 1.8 million had arrived by the year 2000 from destinations in South America as geographically diverse as Colombia and Chile. When considered within the context of mounting debt and a severe downturn in the economic climate throughout the continent starting in the 1980s (when Latin America's GDP fell almost 10 per cent), together with the debilitating effects of civil war, military coups and the rise in violence associated with the massive international drugs trade, the northward migration phenomenon became for many a matter of basic survival.[7]

As the absolute number of immigrants began to exceed the totals for the early twentieth century, and as the Spanish language was heard increasingly on buses, in bakeries and other public places, renewed concerns emerged over the perceived failure of immigrants to assimilate into the American mainstream. Unsubstantiated allegations that immigrants from Latin America used a disproportionate share of public services and welfare benefits began to have a negative impact on public policy. Federal and state governments started to limit immigrants' access to a host of social programmes. In perhaps the most controversial move, California voters in 1994 passed Proposition 187, effectively denying undocumented residents access to state schools and medical care. It may have been appropriate to employ these residents to harvest the nation's produce and to clean its hotels, but the new law required public employees and law enforcement professionals to report suspected illegal residents to the US Immigration and Naturalization Service. On suspicion that immigrants did not 'pay their way', two years later the federal government passed a Welfare Reform Act that withdrew benefits such as Medicaid and food stamps from non-citizens. And in the aftermath of 9/11 new security protocols placed even greater barriers to immigration.

During 2006, as Congress wrangled over additional immigration reform legislation, citizen groups calling themselves 'Minutemen' began patrolling the border with Mexico as unwelcome adjuncts to the official border police. The target population of the extralegal surveillance was a Mexican workforce eager to take on the abundant low-wage jobs in America's agricultural, construction and service sectors, the very types of jobs that Americans consistently avoided. With 33.5 million foreign-born residents in the country, or almost 12 per cent of the total population, the 'nation of immigrants' label still applied, but the national political climate was anything but welcoming. Yet even in the face of a harsher public attitude, the United States remained the golden door for Latin America's economic and political migrants. In July 2001, the US Census Bureau announced that residents of Hispanic origin had surpassed the African–American population for the designation as largest national minority. Almost 39 million Latinos, a figure greater than Canada's total population, resided in the US. And a full 30 per cent of these Latinos were non-citizens.[8]

Mexican–Americans

The history of ethnic Mexicans in North America can be traced back some four centuries, to early settlements like St Augustine, Florida, and Santa Fe, New Mexico. Of course, the so-called 'northern territories' of Arizona and New Mexico, together with large sections of present-day California, Nevada, Utah, Wyoming, Kansas and Texas, were part of the Mexican Republic until they were lost to revolutionary Texas in 1836 and to the US in the war of 1846-8. The Treaty of Guadalupe Hidalgo that ended the war rearranged the boundaries between the two nations 'and made parts of the Southwest previously open to Mexicans technically off limits'.[9] The westward expansion of the US involved the incorporation of some 75–100,000 Spanish-speaking residents before the mid-nineteenth century. More recently, Mexicans have crossed the 1,900-mile common border into the US for economic reasons. Beginning in the 1870s, railroad contractors and agricultural concerns recruited low-wage workers who were easily discarded when the business climate was unfavourable. The chaos experienced during the Mexican Revolution of 1910–19 drove additional thousands northward for political reasons.[10] The Immigration Act of 1917 imposed a literacy requirement and a fee on prospective migrants, but this had little impact on the considerable flow of illegal workers who were hired with impunity by American firms. After the US entered World War I in April 1917, President Woodrow Wilson authorized the US Employment Service to act as contractors with Mexican workers as they entered the country. Historians estimate that as much as 10 per cent of Mexico's population (or 1.5 million people) migrated north to the US during the first three decades of the twentieth century.[11]

By 1929 the overwhelming majority of Mexican workers were located in the border states of Texas, New Mexico, Arizona and California. During the Great Depression there was a large (perhaps as high as 350,000) repatriation as job prospects in the US collapsed, but with America's entry into World War II the need for domestic labour again increased. A major bilateral agreement established the 'Bracero Program' (1942–64) whereby thousands of Mexican agricultural workers were admitted on a temporary basis to maintain domestic food stocks. Supply soon outstripped demand, however, and large numbers of illegal migrants competed with official Bracero participants for low-wage agricultural work in the US. By 1954 the first of many backlashes against undocumented workers led to 'Operation Wetback' in which federal agents of the Immigration and Naturalization Service deported thousands to Mexico. The Bracero Program officially ended in 1964; over 4.5 million Mexican workers had participated during the twenty-year experiment and, despite the new restrictions, the attraction of employment prospects in the US fuelled a continuing trend towards temporary labour.[12]

The outflow from Mexico is somewhat paradoxical in light of the fact that the country's post-war economic development was in large measure successful. In the 1960s and '70s the Mexican government exploited the country's vast oil reserves and invested in a variety of job-producing public projects in road construction, communications, transit and irrigation. Advances in education, health care and electrification improved the lives of millions of Mexicans, creating what some referred to as the 'Mexican miracle'. But a doubling of the population from 20 to 40 million between 1940 and 1970, together with government inefficiencies, cronyism and corruption, hampered efforts to create jobs fast enough.[13] A slump in world oil prices beginning in 1981 reduced dramatically projected foreign exchange earnings, forcing the government to borrow heavily in overseas markets. As a major fiscal crisis loomed, emergency loans from the US and the IMF were made available on condition that a severe austerity plan be implemented. The plan included phasing out subsidies on food and public utilities, thus exacerbating the gap between rich and poor. By 1985 real wages had fallen by 40 per cent from their 1982 level, prompting a further movement north.[14] In the US, efforts to penalize employers who hired undocumented workers were lacklustre; despite a growing anti-immigrant sentiment during the inflationary 1970s, powerful business interests – especially in agribusiness – were successful in efforts to deflect federal attention from the issue.

As noted above, in 1986 the US Congress passed the Immigration Reform and Control Act, giving undocumented workers an opportunity to legalize their status. The legislation granted an amnesty for businesses that had circumvented earlier laws, but imposed tougher sanctions on employers who knowingly hired illegal migrants. Instead of decreasing immigration, however, many newly legalized residents took the opportunity under provisions in the law to bring their families to the US. In 1980 the US Census Bureau reported approximately 2 million Mexicans living legally in the country, and a decade later the figure had doubled. It doubled again in the 1990s. Although controversial in both countries, the 1992 North American Free Trade Agreement (NAFTA) had as one of its goals the stabilization of Mexico's economy through direct foreign investment and job creation. And some US companies were attracted by the possibility of accessing Mexico's low-wage labour force by moving operations south of the border. But in the end NAFTA had limited short-term impact on domestic job creation, and by 2000 almost 8 per cent of Mexico's population, approximately 8.5 million people, resided and worked in the US, making this the single largest out-migration in the world at the beginning of the new century.[15]

Although better-educated and highly skilled Mexicans were hired in the US, the vast majority of newcomers were poor, and 3 million remained undocumented. Almost all of them immediately found work in an expanding economy. Between 1993 and 1997, nearly 11 per cent of Mexicans who departed for the US had been unemployed at home, and from 1998 to 2000 the total increased to 17.3 per cent. By the latter date almost 10 per cent of Mexico's entire labour force was resident in the US.[16] A strong network of social contacts in the source country made it easier for new migrants – including illegals – to find lodging and assistance with the job search. Traditional destinations in the Southwest expanded to include newer receiving states like Mississippi, North Carolina, Georgia, Kansas and New York.[17] While still concentrated in the less secure agricultural sector, Mexican migrants were increasingly found in urban centres, working in construction, meatpacking and the omnipresent domestic service industry. In Illinois, for example, 1.1 million Mexicans were employed in a variety of sectors at the start of the twenty-first century.[18]

The scale of recent Mexican migration to the US had an enormous impact not only on the lives of the newcomers, but also on the economic well-being of those family members who remained behind. Even though Mexican workers were situated almost exclusively in the low-pay job sector of the American economy, remittances during the 1990s totalled over $45 billion, affecting over a million Mexican families and often providing the difference between life on the margins and a modest standard of living. The strength of the American economy during the 1990s and the availability of work was a powerful incentive to prospective migrants from virtually every state and locality in Mexico. When newly elected presidents Vicente Fox and George W. Bush took office at the start of the twenty-first century, both men were eager to conclude a comprehensive policy that would better accommodate the needs of both countries. The Bush administration supported a flexible labour supply model, making it easier for Mexican guest workers to enter the US legally in order to work at jobs that did not attract sufficient numbers of American workers.

But the terrorist attacks of 9/11 intervened, and security interests suddenly took precedence over economic partnerships and cross-border labour opportunities. Significant numbers of undocumented Mexican migrants turned to people smugglers as US border security tightened. Whereas thousands of immigrants once returned home on a regular seasonal basis, high-profile tragedies involving the deaths of undocumented migrants in transit strengthened incentives to stay in the US on a permanent basis. American efforts to tighten border security had the undesired effect of creating a stronger rationale for permanent as opposed to seasonal migration, and strengthened the position of criminal organizations that transported undocumented workers across the border. As families living in poverty in Mexico rose from 34 per cent in 1980 to 40 per cent in 2000, and as trends towards an even greater unequal distribution of income persisted, the incentives to enter through the golden door, even by illegal and dangerous means, only multiplied.

Cuban Politics in South Florida

In the aftermath of the Spanish–American War of 1898, US interference in the government and economy of Cuba was both regular and one-sided. Repeated military interventions were designed to foster pro-American administrations, while US businesses and investors controlled extensive areas of the lush countryside. Havana emerged as an important American tourist destination, and an open-door policy was afforded to Cubans, who moved back and forth without hindrance between the two countries.[19] Travel links between the US and Cuba remained strong throughout the first half of the twentieth century, with those Cubans who resided in the US representing mainly well-to-do business elites. Only after Fidel Castro's successful revolution against the corrupt regime of Fugencio Batista in 1959 did a dramatic burst of emigration occur, with subsequent waves of new departures taking place periodically over the next 40 years. Because of Cuba's unique status as a locus of Cold War conflict, those Cubans who arrived before 1980 were afforded a privileged status that was unavailable to every other Latino immigrant group.

It did not take long after Castro's assumption of power in 1959 for many Cubans to grow disillusioned with the Marxist orientation of their new government. As the Communist regime nationalized foreign-owned businesses and cracked down on all forms of dissent, the exodus grew, cutting across the social and economic spectrum of Cuban society to include middle-class professionals, factory workers and semi-skilled labourers. In January 1961 the Kennedy administration waived all visa requirements and, within twelve months, over 100,000 Cubans fled to the US. The old elite abandoned their property assets as they departed, leaving behind windfalls that the government quickly redistributed. By the close of the twentieth century nearly one-tenth of Cuba's population was living in exile abroad, with the overwhelming majority situated in the US. Welcomed until the 1980s by Americans who, in a Cold War context, chose to consider Cuban residents as exiles rather than immigrants, the newcomers believed that their stay would be temporary. Even after the Bay of Pigs disaster of April 1961, they were convinced that the US government would restore democracy and a free market economy to their homeland. As the wait extended, Cuba's exiles set about transforming the demographic and political profile of South Florida.[20]

Miami was a medium-sized resort town in the early 1960s. A small Cuban community was resident in the area prior to the Castro revolution, and Miami's proximity to Havana (a short 50-minute flight) made it the preferred destination of the initial political exiles. Cuban communities later developed in larger urban centres further north such as New York and Chicago, but South Florida offered both proximity and a familiar climate for residents who hoped to make the return passage to Cuba before too long. The Catholic Church provided much needed aid during the early years, with the Kennedy administration subsequently establishing a special Cuban Refugee Program under the Department of Health, Education and Welfare. During the 1960s and '70s Cuban–Americans benefited from a variety of federal initiatives that helped the community to prosper. The 1966 Cuban Adjustment Act, for example, provided additional public assistance in the form of Medicaid and food stamps. Business credits and start-up loans facilitated the growth of Cuban–American businesses. Bilingual education, scholarship programmes for college-bound students, certification classes for Cuban teachers and even special courses that enabled Cuban doctors to secure their medical licence in the US allowed the fiercely anti-Castro community in South Florida to gain a foothold in American political and economic life that was not available to other Latino groups.[21]

By the time the Cuban Missile Crisis of October 1962 finally put an end to all commercial flights between the two countries, the city of Miami had become home to over 200,000 exiles. Migrants continued to arrive via third countries and on makeshift boats and rafts, and in 1965 Castro permitted relatives of those already living in the US to leave the island. By April 1966 another approximately 300,000 Cubans, from mostly working-class backgrounds, were admitted to the US. Clandestine departures from the island continued in subsequent years until by the late 1970s there were just over 665,000 Cubans living in the US as political refugees. A third, and far more controversial, official wave of refugees numbering over 120,000 people left Cuba in 1980 as Castro attempted to rid his country of convicted criminals and the mentally ill. Announcing in April 1980 that all who wished to leave the country were free to do so through an embarkation point at the port of Mariel, hundreds of small craft from the US sailed across the Florida straits to collect relatives and loved ones. The Cuban authorities forced each vessel to take on additional passengers, and it was through this method that Castro offloaded thousands of 'undesirables' on US authorities. The Carter administration demanded that Castro take back the hardened criminals, but all communications were ignored.[22]

While the vast majority of Mariel emigrants were law-abiding people who sought to be reunited with their families in freedom, the popular press in the US focused attention on the criminal elements who were now overextending prison resources around the country. The Mariel migrants received none of the sympathy or assistance that had been extended to earlier refugees; indeed, the US government, responding to public disillusionment with the open-door policy for citizens of communist-controlled countries, refused to accord the entrants refugee status.[23] Even members of the established Cuban community in Miami were sceptical that the new migrants could successfully navigate the transition to American culture.

With the collapse of the Soviet Union in 1991, Moscow's long-standing subsidy to Cuba of almost $6 billion per year came to an end. Oil imports fell and stocks of imported food plummeted. Shortages in basic consumer items became the norm across the island as the economy tottered on the brink of an economic disaster greater than any experienced in Latin America. Castro called for new austerity measures but refused to make any concessions to political opponents at home or abroad. It was in this climate that additional illegal emigration to the US occurred during the 1990s. American efforts to formalize a new migration accord with Castro failed repeatedly, and by the start of the new century it had become obvious that a fundamental change in the acerbic bilateral relationship would not take place before the end of Castro's personal rule.[24]

South Americans in the United States

When studied in comparison with Mexicans, Puerto Ricans and Cubans, who together constituted three-quarters of the US Latino population at the start of the twenty-first century, immigrants from South America were comparatively few in number. Originating in nine countries, the 2 million resident migrants represented less than 5.2 per cent of the total US Latino population. The largest source country was Colombia, with over 650,000 citizens residing in the US in 2000, while immigrants from Paraguay were fewer than 13,000.

The average socioeconomic background of South American Latinos differed markedly from immigrants from Central America in general, and from Mexico in particular. In 1990 fewer than 45 per cent of Mexican immigrants to the US had graduated from high school and only one in sixteen held a bachelor's degree; for South Americans, on the other hand, the figures were 70 and 20 per cent respectively.[25] Doctors, engineers and scientists moved to the US in the post-war period in order to maximize their economic rewards, while some members of the urban elite sought to escape civil unrest and repressive military rule at home. The rise of the Pinochet regime in Chile in the early 1970s, the ascendancy of military rule in Argentina in the early 1980s and, more recently, the left-wing populist rule of Hugo Chavez in Venezuela all prompted higher levels of emigration north among those with financial means and professional skills. In the case of immigrants from the Southern Cone countries, Chile and Argentina, the 200,000 identified in the 2000 US Census tended to hold professional and managerial positions in the destination country. Travel to the US was too costly for poor people, and the distances involved made the sort of seasonal labour opportunities, common in the case of Mexican migrants, virtually impossible for unskilled workers from South America.[26]

ADJACENT BORDERS: MIGRATION WITHIN LATIN AMERICA

With thousands of miles of poorly secured borders separating the countries of Latin America, there was and remains a great deal of undocumented international migration (most of it temporary) by unskilled workers. Moving in response to shifting employment conditions, especially in agriculture and textiles, rural peoples who share a common language and religious culture accept the prospect of repeated labour migration as a condition of survival. In such cases borders are no more than an inconvenient nuisance. As Argentina, Brazil and Uruguay began the process of industrialization in the nineteenth century, they became receiving zones for upwards of 14 million Europeans. Prior to the 1940s, successful immigrant communities were prominent in cities such as Buenos Aires, São Paulo and Montevideo, but the outflow from Western Europe ceased after economic prosperity returned to the continent in the 1950s. In the post-war decades international migration within Latin America has been prompted by economic and security imperatives. As in Africa, destination states in Central America are often poorly prepared to assume responsibility for refugees who cross borders from war-torn neighbouring countries. In South America, on the other hand, most international migration is the result of economic hardship and the prospect of meaningful employment abroad.

Argentina: From Destination to Source Country

A sparsely populated region of South America before and during the age of Spanish colonization, independent Argentina welcomed immigrants throughout the nineteenth century. Thanks to the confluence of British investment capital and the arrival of immigrants from Southern Europe, this Southern Cone country became a major exporter of meat and grain to Europe and North America beginning in the 1870s. By 1914 almost 30 per cent of the country's population was foreign-born, with the largest communities arriving as unskilled labourers from Spain and Italy. In the early twentieth century three-fifths of Argentina's working class held citizenship in a European country. And this remarkably high percentage of foreign-born did not include the so-called *golondrinas*, or swallows – those who traversed the South Atlantic on an annual basis via steamship, working on the Argentine pampas for part of the year before returning home to farms in Italy during harvest season.

Owing largely to the influx of foreigners, the county's population grew from 1.7 million in 1869 to almost 8 million at the start of World War I.[27] The rate of European migration began declining during the interwar years, and Western Europe's economic recovery after World War II undermined further Argentine efforts to recruit additional immigrants from traditional sending areas. Most of the post-war migration involved neighbouring states in the Southern Cone with less successful economies such as Bolivia, Uruguay, Chile and Paraguay. Thanks to the establishment in 1991 of a South American Free Trade Zone between Argentina, Uruguay, Paraguay and Brazil, crossing member-state borders for work was fairly convenient.

The new arrivals tended to be employed in rural labour, taking the place of native Argentines who sought better opportunities in urban areas. At the start of the twenty-first century, Argentina was host to over half of South America's total migrant population; more than 65 per cent of the country's foreign-born population were citizens of nearby states. While this regional influx meant that Argentina remained a net immigration country, a high level of emigration amongst educated Argentines complicated the drive for modernization and economic development. Beginning in the 1950s, as a series of military dictatorships and unstable economic conditions dimmed prospects for a healthy democratic future, Argentina's professional class began to leave for destinations in Spain, Italy, North America, Mexico and Venezuela.

During the military dictatorship of 1976–83, some 300,000 dissidents were 'disappeared' by the government, prompting a further exodus by members of the highly skilled elite. Half a million Argentines were living abroad in 1985, and the figure had doubled twenty years later.[28] Economic restructuring during the 1990s failed to lift Argentina out of its fiscal crisis, and at the start of the twenty-first century the government defaulted on $141 billion in foreign debt. Unemployment peaked at over 20 per cent, and more than half of the country's 37 million citizens were living below the poverty line. Over a quarter of a million Argentines left their homeland in the first two years of the new century, with most heading across the Atlantic to Spain and Italy where they claimed citizenship through descent.

Brazil's Status Quo

With 184 million people, Brazil stands as the second most populous country in the Americas after the United States. A Portuguese colony from the early sixteenth century until the 1820s, the importation of approximately 6 million African slaves to work on sugar and coffee plantations ensured that European settlement would not be extensive before the late nineteenth century. Indeed, during the colonial period, Portuguese authorities forbade immigration from rival European states. Only after 1808, when the Portuguese king fled to Brazil in the wake of French aggression under Napoleon Bonaparte, were non-Portuguese settlers welcome in the enormous colony. And only with the end of slavery in 1888 did Brazilian authorities and planters begin a programme of actively recruiting European immigrants. Government subsidies were provided to planters so they could bring field hands from Europe, but living conditions for the newcomers remained difficult. As late as 1885 the Italian government was cautioning prospective emigrants to avoid the country as it was considered inhospitable and unhealthy. Just over 1.9 million migrants arrived in São Paulo between 1880 and 1903, with travel subsidies available to entire families with at least one working-age male in an effort to lessen the type of return migration that was prevalent in Argentina.

Most of the immigrants came from Italy, Germany, Spain and Portugal, and their arrival made Brazil the third largest recipient of European settlers after the US and Argentina. The settlers, many of them working under indenture contracts, managed to preserve their linguistic heritage while creating fraternal organizations and a variety of social clubs. Brazil also opened settlement to Japanese migrants in 1908, just at the time when racist policies in the US were excluding Asian newcomers. By the start of World War II there were almost 200,000 Japanese resident in the Portuguese-speaking country. Another 2 million Europeans made the passage to Brazil from 1904 until the onset of the Great Depression in the 1930s.[29]

In the immediate post-war years, a new influx of European immigrants, some subsidized by the Brazilian government, took advantage of opportunities in nascent industries established by the state under an aggressive programme of import substitution. Almost 700,000 European and Asian migrants entered Brazil during the 1950s and early '60s, but after 1964 the country's military rulers discouraged further immigration and, as the economic fortunes of the principal sending countries eclipsed Brazil's in the 1970s, the number of foreign-born residents declined. There was also a greater volume of rural-to-urban migration within the country during the 1970s, making the need for foreign labour less acute.[30] Economic growth was modest during this inflationary period, and during the 'lost decade' of the 1980s and more recently there was a trend amongst educated Brazilians to emigrate for better economic opportunities elsewhere. Just under 2 million Brazilians were living and working abroad in the 1990s, with the US, Paraguay and Japan serving as the leading destination areas. The Inter-American Development Bank estimated that expatriates remitted over $5 billion to Brazil in 2003.[31] A small number of immigrants from South and Central America entered the country during the 1990s, but in general Brazil had ceased to be a destination of choice.

Venezuela's Oil and Colombia's Labour

Recruitment of immigrant labour to sparsely populated Venezuela began in the 1920s as foreign-owned oil companies and agricultural interests hired Spanish, Portuguese, Italian and Colombian migrants to meet the growing needs of an export-driven economy. By the early 1960s, 33 per cent of the labour force in the capital city of Caracas was foreign-born. The windfall generated by oil exports during the 1970s led to an acceleration of migrants from neighbouring Colombia, a country which had experienced a massive rural–urban transfer of population in the post-war period, but whose inability to generate adequate job opportunities for urban residents led to the outflow. In the early 1980s almost 45 per cent of Venezuela's officially registered foreign population was Colombian.[32] The prospect of better-paying jobs in the oil industry drew workers from as far south as Argentina and Uruguay and as far west as Peru. Employment opportunities expanded in dramatic fashion throughout the 1970s, increasing by 5.5 per cent annually.[33]

Unlike most of its neighbours in South America, Colombia has never been a significant destination country. Political instability and civil conflict wracked the country after independence in 1819 and what immigration did take place was centred on the regional movement of agricultural labourers from neighbouring states, in particular Ecuador and Venezuela. Less than half a per cent of the country's population of 37 million was listed as foreign-born in the early 1990s. During this very violent decade migration was very much in an outbound mode. More than 40 years of low-level conflict escalated in the 1990s, involving the national government, leftist guerrilla forces and right-wing paramilitary groups. Most of the latter were deeply implicated in Colombia's notorious drugs trade, and their tactics included indiscriminate killings, kidnappings, torture and the expulsion of civilians from lands that were appropriated for the expansion of coca crops.

The Colombian government received financial support from the US in its efforts to eradicate the drugs trade, but its opponents were well funded and heavily armed. In addition to skyrocketing unemployment, heightened personal insecurity and the internal displacement of over 1.5 million people during the 1990s, approximately one out of every ten Colombians left the country, either as officially recognized refugees or as undocumented migrants. Most crossed the borders into Ecuador and Venezuela, but at the start of the new century the US Department of Homeland Security indicated that Colombia had become the fourth leading source of illegal immigration to the US. With ongoing demand for illegal coca in the developed states of the North, prospects of an early resolution to the civil conflict were dim.[34]

DISCORD AND FLIGHT FROM CENTRAL AMERICA

There had always been a modest level of regional and rural-to-urban migration in the small countries of Central America, but the disruptions caused by civil wars in El Salvador, Guatemala and Nicaragua during the 1970s and '80s produced significant cross-border refugee relocations. Panama and Costa Rica were spared civil strife but as a result they became receiving zones for those fleeing repression and military violence in neighbouring states. For the first group of countries, the promise of a better life after independence from Spain had never been realized. Throughout the better part of two centuries, powerful oligarchies had dominated both landownership and control over the armed forces. They focused their commercial estates on cash crop exports like coffee and bananas over subsistence agriculture, relegating the vast majority of the peasantry to lives of chronic poverty as landless labourers well into the twentieth century. During the early 1900s, periodic popular protests against harsh working conditions and low wages were most often met by repression under authoritarian governments put in power by landed elites.

The autonomy of the small states of Central America was compromised throughout the better part of the twentieth century by the expansive power of the US. American influence in the region can be traced back to the early 1900s when large companies began investing in export-driven plantations. The opening of the Panama Canal in 1909 heightened the region's importance as the US assumed a more active presence in global trade. On more than one occasion, political pressures and military intervention were employed on behalf of US financial interests in the region. Nicaragua, for example, was occupied in 1912 and US marines remained in the country until early 1933. Real power rested with the US-trained National Guard, and in 1937 its ruthless leader, General Anastasio Somoza, assumed the presidency and founded a tyrannical regime that would remain in power until 1979.

The corrupt Somoza dictatorship enjoyed strong support from the US as an ally in the Cold War, and when it collapsed in the midst of a civil war that claimed 50,000 lives between 1977 and 1979, the new Nicaraguan government embraced a non-aligned foreign policy. The conservative Reagan administration, however, wary of Cuban support for the victorious Sandinista government, immediately imposed a trade embargo against Nicaragua and extended enormous covert aid to a counter-revolutionary exile army led by ex-Somoza officers. These so-called 'Contra' fighters engaged in a brutal guerrilla campaign against the government and civilians who supported the country's reform programme. Internal displacement and flight across borders became commonplace during the conflict.

President Reagan also threw his support behind the brutal military dictatorship in Guatemala and backed a despicable military regime in El Salvador that was responsible for the operation of notorious death squads. Guatemala's civil war raged for over three decades, ending only in 1996. With a total population of 14 million, the International Organization for Migration estimated that more than a million Guatemalans were living in the US alone by 2000.[35] The same agency claimed that approximately 60,000 Guatemalans were deported from Mexico annually towards the close of the century. Many of the latter were seasonal workers attracted by higher wages in the coffee fields of Chiapas. El Salvador's civil conflict was especially violent. In 1980 the Roman Catholic Archbishop of El Salvador, Oscar Romero, called for an end to attacks against innocent civilians, but he too was assassinated. Despite the officially sanctioned violence led by off-duty military and police, El Salvador was the recipient of over $6 billion in aid from the US from 1979 to 1989.[36] As a result approximately 1 million Salvadorans had fled abroad by the mid 1980s, representing almost 20 per cent of the country's total population.

Fewer than 300,000 migrants from Central America, mostly drawn from the middle classes, had arrived in the US during the 1960s and '70s, but with more than a million inhabitants fleeing government-sponsored death squads, war and lawlessness during the 1980s, the number of political refugees surged. The Reagan administration was loath to recognize the immigrants as political refugees since they were mostly fleeing the very regimes that the US was funding. The approval rates for Guatemalan and Salvadoran asylum was less than 3 per cent for 1984, compared with a 60 per cent rate for Iranians and a 40 per cent rate for those fleeing Soviet-controlled Afghanistan.[37] In 1990 the US Census indicated that over 1.3 million people of Central American ancestry were in residence, with the vast majority of them recent arrivals from poorer backgrounds. Not surprisingly, given the civil unrest at home, more than half of the total came from El Salvador, Nicaragua and Guatemala.

The immigrants tended to settle in major urban areas across the US and, as new arrivals joined them in chain migration during the 1990s, they established strong communities that provided social support and job placement.[38] By the year 2000, the total foreign-born population from Central America had reached 2 million, 40 per cent of whom were from El Salvador. A sanctuary movement, organized and led by Christian church groups in the US, sponsored and housed undocumented refugees in defiance of the government. A few even worked with activists in Mexico to smuggle refugees into the US. Most of the migrants initially viewed their status as temporary, but as economic conditions in the region continued to deteriorate even after the return of peace in the 1990s, permanent residence became an important economic lifeline to family members left behind.

The Remittance Lifeline

With civil conflict undermining the already fragile economies of El Salvador, Guatemala and Nicaragua during the 1980s, remittances became the economic lifeblood of many families whose loved ones had fled to the US. And the importance of remittances at the microeconomic level continued to grow during the early years of the twenty-first century. The Inter-American Development Bank estimated that the region had been the recipient of $7.8 billion in remittance income in 2004, a dramatic 17 per cent increase from just one year earlier. And this figure did not include what was assumed to be a sizeable flow (estimated by the World Bank at between 5 and 15 per cent of the official flow) of unofficial currency through informal channels and return visits. In El Salvador, for example, 40 per cent of the tourist trade involved return visits by nationals living in *El norte*.[39] For Honduras, El Salvador and Nicaragua, remittances at the start of the twenty-first century totalled between 15 and 17 per cent of each country's Gross Domestic Product.

According to the World Bank, by the year 2003 formal remittances to the region overall totalled three times the amount of foreign direct investment. In 2000 the Salvadoran government officially acknow-ledged the central role of remittances to the national economy by adopting the US dollar as its legal tender. Clearly the 2 million Central Americans living in the US and Mexico were dedicating a substantial portion of their hard-earned savings to cover the basic necessities of relatives at home.[40] Economists debated whether remittance income actually contributed to domestic economic development (as opposed to immediate consumption of basic necessities), with sceptics arguing that the large import of wage capital merely highlighted the dire economic situation of states in the region. But few questioned the value of job acquisition in the US to migrants who faced dire economic prospects in their own countries.

El Salvador provided the best test case. Twenty per cent of the tiny country's population of 6.2 million lived abroad at the start of the new century, and remittances of $2.5 billion in 2004 represented the single most important source of income for more than one-fifth of Salvadoran households. At one level it appeared that emigration had improved the quality of life for the country's citizens. A study conducted by the UN Development Program in 2005 concluded that Salvadorans resident in the US, almost half of whom were women, had improved their life expectancy, literacy and school enrolment rates over citizens who remained at home. In addition, remittance income enabled recipient families to provide for their children's education, improve their housing accommodation and save modest amounts for retirement. On the basis of telephone traffic and airline passenger data, some emigrants remained in very close contact with relatives and were able to visit with a level of regularity that made the emigration experience less disruptive and final. On the other hand, the export of human resources and the influx of remittance funds did not seem to have a major impact on the overall economy of El Salvador. There was no significant boost in investment activity and job creation at the national level, and despite pockets of improvement for families who were supported by those who worked abroad, the macroeconomic results of large-scale economic migration were extremely modest.[41]

DEMOGRAPHICS AND DEVELOPMENT

In the end the volume of international migration within Latin America and to North America hinged on the ability of governments and international financial institutions to effect meaningful and sustainable economic improvement in the lives of common people. Latin America has remained at the periphery of the global economy for centuries. In the late 1800s industrial Europe's rising demand for foodstuffs and raw materials brought many Latin American economies into the transatlantic trading network. The Argentine pampas provided wool, wheat and beef; Brazil and Colombia became major coffee producers; Peru exported sugar and silver; and Chile turned to the extraction of copper.

Latin America's small political elite, largely descended from European stock, embraced economic liberalism and free trade as strategies that would maximize profits for landowners. Assuming the racial inferiority of native peoples, most countries encouraged maximum European immigration. Between the 1880s and the 1920s Latin America's ruling class presided over a long period of growth and political consolidation, while the working classes began tentative efforts to organize and demand better wages. During the first three decades of the twentieth century a number of major cities emerged across Central and South America, drawing significant numbers of rural workers and foreign immigrants who formed the backbone of a nascent industrial working population.[42]

The Great Depression had a devastating impact on these export-orientated economies, as demand for Latin America's primary products evaporated after 1929. Civilian ruling elites were discredited and military governments took power across the continent from Argentina to Mexico. In general, these unelected leaders sought to jump-start industrialization in an effort to free their countries from reliance upon developed states. Called 'import-substitution', the effort to build indigenous manufacturing capacity turned on the erection of tariffs against foreign imports, the provision of generous subsidies to local producers and investment in and operation of large government-owned enterprises.

Modest successes were realized during the war years and into the 1950s, but as prices for Latin America's traditional exports – foodstuffs and raw materials – declined in the global markets, the ability of states to purchase capital goods that were needed in factories was undermined. And, lacking a large consumer market due to the fact that so many remained in poverty, manufacturers were faced with growing inventories and few buyers. Heavy borrowing on international markets for domestic infrastructure projects during the 1970s placed many states at risk should global markets contract. Between 1970 and 1980 Latin America's external debt ballooned from $27 billion to $231 billion. When a major economic downturn occurred in the early 1980s, most Latin American states found themselves shouldering enormous debt and without adequate resources to meet basic debt service payments.

The result was a decade-long economic crisis. Before additional funds were made available, private banking institutions and the International Monetary Fund insisted on a package of severe austerity measures and the abandonment of import substitution. Continent-wide economic output declined by 10 per cent during the 1980s, and despite the reform mandates, total debt surged to $417 billion by 1990. A gigantic transfer of wealth from the South to the North occurred as Latin American countries struggled to make interest payments on existing loans. According to one historian, during the period 1982 to 1987, 'the net transfer of resources from Latin America to the West totalled $148 billion. This was equivalent in real terms to two Marshall Plans – but with the United States as the recipient rather than donor.'[43] US companies operating in Latin America produced a third of the continent's exports and paid a quarter of its taxes. Overall per capita income in Latin America declined by 6 per cent between 1980 and 1987 and, with falling incomes in most households, the possibility of a major social upheaval across the continent seemed imminent. The only upside to the protracted fiscal crisis of the 1980s was the discrediting of right-wing military and left-wing Marxist governments. Democratic civilian rule was embraced once again in Argentina, Brazil, Peru and Chile, and the economic picture slowly improved by the early 1990s.

Despite the infusion of foreign investment after 1990, however, serious social and economic problems remained. Approximately 40 per cent of all Latin Americans continued to live in poverty in the mid-1990s, and the income gap between the continent's richest 10 per cent (who controlled 40 per cent of income) and the poorest 20 per cent (who controlled less than 4 per cent) was the widest in the world. Burgeoning shantytowns on the periphery of large, increasingly polluted cities stood testimony to lost hopes and expectations. Civil institutions – the courts, legislatures, regulatory agencies – remained weak in many countries, and the scourge of the drugs trade enabled criminals to intimidate and corrupt police officers, local and regional politicians, and in some cases the national security apparatus itself.[44] Thanks to a seemingly insatiable appetite for drugs in the US, more than half a million Colombians were involved in some aspect of the illicit trade in the early 1980s.[45] On more than a few occasions, officials in Mexico, Bolivia, Peru and Colombia who fought the drug barons were targeted for assassination.

Of course, economic success and jobs creation has always been intimately tied to population growth. In the immediate post-war period the population predictions for many Latin American countries were troubling. Large families were encouraged in traditional rural societies, and the powerful Roman Catholic Church remained adamantly opposed to family planning and artificial birth control. There was even a feeling in some leftist political circles that calls for population control were part of a nefarious plot by North American imperialists to continue their domination over the continent. The birth rate in South America's two most populous states, Brazil and Mexico, did moderate during the final two decades of the century, bringing some relief to overburdened public services. But with youthful, and increasingly urban, populations placing additional strain on the social fabric as they sought to enter the workforce, the question of whether neo-liberal market economics could improve the continent's position in world trade remained unanswered. In the meantime labour-surplus countries like Mexico and Brazil continued their roles as sending zones, irrespective of the heightened fears of security-conscious destination states.

Terms of Reception

For the receiving countries of El norte, the demographic and economic challenges facing Central and South America were not to be wished away by more stringent rules of entry. In the case of Canada, geography and labour markets dictated that selective admission policies could be pursued with relative ease. During the 1980s, as the Reagan administration viewed asylum applications from Central America with suspicion, Canada admitted almost 16,000 refugees from the war-torn region. Salvadorans and Guatemalans whose applications for asylum were rejected in the US found a much higher acceptance level in Canada. But tougher criteria for asylum and resettlement were adopted in 1993, reflecting a growing level of public mistrust over the country's willingness to embrace those who had been rejected by US authorities.[46]

Indeed Canada's immigration policy shifted to advantage so-called 'designer immigrants' of the 1990s, women and men who were admitted to the country on the basis of entrepreneurial skills, control over capital or specialized skills, complementing the government's emphasis on reducing the burden of assimilating newcomers. During the 1990s, refugee admittance and family reunification were downplayed, social service costs were reduced and maximum short-term benefits were realized as 'made-to-order' newcomers had an immediate positive impact on economic development. The points-based immigration system adopted in the mid 1960s, whereby admissions decisions were governed by social and economic criteria, including language and occupational skills, remained firmly in place after 2000, with bonus points available to prospective migrants with skills in high demand areas. For the typical migrant from Latin America, the formula for admission to Canada, together with the paucity of jobs in the low-wage, unskilled sector and the cost of travel all conspired against the formation of a significant Latino presence.[47]

That presence was destined for the US, irrespective of the perceived security imperative, growing public hostility towards undocumented workers and the post-9/11 folding of the old Immigration and Naturalization Service into the new Department of Homeland Security. As long as demand for labour in the North remained strong and supply in the South remained abundant, international South–North migration, especially the illegal variety, would continue to shape the relationship between the world's wealthiest country and the much poorer republics of the Spanish and Portuguese-speaking South. The work of closing the productivity and income gap between the two continents through 'neo-liberal' market mechanisms and freer trade had proved disappointing in the short term, but no viable alternatives were on the horizon as politically acceptable options.

In Venezuela, the populist government of President Hugo Chavez opted for a revamped socialist alternative funded by oil revenues, but he had few supporters among the middle class. At any rate, the petrol 'solution' was a one-off, non-renewable option for a single small country in the region. As long as widespread poverty persisted in Latin America, there was little prospect that current emigration trends would shift. Sadly, US interest in the economic betterment of its southern neighbours had been less than robust during nearly two centuries of independence from Europe. The rhetoric of hemispheric partnership had always been attractive, but in a Cold War environment, it was deemed more important to support authoritarian regimes that took a strong anti-communist line. Too often such support was forthcoming even when those regimes ignored human rights and failed utterly to improve the lives of its citizens. The new century held promise for a more constructive relationship, but other than descrying the anti-free market 'excesses' of the Chavez administration, by 2007 there were few signals from Washington that a new partnership with Latin America was in the immediate offing.

Chapter 3

Africa: The Displacement Continent

Although Africans constitute a mere 13 per cent of the world's total population, it is estimated that they currently make up 30 per cent of the world's refugees and 60 per cent of its internally displaced persons.[1] Thus at the beginning of the twenty-first century not only does Africa have the most mobile population on earth, it has the ignominious distinction of being home to the largest number of involuntary migrants. The approximate number of refugees and asylum seekers reached 13.5 million in 2001, up by a stunning 5 million from 1998. This figure included over 3 million protracted refugees, men and women who had lived outside their home country for more than five years without hope of voluntary repatriation, permanent reception in the country of asylum or resettlement in a third country.[2] In addition, another 21 million Africans fell into the category of internally displaced persons (IDPs), forced from their homes but still living in the country of their birth.[3]

These distressing statistics reflect poorly on the history of independent Africa, especially in light of the optimism about the future expressed by nationalist leaders who played key roles in post-war independence struggles. Many of those struggles continued after independence, with debilitating internal conflict, ethnic and religious pogroms and violent regime change a troubling feature of post-colonial life. Between the early 1960s, when independence movements in sub-Saharan Africa first gained momentum, and the 1990s, when the whole continent won its freedom, there were more than 80 violent changes of government at the national level.[4] Military coups against democratically elected leaders began soon after independence, while at the start of the twenty-first century armed conflict afflicted more than a quarter of Africa's 53 nation states. With conflict, of course, came massive displacement and homelessness, the involuntary flight of millions and the further impoverishment of whole countries.

It is easy to blame the policies of post-colonial states for the tragedy of displacement, but in reality the roots of the ongoing crises in many African countries go much deeper than instances of mismanagement and malfeasance. Indeed the post-war migration experience in Africa can be understood only within the context of an enormously damaging colonial precedent. In particular, the territorial partition of sub-Saharan Africa by the major European powers that began in the 1880s disrupted traditional patterns of political organization, pushed the indigenous population to the political margins and set the stage for the subsequent emergence of weak and vulnerable nation states. In the main, most Africans were ill prepared for the responsibilities of democratic governance when the colonial powers withdrew or were forced out. Many of the continent's most serious challenges, including the involuntary displacement of peoples, can be traced directly to the formation of nation states in which boundaries were set by colonial elites whose primary interest in Africa was neither internal development nor domestic governance, but economic aggrandizement.

During decades of colonial rule, most indigenous African leaders were denied both the educational resources and the experience to address the demands of a long-suffering public. When independence finally was achieved, democratically elected leaders, who in many cases lacked the training available in Western countries, were forced to deal with rapid population growth, environmental crises, high rates of unemployment, ethnic rivalries and civil conflict. Nationalists who had rallied support for independence with the claim that colonialism alone stood in the way of economic growth and modernization now faced the unenviable task of providing a 'quick fix' to myriad social and economic problems. And they were obliged to do so while working to cultivate a sense of national identity that transcended local, regional and ethnic boundaries. The struggles, and the failures, of these efforts lay at the core of Africa's recent migratory phenomena.

FROM COLONIES TO NATION STATES

The post-war history of migration in Africa is intimately connected to the inter-ethnic quarrels of the pre-colonial era, and to the experience of foreign rule and its immediate aftermath. For centuries before the arrival of the first Europeans, Africans relocated in the wake of environmental degradation and catastrophe, in flight from war zones, oppressive rulers and slave traders, and in search of subsistence and better grazing land. Individual nomads and traders, together with entire villages and ethnic groups, moved long distances across what later became national borders in response to myriad threats and opportunities. The continent was dotted with thousands of political structures that ranged from expansive territorial kingdoms like those erected in Ghana, Mali and Songhai, to loose aggregations of warriors who claimed authority within constantly shifting frontiers. As a result, ethnic conflict was endemic in pre-colonial Africa. At the start of the colonial period, low-level clashes were commonplace, with ascendant militarized groups imposing their will on subordinate peoples by force and intimidation. Warrior culture, centred on the kinship group and the larger ethnic alliance, was highly regarded, with elaborate initiation rituals signalling the emergence of new leaders whose first priority was the expansion of the group's power and territory. Since settled frontiers were rarely agreed, the aggressive warrior was acknowledged as the bulwark of social order and economic survival.[5]

European colonial rule drastically altered the political calculus, imposing arbitrary territorial boundaries and centralized control over peoples of widely varying cultures, and dividing other ethnic groups who shared a common language and culture into two or more rival colonies. This cynical carve-up of Africa began in earnest during the 1880s, and before it was over 'the new boundaries cut through some 190 culture groups'.[6] By the early 1900s, after resistance movements were crushed by superior force and their leaders executed or sent into exile, the major European powers had subordinated both the peoples and the economies of Africa to the demands of the West.

Driven to maximize the economic productivity of the colonies, few colonial administrators took the time to understand the complexities of ethnic pluralism and age-old divisions. Traditional African leaders were either undermined or co-opted by the colonial elite, while subsistence farmers faced new taxes and obligations to support the imperial administration. Male labour migration to settler-owned coffee, cocoa, groundnut, palm oil, cotton and rubber plantations, to the site of extractive industries like mining, and to urban colonial capitals, threatened the cohesiveness of family and ethnic community. Millions of rural Africans were drawn into the commercial economy – and the imperial tax regime. All of this was of little moment to the colonizers who, as a rule, saw little to value in traditional African culture and who vigorously supported Western administrative practices and Christian evangelization as principal civilizing agents.[7]

Still, no two areas of Africa experienced the same colonial regime. The seven powers that divided up the continent – Britain, Germany, France, Spain, Portugal, Italy and Belgium – each adopted a different imperial profile. Europe's contact with North Africa, for example, was both centuries-old and complicated by the historic antipathy between Muslim and Christian traditions. In Somaliland, for example, sheikh Muhammad 'Abdille Hassan led Muslim resistance fighters against the British until 1920.[8] Portions of East Africa, especially Kenya, attracted white settlers who presided over plantation economies, while in Southern Africa the beginnings of minority rule could be traced back to Dutch settlement in the early seventeenth century. The British transfer of power to a white Afrikaner government in 1910 ultimately set the stage for South Africa's reactionary apartheid regime. West Africa suffered from the predatory actions of European slave traders for more than three centuries, and after 1870 the export-led economies of coastal colonies like Gold Coast and Côte d'Ivoire became net receiving zones. In these colonies millions of impoverished migrants from the interior took up seasonal positions on cash crop farms and in commercial mines.

During the height of the colonial period, African migrants were most often victims of those who sought to exploit the continent for its considerable human and natural resources. Colonial regimes brought relative peace to regions where migration had previously been prompted by internecine ethnic warfare and the search for food, but in the place of this was erected a migration flow regime dictated by the economic priorities of the metropolitan power.[9] The confiscation of African land and the subsequent expulsion of whole communities; the recruitment of African males to work in copper, gold and diamond mines; forced employment on cash crop plantations and on public works projects; and the failed resistance movements of indigenous peoples all contributed to involuntary migration and refugee crises.

During World War II, the forced labour and redoubling of colonial efforts to maximize cash crop production led to food shortages in British-controlled Kenya, Tanganyika, northern Nigeria and French West Africa. One result was the massive flight of rural dwellers to the towns, where new job opportunities were available due to the war, but where housing and food were often lacking, and where sanitation was minimal.[10] After independence was achieved, the economic, ecological, ethnic and political problems that hampered so many fledgling governments drove migrants to seek better opportunities, greater security and, in many cases, basic food and shelter outside their natal lands. In 1960, for example, just as the process of decolonization was starting, an estimated half a million men entered Gold Coast and Côte d'Ivoire each year in search of temporary labour. Most seasonal migration was from north to south, out of the savanna towards the forest and coastal zones.[11] More than a century of European interference in Africa's affairs set the stage for a post-colonial environment in which the displacement of people became a disturbing constant of daily existence.

Independence

In the decade after World War II it became clear to most observers that the age of European control over Africa was nearing its finish. African troops from British and French colonies fought in a variety of theatres during the war and returned home with a renewed sense of nationalism. The charter of United Nations Organization affirmed the right of popular self-determination for all peoples, and both emerging super-powers were opposed to the colonial project. By 1965 the entire continent had achieved independence with the exception of Portuguese-controlled areas and the Spanish Sahara. Obdurate white minority regimes in Rhodesia (contemporary Zimbabwe), South Africa and South West Africa (contemporary Namibia) represented local forms of colonialism, but elsewhere Europe's direct rule ended fairly quickly.

In those areas where white settlement was sparse and where the economic bonds between the metropolitan power and the colony were strong, decolonization took place in a largely peaceful and orderly manner, although a de facto dependent relationship remained. Europeans recognized that independence would conveniently shift the responsibility for costly social programmes and development projects to Africans, leaving the former imperial power to economize and focus solely on trade relations. In areas where the colonial power attempted to maintain control, however, bloody independence struggles and atten-dant civil unrest undermined efforts to build stable and prosperous countries. In Kenya, a settler colony where the best land was under the control of whites, an uprising by the Kikuyu people during the 1950s was put down at considerable expense and bloodshed by British author-ities, but the conflict further eroded public support for continued colonization, and independence was granted in 1962. Wars of liberation in Congo, Algeria, Angola, Guinea-Bissau, Zambia (formerly Northern Rhodesia), Zimbabwe (formerly Southern Rhodesia) and Mozambique led to the flight of hundreds of thousands, creating refugee emergencies across the continent. There were fewer than 79,000 refugees in Africa in 1960; 35 years later the number had mushroomed to 6.4 million.[12]

At a Pan-African Congress held in Manchester in 1945, delegates condemned 'the artificial divisions and territorial boundaries created by the imperialist powers'.[13] Representatives in attendance from the United States, Europe and Africa envisioned a future for independent Africa where continent-wide political and economic cooperation would end the misery of millions. But the staying power of arbitrary colonial boundaries was too great. When the newly founded Organization of African Unity (OAU) decided in 1964 to accept the inviolability of state borders created by the old colonial powers, it meant that in many parts of the vast continent, ethnically and linguistically homogeneous peoples would continue to be separated by arbitrary national frontiers. Many ethnic groups found themselves split by new international boundaries, including the Yoruba of Nigeria/Benin, the Kakwa of Uganda/Somalia/Zaire and the Makonde of Mozambique/Tanzania.[14] Some of the new states were barely viable; in the mid-1960s more than twenty new countries had populations of less than 5 million, and four sovereign states had under 1 million citizens.[15] Europeans left behind a continent where the majority lacked access to basic education or primary medical care, where disease proliferated and where average life expectancy was barely 39 years.[16]

Following precedents set by the former colonial powers in Europe, most of the newly independent states adopted laws regulating the entry, employment and residence status of foreign nationals through passports, visas and temporary work permits. In some cases white colonial administrators stayed on to work in key sectors, but most returned home as nationalization of the bureaucracy gathered momentum. And white Europeans were not the only ones to leave; Ghanaians from Sierra Leone, Nigerians from Ghana, Dahomeans from Upper Volta – all were repatriated in the years immediately following independence.[17]

Employment protocols, categories of authorized immigrants possessing needed skills and the recruitment and regulation of unskilled labour for seasonal work all signified the importance of formal national boundaries. But policing those long borders and prosecuting undocumented migrants proved difficult, especially in the case of tribal peoples who understood little of the meaning of international borders and whose movements were informed by ethnic ties. Most of the newly formed states retained their links with metropolitan economies, while the first generation of elected political leaders accepted the cultural and linguistic practices of the colonial elite.[18] Ties with the developed West and a focus on cash crop production for export placed the economies of many fledgling states at the mercy of fluctuations in global markets and hindered the development of sustainable farming for domestic needs.

And those needs were becoming acute. Despite the disease factor, the African continent experienced unprecedented population growth in the post-colonial period. From approximately 200 million people in 1950 to 600 million four decades later, the total reached 840 million by the year 2005. Most of the increase occurred in rural areas, where access to educational services was least likely. Whether they embraced some form of socialist planning or followed more traditional market-based strategies, sub-Saharan African governments did not, as a rule, pay close attention to food production for domestic consumption as part of their overall development strategy. Rather, agriculture was viewed as a means of generating export revenue that could in turn support rapid industrial development and urban infrastructure. Unfortunately, during the late 1950s and '60s, just as many African colonies were securing independence, commodity prices for key agricultural products were in decline. Smaller states with mono-crop strategies were especially vulnerable when global markets did not favour their export product. Regional integration efforts were attempted over the years, such as the Economic Community of West African States and the Southern African Development Coordination Council, but the colonial legacy of economic dependency was never effectively addressed.

Disappointing revenues from the export of primary products, coupled with overly ambitious development projects and inefficient (and sometimes corrupt) bureaucracies meant increased national indebtedness. As early expectations for a better life went unrealized, democratically elected governments were replaced – sometimes violently – by military regimes. This situation was exacerbated during the 1970s when many countries, encouraged by Western experts and Western bankers, borrowed heavily to finance basic infrastructure development. As interest rates (and inflation) soared, debt servicing took up an increasing percentage of export earnings. By 1979, 25 of the 39 countries in sub-Saharan Africa were among the poorest in the world.[19] To compound these economic reverses, severe drought affected much of the continent in the 1980s and food production per capita declined. In the words of one commentator, sub-Saharan Africa during the 1980s became a land where people had little occasion to speak of 'meaningful development, of supply or abundance, of leisure or happiness'.[20] During the final decade of the twentieth century, as sub-Saharan Africa experienced the fastest growth in population of all developing regions of the world, the importation of basic foodstuffs became commonplace. Drought conditions, soil exhaustion, poor planning and political instability hampered efforts to reverse the trend, making food insecurity a major factor in the process of involuntary migration.[21]

And despite the colonial interlude, ethnicity still mattered in sub-Saharan Africa. Given the fact of ethnic pluralism and the separation of peoples at the moment of independence, federal political systems, with some degree of autonomy for ethnic groups, may have allowed for greater stability. Too often Africa's ruling elites attempted to govern from their own ethnic base, and were quick to adopt repressive measures when resistance emerged.[22] There were 53 sovereign states on the continent (and on offshore islands) at the start of the twenty-first century, but in reality several of these countries were in fact no more than congeries of competing ethnic and tribal interests, torn by civil conflict, plagued by economic instability and bereft of responsible leadership. A number of key defining characteristics of the state, including unchallenged control over territory within defined borders, a monopoly over the legitimate use of force within and beyond those borders, and acceptance of the rule of law in government, were absent in some of Africa's post-colonial states. Enduring tribal antipathies and politically inspired tribal violence frustrated efforts to cultivate nationalist sensibilities, while the ambitions of warlords and corruption at the highest levels of national government undermined the rule of law – and public support for nascent democratic institutions.

Virtually all of the wars that affected the continent in recent years involved ethnic and communal components. Of course political instability and civil conflict intensified the level of involuntary migration, both within states and across borders, leading to more dislocations and humanitarian crises that often overwhelmed the capacity of national governments and international aid organizations. By the end of the 1960s, the Office of the United Nations High Commissioner for Refugees (UNHCR) was spending almost two-thirds of its total relief funds in Africa, even though only 1 per cent of international migrants in Africa were refugees. Still the displacements continued, and by the start of the twenty-first century, Africa was home to over 13 million internally displaced persons, and approximately 3.6 million international refugees, or 33 per cent of the total migrant stock.[23]

INDEPENDENCE AND RELOCATION IN MUSLIM NORTH AFRICA

Within a few years of the end of World War II, most of North Africa, including Egypt, Sudan, Ethiopia, Somalia and Libya, had achieved independence. These mainly Muslim peoples witnessed the post-war dismantling of the European mandate system in the Middle East and acted in conformity with the principles of the 1941 Atlantic Charter, whereby Britain and the United States affirmed 'the right of all peoples to choose the form of government under which they will live'. As early as 1922 the British had recognized Egypt's sovereignty, but with the acquiescence of King Fu'ad and his successor, the dissolute King Farouk, British forces maintained a presence in the Suez Canal zone. World War II disrupted plans for the withdrawal of these troops to a narrow base around the Canal, but the allied victory in the war, including the destruction of Italy's empire in North Africa, meant that the process of disengagement would continue. Libya and Eritrea were placed under temporary military governments, and by 1951 the former had achieved its independence. Eritrea became a province of independent Ethiopia in 1952, only to be absorbed by its neighbour ten years later. Somalia was assigned to Italian and British supervision, and in 1960 an independent Somali Republic was founded.[24]

Efforts to secure full Egyptian autonomy from Britain were complicated by a disagreement over the status of Sudan, with Egyptian nationalists claiming that expansive territory for a larger Egyptian state and the British insisting that the Sudanese be allowed to determine their own status. Only after a military *coup d'état* and the abdication of King Farouk in 1952 did the new government come to terms and accept the principle of self-government for Sudan. General Gamul Abdel Nasser successfully negotiated the withdrawal of British forces from the Canal zone, a major victory for Egyptian nationalists that made it easier to accept Sudanese independence in 1956. Nasser's programme of nationalization, which limited a company's alien staff to one-tenth of the total, led to the departure of about 140,000 Greek and Cypriot nationals, but otherwise the new government's policies did not prompt large-scale emigration. Egyptians who chose to migrate during the post-war period typically left for destinations in Europe or, beginning in the 1970s, to the oil-producing countries of the Middle East.

Sectarian Sudan

Independent Sudan faced its own internal ethno-religious strains, as the historic north–south divide between Muslim and Christian inhab-itants descended into five decades of intermittent civil war and forced displacement beginning in 1955. Although the largest country in Africa, the majority of Sudan's estimated 32 million inhabitants were divided along religious and regional lines. The south, sparsely popu-lated and multilingual, embraced a variety of traditional African religions and was home to a minority Christian community, while the Arabic-speaking north was predominantly Muslim. During the colo-nial period, British authorities tolerated Arab–Islamic mistreatment of non-Muslims in the north – including the practice of forced labour – while emergent views of nation building became associated not with residency within colonial borders but with being Arab and Muslim. From the moment of independence, then, the largely Christian and animist southern provinces resisted efforts by Muslim rulers in Khartoum to consolidate power and demanded the adoption of a federal structure of government that would reserve considerable autonomy for the south. When northern delegates to a constitutional committee produced a draft document that privileged Islam and Arabic over other religions and languages, the stage was set for conflict.

The military seized power in a *coup d'état* in 1958 and began a campaign of Islamization in the south (which included, by 1964, the expulsion of all Christian missionaries). Sharia law was proclaimed across the country in 1983. Clashes between southern resistance fighters based in Congo and Uganda and Sudanese government forces led to the flight of tens of thousands of civilians into neighbouring countries.[25]

After another military coup in 1989 brought a stridently Islamic regime to power, a policy of *jihad* against the south was undertaken, with the aggressors being accused of reintroducing slavery in certain areas. Government bombing of civilian targets led to the flight of a million southerners into neighbouring countries, while another 3 million relocated to the north of the country. Those who repaired to refugee camps around the capital of Khartoum were forced to renounce their faith before receiving food aid, and churches built by the dispossessed were destroyed by government authorities.[26] During the course of a conflict that continued into the twenty-first century, international human-rights organizations criticized all parties for forcing displaced persons into labour on commercial farms, recruiting child soldiers in refugee camps and even bartering refugees in exchange for emergency food relief.[27] Finally in 2005 a peace settlement was agreed, but not before a new and more brutal government-sponsored offensive started in the west of the country.

In the early years of the twenty-first century, the government singled out the western Darfur region of the country as the major source of rebel activity. Claiming that local tribal peoples were supporting the rebels, the authorities in Khartoum started arming Arab militiamen known as Janjaweed, who in turn set upon civilian populations, beating and raping, destroying cattle and burning entire villages. The butchery quickly took on a religious and racial tone, with the black African victims of Janjaweed gunmen appealing to the international community for protection. By the end of 2005 more than 250,000 Darfur refugees had crossed the border into Chad, a nation that declared war on Sudan in December 2005, while another 2 million residents were displaced internally and living in some 200 makeshift refugee camps. A lack of cooperation on the part of the Sudanese government frustrated efforts by international relief agencies to provide food and medical assistance to those who had been attacked and displaced. Western observers accused the government of promoting genocide in Darfur, and in response President Omar Hassan al Bashir declared that alleged international concern was no more than an assault on a Muslim state. By 2006, over 7,000 African Union (AU) troops were stationed in Darfur as AU-mediated talks between rebels and the Sudanese government took place, but President al Bashir refused to allow the expansion of this peacekeeping force under UN auspices. In April of 2006 the UN Security Council imposed sanctions against four individuals accused of war crimes in Darfur, but attacks by government aircraft and militias on both sides continued to force civilians from their homes, prolonging the suffering and presenting the international community with a seemingly intractable humanitarian crisis.

Violence in French Algeria

Creating a strong consensus for independence after World War II was not difficult to achieve in colonies with minuscule European settler populations. But where the European presence was significant, as it was in French-controlled Algeria, an indigenous nationalist movement encountered stiff opposition from those who controlled the best land and held the most lucrative positions. French citizenship had been accorded to Algeria's 7.5 million Muslims in 1947, but representation in the local territorial assembly and in the French parliament was equally divided between Algeria's Muslims and approximately 1 million settlers.[28] Stung by its humiliation during World War II, France was unwilling to concede independence to its most valuable African possession and created the fiction that colonies were not separate territories but rather part of *la plus grande France*. Hundreds of thousands of unemployed Algerians migrated to France after 1945 in search of work, while nationalist leaders who remained behind concluded that armed struggle was the only option remaining in the drive for independence.

The triumph of Algeria's National Liberation Front (FLN) over France in a brutal eight-year conflict (1954–62) resulted in the deaths of some 300,000 Algerians, the flight of over a million European settlers and the creation of refugee emergencies in the neighbouring states of Morocco and Tunisia. During the height of the conflict, French military forces – which reached the level of over 500,000 men – forcibly relocated Algerian peasants who were thought to be sympathetic to the insurgents, and by 1960 over a million people were displaced from their homes and held in rural detention camps. In order to avoid a similar fate, thousands of Algerians crossed the border into Morocco and Tunisia, countries that had secured independence from France in 1956. In a controversial move that angered French authorities, UNHCR entered both countries to provide humanitarian assistance to the refugees, and continued its work once the fighting ended in 1962 and the refugees began to return to their war-torn homeland. In addition to the 1 million embittered French colonists who left Algeria for France after the war, another 160,000 Algerians who had fought for the imperial power were transported to France and awarded citizenship, although they faced a significant measure of discrimination in their adopted land.[29] UNHCR intervention in Algeria set the stage for a dramatic expansion of the UN's peacekeeping and refugee assistance roles. Focusing its efforts on European refugees during the immediate post-war period, the agency now directed its attention to the displacements associated with independence movements throughout sub-Saharan Africa.

Clan Violence and the Implosion of Somalia

Securing independence from Britain and Italy in 1960, Somalia's mostly homogeneous population (in terms of language, religion, and major cultural traditions), was rent along clan, sub-clan and family lines. Many political parties emerged during the first decade of independence, each claiming to represent its own provincial group. After a military coup in 1969 ousted the elected government, General Mohammed Siyad Bare attempted to unify the country by officially banning clan affiliations, nationalizing much of the economy and resettling pastoralists on state farms.[30] Despite significant Soviet military and economic assistance, a severe drought in the mid 1970s hampered the government's efforts to create a socialist state, and when Bare attempted to whip up nationalist sentiment by claiming the Ogaden region of Ethiopia for Somalia, the resulting 1977–8 war led to a flood of Somali-speaking refugees from Ogaden into the north of the country. Somalia eventually lost the war against the authoritarian regime of Ethiopia's Haile Selassie, but the refugees kept coming, an estimated 1 million by 1981. The resulting strain on the nation's meagre resources, coupled with Bare's tendency to fall back on his own clan for support in efforts to silence dissent, plunged the country into fratricidal conflict that resulted in the breakdown of state authority and a tragic return to clan-based warfare.

By 1988 almost 400,000 Somali refugees had fled to Ethiopia, and another 400,000 were displaced in the countryside.[31] Bare was finally ousted in 1991, but the opposition failed to unify the country, propelling even more residents into foreign exile.[32] Those who stayed behind often sought refuge in hastily constructed relief camps, where outbreaks of infectious diseases claimed the lives of thousands. An attempted UN military intervention in 1993, led by US forces, failed to put a stop to the clan violence, and after UN troops were killed in clashes with gunmen, the peacekeepers were hastily withdrawn. Two years later the UN estimated that 4.5 million people were still in urgent need of food relief.[33] Regional governments declared their temporary sovereignty in the late 1990s, but they did not receive recognition by the international community. The ongoing violence uprooted approximately 1.7 million people in the south of the country, whose only recourse was the refugee camp.[34] As the endemic fighting destroyed virtually all public services and institutions, including roads, telecommunications, air and seaports and power generation, the developed world remained largely aloof from a society that seemed incapable of embracing the nation-state ideal.

VIOLENCE AND FLIGHT IN WEST AND CENTRAL AFRICA

Unlike so much of Muslim North Africa, the European colonies south of the Sahara were never directly involved in the military campaigning of World War II, but their Western-trained nationalist leaders were fully aware of the power of self-determination in the wake of the defeat of Nazism. Unfortunately, at the moment of independence most of these colonies suffered from inadequate educational systems, communal divisions, lack of experience with democratic political institutions and an underdeveloped sense of public service.[35] Leaders of geographically large, ethnically diverse and linguistically plural states like Nigeria and

Congo/Zaire found the challenge of forging a common national identity overwhelming. When economic ills were not addressed, states with shallow democratic roots were quick to fall victim to authoritarian, one-party alternatives – usually military men. After concentrating their power, a number of these leaders moved in the direction of state socialism, often expelling foreigners during difficult economic times. Despite the generally lax enforcement of immigration laws, mass expulsions of undocumented residents took place at one time or another in Côte d'Ivoire, Sierra Leone, Ghana, Zambia, Uganda, Kenya, Senegal and Nigeria. In the cases of Kenya and Uganda, members of the enterprising South Asian community – most of whom were British passport holders – were targets of attack. Aliens were almost always the first to become scapegoats when a host country experienced severe economic difficulties.

West African Crises

At the close of the twentieth century, almost 42 per cent of Africa's international migrants lived in West Africa.[36] And given that the poor and politically unstable West African nations of Liberia, Guinea, Sierra Leone and Côte d'Ivoire were racked by civil war, political corruption, and massive human dislocations during the late twentieth century, it is not surprising that the majority of these migrants were refugees. In the settler republic of Liberia, established in 1822 by American blacks with the support of influential political figures in the United States, tensions between the ruling elite of Americo-Liberians and the indigenous population remained a dreary constant of twentieth-century life. Excluded from meaningful participation in political affairs and dismayed by the corruption of the governing class, the marginalized indigenous majority supported a military coup in 1980, but the new regime of Samuel Doe quickly degenerated into a brutal military dictatorship. Refugee flows out of Liberia began in 1989 and cascaded the following year, with half a million taking refuge in neighbouring Guinea and an additional 270,000 in Côte d'Ivoire. In addition, there were an estimated 500,000 persons who were displaced internally, leaving a situation where approximately half of Liberia's population had become refugees.[37]

Full-scale civil war erupted in 1989 and involved more than a dozen armed ethnic groups. The fighting soon spilled over into neighbouring Sierra Leone before spreading to other countries in the region by the close of the century. Borders were meaningless to the men of violence who perpetuated the conflicts. Recent estimates indicate that as many as 1.1 million people in the region were made homeless for long periods, either as refugees or internally displaced persons. In Liberia, the election of the military strongman Charles Taylor as president in 1997 signalled the prelude to years of widespread corruption and human rights abuses. An insurgency movement took up arms against Taylor's regime in 2003 and inched toward the capital of Monrovia, prompting yet another round of population displacement. Government forces and rebel groups alike attacked refugee camps as aid workers fled, and before the end of the year almost 700,000 Liberians were displaced, with more than 200,000 of these fleeing the country altogether. Disease, malnutrition and lack of access to clean water became the daily reality for an entire nation.[38] Taylor was exiled to Nigeria in 2003, but even with the democratic election of Ellen Johnson Sirleaf as president in 2005, the country faced enormous rebuilding and resettlement challenges.

Nigeria

As sub-Saharan Africa's most populous state, with 42 million citizens at the moment of independence in 1960, Nigeria's political elite had received some administrative experience under British rule, but the multilingual country was sharply divided along ethnic lines. In 1947 a future Nigerian leader, Obafemi Awolowo, wrote that 'Nigeria is not a nation. It is a mere geographical expression. There are no "Nigerians" in the same sense as there are "English", "Welsh" or "French". The word "Nigerian" is merely a distinctive appellation to distinguish those who live within the boundaries of Nigeria and those who do not.'[39] Three main groups, the Muslim Hausa in the north, the Yoruba in the south-west, and the Igbo in the south-east, contested elections, competed for government jobs, sought leadership positions in the military and struggled for control over the national treasury. In the words of one historian, in Nigeria 'tribalism became the ideology of politics'.[40]

In the summer of 1966, junior military officers from northern Nigeria killed Nigeria's military head of state, Major General Johnson Thomas Umunnakwe Aguiyi-Ironsi, who himself had led a successful coup against the corrupt civilian government only months earlier. In the resulting chaos, almost a million Igbo fled from their northern homes to the east of the country where, in the spring of 1967, the military governor declared that the region, renamed Biafra, was now independent. Non-easterners were now the victims of expulsion as the ethnic divide grew more intense. Over the next two and a half years nearly 2.5 million Biafrans died, casualties of intense fighting and hunger, before the secessionist state capitulated to superior federal military forces in 1970. The country experienced an oil boom during the 1970s, and between 2 and 3 million immigrants flowed into the country, attracted by relatively high wages and a growing consumer sector. There was also a considerable north–south internal migration prompted by prolonged drought in the north. Most of the internal migrants relocated to Nigeria's southern cities.

Civilian rule was restored in 1979 under a new constitution that established a federation of nineteen states. With the country now the world's sixth largest oil producer, the opportunity for meaningful economic progress and national consensus seemed to be at hand. But the temptations of new-found wealth were too great for the leaders of the civilian government, and by the early 1980s corruption at the highest levels was endemic. When oil prices suddenly fell, unemployment and recession returned, and the welcome sign for foreign workers was removed. The military again assumed power, and in 1986 accepted a Structural Adjustment Program that called for reduced spending on key public services such as health, education and housing in return for international aid. This difficult decision accelerated the emigration of Nigeria's skilled professionals to more affluent and stable countries. According to a leader of the Nigeria Medical Association, many health workers left 'not only because of money but in search of good values, such as recognition of honesty, truth, equality of opportunity and justice'.[41] For the influential Nigerian novelist Chinua Achebe, the

Nigerian problem was not lack of resources but simply 'the unwilling-ness or inability of its leaders to rise to the responsibility, to the challenge of personal example which are the hallmarks of true leadership'.[42]

Ghana: The Loss of Human Capital

Ghana was the first sub-Saharan state to achieve independence after World War II. A major sending region for the infamous transatlantic slave trade beginning in the sixteenth century, the so-called 'Gold Coast' (encompassing modern Ghana, Togo and Benin) became a highly profitable gold and cocoa exporting region under the British during the second half of the nineteenth century. Formally established as the Gold Coast colony in 1874, male migrants from the neighbour-ing colonies of Gambia, Sierra Leone and Nigeria numbered approximately 40,000 just before the outbreak of World War I, and the total expanded to just under 300,000 in 1931, including migrants from the regional French-controlled colonies of Upper Volta (modern Togo, Côte d'Ivoire, Mali and Benin). Much of the migration was seasonal in nature, with workers returning home once the cash crops were harvested. The constant cross-border migration in colonial West Africa continued a pattern of pre-colonial nomadic exchange and regional trade. Only now the flow of peoples across international borders was dictated by market forces within an emerging global economy.

Winning independence in 1957, Ghana continued to be a net receiv-ing zone. By 1960 almost 12 per cent of the country's total population were foreign-born, with the vast majority entering the country from neighbouring lands where ethnic bonds and, in some cases, a common language made the transition less difficult for the newcomers. Declining economic fortunes, coupled with the ouster of President Kwame Nkrumah in a military *coup d'état* in 1964, prompted a growing number of Ghana's professional elite – teachers, physicians, engineers – to seek employment outside the country. Ghana's immigrant popula-tion was accused of exacerbating the country's economic woes, and in 1969 the government expelled all undocumented aliens, some 200,000 men and women, most of whom worked in the cocoa industry.

Emigration continued throughout the 1970s as a series of regimes failed to restore economic prosperity to what had once been one of colonial Africa's most productive regions. Nigeria, with its booming oil industry, became the destination country of choice for semi- and unskilled Ghanaians during the 1970s, but when oil prices dropped in the early 1980s and Nigeria's economy began to suffer, that government followed its neighbour's earlier example and began to expel undocumented workers. Some 1.2 million unskilled Ghanaians had little choice but to return home, but those with professional qualifications tended to relocate further afield. By the middle of the 1990s, it was estimated that between 10 and 20 per cent of Ghana's 20 million citizens were living abroad. Since many of these migrants possessed the types of specialized training and skills that were in demand in Europe and North America, a significant 'brain drain' complicated the government's ability to reverse the country's economic, educational and health-care difficulties.[43]

Congo/Zaire

The chronic migration crises that have afflicted the former Belgian colony of Congo since independence can be traced in part to the harsh and arbitrary nature of the colonial regime, and to the absence of strong nationalist sensibilities in a country that comprised 1 million square miles, or one-thirteenth, of the entire African continent. Congo's ivory, palm oil, rubber and copper had made the colony a major economic asset to Belgium since it was first established as the personal property of King Leopold II in 1885. Throughout the colonial period political affairs were run from Brussels, where edicts were sent to colonial officials and where punishments for disobedience were harsh. Private companies shared their profits with Leopold until the King was forced to transfer his private empire to the Belgian government in 1908. Before this date, however, the experience of forced migration in Congo had been well established. Companies had engaged in coercive labour practices on a regular basis, and villagers who failed to meet their production quotas – especially in rubber production – were flogged and mutilated. Thousands fled their homes rather than face the imperious demands of Leopold's labour regime.

By the early 1950s, Congo was producing 10 per cent of the world's copper, 50 per cent of its cobalt and 70 per cent of its industrial diamonds.[44] Colonial authorities believed that as Christian missionary efforts and primary education expanded, the Congolese would come to accept Belgian rule. 'The essential wish of the Congolese elite,' wrote the future prime minister, Patrice Lumumba in 1956, 'is to be "Belgians" and to have the right to the same freedoms and the same rights.'[45] No such rights and freedoms were forthcoming, however, and when riots broke out in the capital of Leopoldville in January 1959, the government, fearing an Algeria-style guerrilla war, swiftly pledged to begin a programme of political reform.

A tiny elite of Congolese intellectuals had been at the forefront of calls for independence during the 1950s, but there were no consensus political leaders within the large colony of some 15 million. The Belgian government invited leaders from thirteen political parties to Brussels in an effort to agree a plan for independence. In the run-up to hastily arranged national elections in June 1960, dozens of political parties, each one representing narrow regional and ethnic interests, emerged. The outspoken Lumumba was elected as the country's first prime minister, but his political party held only a quarter of the seats in the new legislative assembly, and most of these representatives came from one province. Never before had the Congolese voted in elections, nor had their indigenous leaders ever held political office. The new nation had only a handful of university graduates, no physicians, teachers or army officers and little sense of national identity. The first government was a coalition of twelve parties, some of whose leaders were divided over fundamental issues of policy and governance.[46]

Before long the new state was facing a mutiny by its own military rank and file, and a de facto division of the country. Whites were attacked and began to flee the country, leaving key administrative offices without trained staff. With civil society imploding around him, Lumumba appealed to the UN for help in restoring order, but when he subsequently asked UN troops to expel Belgian forces, Western support for his government collapsed. Lumumba's decision to seek Soviet logistical aid prompted the Americans to plot his removal from power. Before the CIA could carry out its objective, however, the prime minister ordered a military assault against the secessionist region of Kasai, home to Congo's lucrative diamond fields. Hundreds of local tribesmen were killed in the operation and a quarter of a million people were made refugees. The prime minister was assassinated in early 1961 and, in an effort to prevent the country from becoming a surrogate in the Cold War, the UN maintained its peacekeeping force in the country. It was not enough. In 1964 a rebellion erupted in the eastern half of the country. Former Lumumba supporters ordered the mass execution of civil servants, teachers and other government representatives. Before the rebels were beaten back the next year, an estimated 1 million people had perished. Not until 1965 was a semblance of order restored under the direction of General Mobutu Sese Seko, whose strongly anti-communist regime was propped up by generous Western aid. But the damage to the nationalist ideal had been done: Congo (renamed Zaire by Sese Seko) remained deeply divided amongst rival ethnic groups, many of whom viewed the increasingly dictatorial Mubutu as a puppet of Western interests.

Crises in the Great Lakes Region

'Divide and Rule' policies implemented during the colonial era contributed greatly to the refugee crises in the post-colonial period. Events in Central Africa represent the most tragic illustration of the ill effects of colonial practice. Unlike the situation in West Africa, where Britain and France had provided educational opportunities for the indigenous elite, Belgian policy in the Congo had failed to encourage the formation of an educated Congolese leadership that could command broad national support. While the process of independence in most of West Africa involved fairly brief periods of peaceful struggle followed by the rise to power of Europe-educated and pro-Western African leaders, Congo was beset by internal political struggles and the absence of a managerial class from the outset.

In German- and, after World War I, Belgian-controlled Rwanda, colonial authorities regularly favoured the Tutsi ethnic minority over the majority Hutu population. Belgian relations with the Tutsi deteriorated prior to the achievement of independence in 1962, however, and violence erupted between the two groups, with the Hutu-dominated First Republic sanctioning attacks on Tutsi civilians. An unsuccessful assault against the state by Tutsi refugees in 1963 led to a violent reprisal and the deaths of over 10,000 Tutsi in Rwanda, prompting a further exodus north into neighbouring Uganda. The Tutsi refugee population in Uganda eventually grew to over 200,000, but they were subject to waves of discrimination and persecution during the 1980s. In the autumn of 1990 some 4,000 Tutsi rebels, trained as members of Uganda's national armed forces, invaded Rwanda in the hope of returning to power. The initial clashes and ensuing civil war inflamed the views of extremists on both sides, despite the fact that a power-sharing agreement was signed in 1993 and a UN peacekeeping contingent had been installed to monitor the ceasefire.[47] The UN deployment was not prepared for what followed in the spring and summer of 1994.

Fearful that additional Tutsi refugees would join the rebel army known as the Rwandan Patriotic Front (RPF), hardliners among the Rwandan Hutu leadership pressed for the elimination of the country's Tutsi population. The death of President Juvenal Habyarimana in an air crash in April provided the occasion for Hutu radicals in the capital of Kigali to set upon the Tutsi minority and moderate Hutu who had supported the peace process. Soon the violence spread across the country, reaching genocidal proportions between April and July 1994. Before it was over, an estimated 800,000 civilians had been murdered. The small UN peacekeeping force was unable to protect the victims, and with members of the UN Security Council divided over expanding the peacekeeping mission, most members of the contingent were withdrawn from the country. Those Tutsi who survived the genocide felt, understandably, a deep sense of having been betrayed by the international community. In a dramatic turn of events, the RPF handily defeated the Hutu government's forces during that summer and captured the capital of Kigali, setting off a massive flight of Hutu into neighbouring countries. Over 2 million Hutu – including soldiers and government officials implicated in the genocide – became refugees in neighbouring Tanzania and Zaire. Ethnic civil war also contributed to a massive refugee crisis in tiny Burundi, located directly south of Rwanda. The assassination of the Hutu president in October 1993 triggered mass killings of Tutsi and immediate reprisals. In Burundi approximately a quarter of a million lost their lives while another 500,000 (mostly Hutu) fled into Rwanda, Tanzania and Zaire after Tutsi soldiers took control of the government.[48]

Conditions in the Hutu refugee camps in Zaire were chaotic; in July 1994 a cholera outbreak claimed the lives of thousands. Most of the refugees had been forced across the border by leaders of the Hutu regime. The camps became militarized, serving as bases of operations and recruiting centres for Hutu militants. Cross-border attacks against the new Tutsi government of Rwanda were commonplace. A Rwandan government in exile was declared by exiled Hutu leaders, and UNHCR relief workers found themselves in the difficult position of trying to provide humanitarian assistance in an environment where the former Rwandan regime was using fellow refugees as human shields and political hostages. The Organization of African Unity estimated that as many as 100,000 of the Hutu refugees in Zaire were militants and war criminals.[49]

The Zairean central government wielded little authority in the eastern part of the country, as the corrupt regime of President Mobutu Sese Seko was preoccupied with its own efforts to remain in power. Frustrated by the failure of Zaire or the international community to disarm militants in the camps, or to bring those implicated in the genocide to justice, the Rwandan army launched a series of attacks across the border in the spring of 1995. RFP forces also attacked a Hutu refugee camp within southern Rwanda, where a French-led multi-national force had been assigned by the UN Security Council. Thousands of Hutu civilians were killed in the assault, and once news of the killing reached the camps in Zaire, further repatriation efforts ground to a halt. As political and military conditions both within Rwanda and across the border in Zaire deteriorated, the UNCHR made desperate calls for Security Council action, but the UN remained indecisive. The refugees in Zaire, fearful lest they face further violence in Rwanda should they return, expecting retribution from camp authorities should they express the desire to go home, and lacking basic protection from the host government of Zaire, were largely abandoned by the international community. During 1996 fighting escalated throughout the region, and none of the various refugee camps were exempted from attack. The Rwandan military joined forces with Zairean rebels and compelled the return of large numbers of Rwandan refugees in autumn 1996. By the end of that year UNHCR staff had been forced to abandon most of their posts, leaving behind thousands of vulnerable refugees in a de facto war zone.[50]

Civil war in Zaire and the collapse of the Mobutu kleptocracy in 1997 made conditions for the refugees untenable. During 1997 the majority of Hutu refugees living in Zaire made their way back across the border into Rwanda. UNHCR arranged transportation for 260,000 of the refugees, while thousands of others returned on foot. Repatriation efforts continued over the next few years, but attempts to identify and arrest those who had been involved in the 1994 genocide were largely unsuccessful. After the fall of Mobutu, the Democratic Republic of the Congo (formerly Zaire) descended into military conflict driven by competition over the country's vast natural resources. By the end of the century there were as many as a million people displaced by the regional conflicts that by now seemed endemic in the Great Lakes region.[51] In Rwanda and Burundi, tensions between Tutsi and Hutu remained, the memory of genocide still immediate. Tragically, the enormous loss of life during the 1990s, including the genocide, occurred as an irresolute international community stood on the sidelines.

MINORITY REGIMES IN EAST AND SOUTHERN AFRICA

State-sponsored Relocation in Tanzania

The programme of internal relocation that took place in Tanzania during the mid-1970s was the product of a unique vision of socialism articulated by Julius Nyerere. The first president of independent Tanzania (1962–85), Nyerere was in favour of a programme of 'African Socialism' that ostensibly reflected the communal and family nature of traditional East African society. During the 1960s and '70s, the well-meaning Nyerere sought to discourage urbanization and harmful industrialization with the formation of communal farming villages. He believed that the economies of pre-colonial African society were based on *ujamaa* or 'familyhood' where cooperation allowed self-sufficient villages to provide all the essential services necessary to a meaningful life. According the Nyerere, the colonial experience had encouraged elitism, selfish individualism and economic dependency, and if these harmful tendencies were to be reversed, it was up to the state to provide the appropriate leadership and guidance.

The *ujamaa* communitarian experiment was an effort to lift Tanzania out of poverty without employing the rhetoric of Marxist class conflict. Based loosely on the rural reform projects undertaken by communist China, it began in the late 1960s and continued until 1976, with more than 13 million peasants (or 85 per cent of the rural population) first invited, and subsequently forced, to abandon their individual farms and relocate to communal villages. Some were obliged to surrender their land to the state before relocation, while others were simply rounded up and assigned to new locations. Large plantations were nationalized and capitalist farming practices were brought to a close. Resistance to the collectivization scheme was considerable, especially as decision-making powers were moved from the village to the regional level, leading to food crises (compounded by drought) in 1974 and again in 1976. Tanzania went from being one of Africa's largest exporters of agricultural products to one of the continent's biggest importers. The *ujamaa* experiment never led to the breakthrough in food production that was anticipated, and by the end of the 1970s it had been abandoned. For Tanzania's peasant majority, the democratic and communal rhetoric of *ujamaa* merely masked the increasing authoritarianism of a government that seemed out of touch with its citizens.[52]

Elements of Nyerere's vision were embraced by the Marxist rulers of Mozambique after that country achieved independence from Portugal in 1975. Heavily reliant on development aid from the Eastern bloc, President Samora Moises Machel and his Frelimo Party embraced the compulsory 'villagization' of rural dwellers during the 1980s, together with the rapid mechanization of farms, as the best solution to low productivity in the agricultural sector. Large farms that had been abandoned by Portuguese settlers were the first to be collectivized. As in Tanzania, collectivization was deeply resented by peasant proprietors; by the mid-1980s productivity had diminished to the point where all state farms were operating at a deficit. In addition, the collectivization programme was hampered by the efforts of Rhodesia and South Africa to undermine Machel's government. Both white minority regimes funded Mozambican rebel elements that represented themselves as enemies of villagization. The ensuing conflict led to further displacement in the country and the eventual abandonment of the socialist agenda in the 1980s. Between 1981 and 1992 over 5 million Mozambicans were displaced or became refugees in neighbouring states as a result of the bloody insurgency that had been funded by the white minority regimes, especially apartheid South Africa.[53] By the latter date Mozambique had become, according to the World Bank, the world's poorest country.

Civil War and Dislocation in Angola

Portugal's African colonies originally served as sources for the transatlantic slave trade. Until the middle of the nineteenth century, Angola, Mozambique and Guinea provided slave labour for both an American market and for the Portuguese-controlled plantation economies on the Cape Verde islands, São Tomé and Príncipe. Even after the transatlantic slave trade declined in the second half of the century, slave labour was employed on the coffee and cocoa plantations of the latter two islands. An 1875 decree simply abolished the category of free labour and in its place created a system of compelled labour, thus facilitating the transport of workers to colonial possessions in need of additional workers. By the final decades of the century, Portuguese colonial authorities had introduced a taxation regime that obliged peasants to sell their labour as a means of paying their financial obligations to the metropole. And levels of taxation regularly outstripped wage packages. Indentured labour and even slavery continued into the first decade of the twentieth century, especially in Angola, São Tomé and Príncipe.[54]

The colonial regime in Angola was especially harsh. A source of slaves for over four centuries, Angola came under direct Portuguese control during the second half of the nineteenth century. An onerous 'native tax', payable in Portuguese currency, was imposed in 1908, and by the end of World War II some Angolans were fleeing the colony rather than pay the tax. Forced labour and the expropriation of black-occupied land remained hallmarks of the plantation-based economy until 1962, with farmers obliged to leave their subsistence farms for low-wage work on cotton, coffee, corn and sisal plantations. In 1960 the age of tax liability was lowered to sixteen, forcing additional thousands into indentured labour contracts. Coffee was the leading cash crop in the post-war period, with exports propelling the colony to the status of the world's third largest coffee grower by the 1960s. The profits, of course, went to overseas investors and white settlers whom the government encouraged by offering free transportation, housing and land. By 1960 almost 200,000 white settlers had taken up residence in Angola. Opportunities for black Angolans within the colonial administration narrowed as racist ideology gained greater currency. Diamond mining and oil drilling also began in earnest after the war, and by the early 1970s the sale of oil enabled Portugal to fund its wars against independence movements in its colonies.

Armed resistance to colonial rule in Angola began in 1961, and brutal reprisals led by civilian colonial militia led to the flight of approximately 250,000 refugees across the northern border into newly independent Congo. The 1961 risings signalled the start of a debilitating, destructive and politically fragmented guerrilla war that lasted for fourteen years. Despite the fact that rival nationalist leaders were never able to unite, Portuguese forces were unable to eliminate the insurgency, and when a military coup overthrew the Portuguese government in 1974, a new stage in the struggle for Angolan independence began. Leaders of the three major rebel groups met at the start of 1975 and pledged to seek national reconciliation, but before formal independence was secured in November 1975, both the US and the USSR began sending covert military aid to their preferred nationalist groups. Before long Cuban forces were inserted to bolster the socialist Popular Movement for the Liberation of Angloa (MPLA), while South African troops crossed the border to prop up the National Union for the Total Independence of Angola (UNITA) led by Jonas Savimbi. Angola became the scene of a bloody Cold War conflict by proxy, with the MPLA government declaring its allegiance to Marxist–Leninist principles, while opposition UNITA forces accepted arms and assistance from the South African defence forces, and from the Americans via the government of Zaire. Although the end of the Cold War resulted in the withdrawal of military aid to both sides in the civil war, when the results of free elections in 1992 did not satisfy Savimbi, his UNITA fighters returned to guerrilla activities.[55]

The protracted civil conflict produced one of the world's largest populations of internally displaced persons. Mineral and resource rich, producing the second largest volume of oil in sub-Saharan Africa after Nigeria, and serving as the fourth largest producer of diamonds in the world, 10 per cent of the country's population relied on external assistance to meet basic food needs at the start of the twenty-first century. Thirty per cent of Angolans lacked access to primary health care, and the mortality rate for children under the age of five was the second highest in the world. Fighting between the government and rebel forces involved kidnappings, torture, terrorist assaults and the forced removal of civilians by both sides. In 2001 the UN estimated that the total number of displaced persons over the quarter century of civil war numbered 4.1 million – almost a third of the country's population. A ceasefire was finally agreed after the death of rebel leader Jonas Savimbi in 2002, but the process of rebuilding, reuniting families and establishing basic services to millions who lived below the poverty line was slowed by inefficiencies and poor infrastructure.[56]

Almost half a million Angolans were forced into refugee status during the years of fighting, with the majority fleeing to neighbouring Zambia, Namibia, Republic of Congo and the Democratic Republic of the Congo. In the region as a whole, South Africa's efforts to destabilize the governments of Angola, Mozambique and Namibia, together with the interventions of Cold War antagonists, exacerbated civil conflicts and refugee flows. In the end almost 2 million people fled from Mozambique and Angola, and an additional 6 million became displaced internally. By 2002, almost 300,000 Angolans had returned home, but the returnees faced severe food shortages, a degraded road network and the constant threat of land mines.[57]

Apartheid South Africa

The white-dominated state of South Africa was the most economically advanced country on the continent. In 1950 whites constituted 21 per cent of the country's 12 million inhabitants, and most of these were descendants of Dutch and British settlers.[58] Nominally independent since 1910, the government (under the leadership of Jan Smuts) had entered World War II on the side of Britain, but in the post-war environment the Dutch-descended Afrikaner population, concentrated mainly in the Transvaal and in the cities, began its rise to political prominence. In national elections held in 1948, the Afrikaner-led National Party narrowly won control of the government and parliament began implementing a wide-ranging policy of racial separation known as apartheid. The apartheid government cracked down on illegal urban squatting and severely restricted urban residency. Segregation of the races in education, health care, housing and transport became normative. Even the rights previously enjoyed by Indians and 'coloured' (mixed-race) citizens were undermined.

None of these racist actions was lacking in precedent. Early in the twentieth century the government, operating on the specious theory that all racial groups belonged to separate nations, undertook to create a series of native homelands (called Bantustans) where black South Africans could own land. But since more than 87 per cent of the country's total land was reserved for whites, blacks increasingly sought employment in towns and cities. A significant urban migration had begun during the war years, with 1.8 million blacks resident in the cities by 1946. The owners of South Africa's coal and gold mines continued to recruit male workers from rural areas within the country and from neighbouring colonies (and later states) to the north. Recruiting stations in Angola, Mozambique, Rhodesia and Tanzania organized road, rail and, later, air transport to move men to temporary positions in dangerous jobs. They lived in sparse, single-sex barracks and were afforded few opportunities for recreation. Ethnic mixing in the hostels reduced the likelihood of labour organization, while difficult or activist workers were quickly dismissed and returned to their rural homeland.

For spouses and family members left behind, life was equally difficult. Many rural communities came to depend on the remittances sent by urban migrants for personal survival. By 1960 more than 500,000 blacks from the reserves were away from home as workers in white areas, 'representing 40 per cent of all males between the ages of 15 and 45'.[59] By now the apartheid government was committed to reversing the trend. An elaborate system of passes was instituted, listing where blacks were allowed to work and reside. In order to enforce the interlocking system of apartheid, a large portion of federal funds was devoted to police and military services.

Popular protests against the pass laws in 1960 led to violence in the township of Sharpeville, near Johannesburg, where 69 Africans were killed by the security forces. The government responded by imprisoning thousands, outlawing the African National Congress and the Pan-Africanist Congress, and setting the groundwork for more than three decades of clandestine resistance to the regime. In the 1970s the Bantustans were offered full independence, but only four accepted the offer since it carried with it a renunciation of South African citizenship; not surprisingly, the international community refused to recognize the legitimacy of the move. The worst abuses of the temporary labour system came to an end in 1994, but the phenomenon of temporary rural to urban migration continued as a major feature of South Africa's mining industry.

Southern Rhodesia/Zimbabwe

White settlers in Southern Rhodesia made up 5 per cent of the population (as opposed to only 1 per cent in Kenya) in the 1950s. Enjoying significant domestic self-government since the early 1920s, the minority whites were unwilling to accede to the 'wind of change' that British Prime Minister Harold Macmillan referred to in a speech before South Africa's parliament in 1960. During the period of minority rule, more than half a million blacks had been uprooted from their homes and removed from lands designated as white only. When moderate blacks established their first nationalist organization, the African National Congress, in 1957, the government responded by outlawing it and arresting its leaders. Its successor organization, the National Democratic Party, was similarly banned in 1961. The government became increasingly reactionary and in 1965, under the leadership of its new prime minister, Ian Smith, declared its full independence under white minority rule.[60]

For the next ten years, the regime jailed its opponents and effectively defied the economic sanctions imposed by Britain and the UN. But when Mozambique secured its independence from Portugal in 1975, the Marxist-led government there began to arm and train black Rhodesians who were committed to a costly guerrilla war against the white minority regime. The ensuing conflict was bloody and bitter, and the dislocation of innocent civilians caught in the middle of the fighting created new refugee emergencies. A growing number of whites, living in a climate where the threat of ambush was constant, chose emigration over intransigence. When South Africa began to withdraw its military aid, Smith was forced to accept the inevitability of majority rule. A ceasefire agreement was signed in London in 1979, and the following year Rhodesia held elections that were marred by intimidation and violence. The outcome surprised no one, with the majority of seats in the new Zimbabwe parliament going to the African National Union Party under the guerrilla leader Robert Mugabe. Despite his conciliatory victory speech and subsequent affirmation of the sanctity of private property, many whites departed, and within three years of independence Zimbabwe's settler population declined from almost a quarter of a million to 80,000.[61]

In the end, the voluntary white flight was not enough for Mugabe, who faced increasing pressure from his political backers to dispossess white landowners and redistribute the property to poor farmers. At the time of independence fewer than 6,000 white commercial farmers controlled nearly 40 per cent of all agricultural land, and employed almost 300,000 blacks. After silencing his political critics through a campaign of state-sanctioned violence and systematic starvation in the early years of his regime, Mugabe's one-party state next turned against the remaining white landowners. In 1990 a plan was announced to redistribute half the white-owned land, some 13 million acres, to peasant farmers. The initial plan was not carried out, but threats of expropriation continued throughout the 1990s. In early 2000, after Mugabe failed to win a referendum that would have affirmed his dictatorial powers, armed gangs attacked white-owned farms across the country. Many of the attackers were transported to their destinations in government-owned vehicles, and the police refused to take action against them. Not only white owners, but some 400,000 black farm workers were victimized, with their homes destroyed in the process. Thousands fled, instantly becoming internal refugees in a country whose economic infrastructure was being destroyed by a dictator whose thirst for revenge against the minority settler population was compulsive. Facing economic collapse, some 7 million people – half of Zimbabwe's population – were at risk of starvation in the opening years of the new century. Hundreds of thousands, including large portions of Zimbabwe's educated middle class, fled to escape political repression and politically manufactured material hardship.[62]

THE DEVELOPED WORLD AND AFRICA

The late Myron Weiner once observed that questions concerning human migration, and especially refugee policies, ultimately involved moral judgements. How do societies weigh their own needs against the needs of those who have been displaced; how do prospective host societies wish to define themselves; and what influence can and ought to be brought to bear on societies that impel people to move? Although we have not examined migration trends since 1945 in all African nations, the principal factors involved in relocation are now apparent. Political independence did not insure economic freedom, and democratically elected but inexperienced leaders were unable to fulfil the promise of a better life once independence was achieved. Nation building required a willingness to subordinate ethnic interests to a broader set of mutually agreed principles and values. It demanded honesty and integrity at every level of civil society. And it was contingent upon solid economic footings, where domestic priorities came first and where trade relations with the developed world were reciprocal.

Africa's struggle to throw off the bonds of colonialism was predicated on the conviction, shared by nationalist leaders across the continent, that autonomy would promote individual and collective dignity, material betterment, longer and healthier lives and a position of equality within the community of nations. Some believed that the goals could be achieved most rapidly within a pan-African political context; most, however, gave priority to the national path. When not one but virtually all of these goals proved elusive, the national idea began to lose its attraction, and more provincial allegiances – religious, ethnic, regional, clan – returned to the foreground, with tragic consequences in country after country.

Relocation, either voluntary or – more typically for Africans – involuntary was one of these consequences. And the displacement continent seemed of little moment to the developed world. Especially since the end of the Cold War, when Africa lost much of its strategic importance to the developed West, the response of the international community to ethnic, religious and regional conflicts, and the resulting displacement of peoples, has been less than urgent. With ongoing civil conflicts, deteriorating health and education systems, population expansion and rising poverty levels, declining human resources due to the AIDS pandemic, drought and environmental degradation in rural areas and the emigration of skilled professionals, Africa stands at a crossroads. Today the viability of the state is in question across wide areas of the continent. And this was the context prior to the onset of the terrible epidemiological disaster known as Acquired Immune Deficiency Syndrome.

HIV/AIDS and Human Trafficking

There is a broad consensus that the great scourge of the late twentieth century had its origins somewhere in central Africa. Most likely a species jump from monkeys to humans occurred at some point, with HIV subsequently spreading along major transport routes. By the mid-1990s Africa was the hardest hit of all areas of the globe, with upwards of 70 per cent of the world total of infected people living in this one continent. In 2003 an estimated 28 million Africans were living with HIV, representing 65 to 70 per cent of the world's total.[63] By 2004 approximately 20 million people had died from the disease and 3 million new cases were identified each year. Some governments, already facing pressure from the International Monetary Fund and the World Bank to scale back social services in the interest of debt reduction, downplayed the extent of the pandemic well into the 1990s, further complicating efforts to address this public health emergency. In the meantime hundreds of thousands of children were left destitute as parents died from the disease.

Rural to urban migration, refugee flows, trafficking and regional trade patterns have all been linked with the spread of HIV/AIDS in Africa. Rapidly growing cities in particular tend to have higher rates of infection, doubtless due to the fact that residents come from a wide variety of sending areas. In South Africa, where migrant labour remained important after the end of apartheid, HIV/AIDS in rural areas has been aggravated by men returning from single-sex hostels, where access to the services of sex workers is commonplace. A strong correlation exits between war-related refugee displacement and HIV infection. The forced sexual relations that too often accompany the displacement caused by warring armies and militias exacerbate the spread; a sharply higher incidence of the disease among military men has been recorded in a number of sub-Saharan countries. Clearly, the deaths of an estimated 12 million people during the 1990s due to AIDS was not unrelated to the forced displacement of Africans from across the continent and the predatory actions of military forces.[64]

As if the AIDS epidemic were not devastating enough, in many African countries new forms of inhumanity have emerged in recent years. In particular, reports of trafficking in women and children have been on the increase, and no country is exempt from the phenomenon. The most common form involves rural to urban movement for purposes of child labour and adult prostitution. Criminal syndicates sometimes had international connections as far away as Asia, but in most cases the exploitation occurred regionally or internally. UNICEF estimated that, in 2003, 32 per cent of all trafficked children worldwide were African. Children were victims of sale, prostitution, debt-bondage and slavery, In war zones, children were abducted and forced to train as soldiers, while women were subject to forced marriages and physical and sexual abuse.[65] No longer exclusively the product of warfare and economic want, late twentieth-century trafficking brought the phenomenon of involuntary migration full circle with the age of slavery, when a similar commodification of humans again testified to humankind's potential for malfeasance.

Rural to Urban

Whatever the reason for human relocation in Africa after 1945, urban centres served as destination points for ever-larger numbers of migrants. During the colonial period, cities and towns in Africa functioned principally as administrative and commercial centres. Capital cities in particular tended to attract educated Africans seeking employment in the colonial bureaucracy, but most rural to urban migration remained temporary and seasonal in character. In 1945 fewer than 50 cities in Africa had populations that exceeded 100,000, and half of these were long-established commercial and cultural centres in Muslim North Africa. Indeed, by the middle of the twentieth century, only about 15 per cent of the continent's inhabitants lived in urban areas.[66] With their citizenry eager to escape the endemic poverty of the countryside, however, African leaders could not prevent the surge of migration to cities and towns that began after independence.

Population growth, together with drought and resulting environmental degradation, were important 'push' factors in rural to urban migration. Many newly established governments invested heavily in urban infrastructure, fostering employment opportunities in construction, while expanding civil bureaucracies boosted the need for government workers. Lagos, Nigeria, for example, had a population of 312,000 in 1955, but by the early 1980s the total exceeded 3 million. Similar patterns emerged in places like Leopoldville (Kinshasa), Zaire, Addis Ababa, Ethiopia and, in Monrovia, Liberia. In France's former West African colonies, 'almost half the urban growth between the mid-1960s and the mid-1970s came from migration, mostly from the rural areas, but some from smaller urban centres and some international'. Overall between 1950 and 1990, sub-Saharan Africa's capital cities grew by 1,000 per cent.[67] Unskilled male migrants, desperate to diversify sources of household income, generally came in search of construction, service and casual employment. Newcomers always faced uncertain job prospects, however, not to mention the challenges associated with housing and transportation. But in an overwhelmingly rural and impoverished continent, where land shortages were increasingly common, the exchange of 'misery without hope in the rural areas for misery with hope in the cities' was a rational choice for many.[68]

Most of Africa's post-colonial cities were alike in their general unpreparedness for growth, with newcomers from the countryside generally lacking access to clean water, sanitation and decent accommodation. Shantytowns emerged at the periphery of many urban centres and, as more women and children followed their husbands out of the rural setting, a pressing need emerged for basic education and social services. As late as 2004 it was estimated 'that roughly 75 per cent of basic needs are provided informally in the majority of African cities, and that processes of informalization are expanding across discreet sectors and domains of urban life'.[69] Unfortunately, Africa's marginality in the world economic system, and the economic reverses that the continent suffered during the 1970s and '80s, did not allow for costly and long-term urban strategies. In the meantime, urbanization continued apace – despite the threat of AIDS. While the rate of natural population increase for Africa was 2.7 per cent during the early 1970s, the urban growth rate was nearly double this figure. By the final decade of the twentieth century, about a third of the continent's population was urban based, as compared to a quarter in 1975. Some projections indicate that by 2030 approximately 54 per cent of Africans will live in urban areas, even though it is unlikely that urban infrastructure will keep pace with such dramatic change.[70]

Feminization

Labour migration was traditionally the province of African males. During the colonial period, most major employers, including government agencies, mines, commercial farms and missions, limited their labour recruitment by sex. When the male head of household departed, the wife normally assumed the dual responsibilities of child rearing and agricultural work on the small family farm. Smallholder agriculture thus became increasingly feminized during the colonial and immediate post-colonial periods. Cities were out of reach for most rural women. Even in urban occupations traditionally associated with women – domestic servants, secretaries, nurses – African men predominated. Male migrants, it was argued, placed fewer strains on colonial urban infrastructure, especially housing provision. As we have seen in white settler colonies like South Africa, accommodation was only provided for males, most of whom were accorded short-term labour contracts at very low wages. This encouraged a pattern of circular migration for males, whereby a period of urban labour lasting from a few months to a couple of years was paired with an extended stay on the family or communal farm. Return transportation was occasionally provided by one's employer, but more often such costs were borne by the contract worker. The social and familial strains associated with protracted migrant labour were enormous, but with poor wages and few opportunities for decent housing, family reunification in urban settings was impractical.[71]

In 1960, Africa had the lowest proportion of female international migrants of all major sending areas.[72] With independence came higher wages for many workers in towns and cities and as a result more women and children relocated with their husbands, while maintaining the hope of someday returning to their family lands. In addition to family reunification, significant numbers of young, single women began moving into urban centres. Those lacking education entered the temporary domestic servant market, hoping for modest earnings before returning to their village during harvest season. Greater opportunities for permanent work, together with the prospect of economic independence from family and village control, also attracted younger women to the expanding cities.

By the end of the twentieth century, increasing numbers of African women were relocating to cities at home and abroad in pursuit of personal economic advancement. Forty-six per cent of African migrants in 2000 were female, just slightly below the world average of 49 per cent. But opportunities for women always came at high cost. The village environment at least provided a modest level of security for single women, while family land, no matter how tiny the plot, offered the prospect of food and comfort. Very few urban workers in Africa, and fewer women still, secured jobs that offered pensions or lived in homes that could provide income or food from the land. Still, research conducted in the 1980s and '90s for Sierra Leone, Ghana, Nigeria and Congo indicated that more women than men planned to remain in cities over the long term, despite the considerable difficulties associated with urban life.[73] It was a considerable shift in gender relations over the course of one generation. But while greater female mobility may be viewed as a bright spot in an otherwise gloomy picture of rural to urban migration, the larger fact remained that Africa's cities were in the main poorly prepared to accommodate the massive influx.

The Talent Exodus

What then for those Africans whose skills were in demand elsewhere, and for whom prospects of meaningful employment at home seemed dim? By the late 1980s, as many as 70,000 highly skilled professionals from sub-Saharan Africa (30 per cent of the total) were living outside the continent.[74] Professional women in particular were likely to relocate overseas, as nurses, physicians and teachers commonly found more attractive employment options in wealthy countries. Most of the emigrants relocated to Europe, with France and Britain recruiting and hosting the largest numbers. Perhaps not surprisingly, many migrants who left to pursue specialized university or technical training – often at the expense of their government – elected to stay on in the former colonial power.

During the 1990s, the number of African-born residents in the United States increased by 142 per cent, from just under 364,000 at the beginning of the decade to 880,000 in 2000. The major portion (37 per cent) of these newcomers were from countries in Western Africa, especially Nigeria, Ghana and Liberia. More than two of every five migrants in the US were college educated, and the majority of these were employed in professional-level occupations that offered higher median salaries.[75] Receiving countries in the demographically stagnant North actively recruited African nurses, physicians, educators and business professionals in order to compensate for local skills shortages. With a growing and youthful population (nearly half of the population of sub-Saharan Africa is under age fifteen) and with a labour force that is projected to grow to over 477 million by the year 2025 (matching the region's total population in 1990), the emigration of skilled workers is bound to intensify.[76]

An African Solution?

During its 40 years of operation, the Organization of African Unity attempted to serve as a focus for pan-African interests and continent-wide cooperation. But the organization's commitment to the principle of national sovereignty, together with its high percentage of heads of state who rejected democratic values, severely undercut its ability to prevent massive human dislocations and the hardships associated with forced removal. In 2001, a successor organization was inaugurated with the support of 53 states. The new African Union pledged to work towards the protection of human rights, the advancement of democracy and the creation of stable economic conditions across the continent. The organization boasted a parliament, a court of justice and an African central bank, all instruments of greater centralization and integration. Although signatories pledged to defend 'the sovereignty, territorial integrity and independence of its Member States', they also committed to work towards 'the political and socio-economic integration of the continent'.

Significantly, the Union's foundation document allowed for intervention in the affairs of a member state if the Assembly of the AU (composed of all heads of state) determined that war crimes, genocide or crimes against humanity were taking place. The organization also called upon its members to develop a strategic vision for a continent-wide migration policy. The so-called 'Lusaka Declaration' of 2003 set the ambitious goal of free movement of peoples across borders and a renewed focus on economic development as a key element in reversing Africa's brain drain. Efforts have also been made to better coordinate interstate migration through the formation of regional economic partnerships. The Economic Community of West African States (ECOWAS), the East African Community (EAC) and the South African Development Community (SADC) have achieved modest successes in regulating seasonal and temporary migration flows.

But it has not been enough. Inheriting both the structure and the limited fiscal resources of its predecessor, the AU wielded little practical influence over member states that jealously guarded their sovereignty. Too many of the signatories had long track records as dictators and abusers of human rights. The promise of democracy continued to ring hollow across much of independent Africa at the start of the third millennium. Military dictatorships and authoritarian cliques dominated wide swaths of the political landscape; corrupt and ineffective leaders cynically raided public funds and moved them to private accounts offshore. In 2002 the AU commissioned a report on public corruption whose results put the annual cost at $148 billion, 'more than a quarter of the continent's entire gross domestic product'.[77] Average per capita national income remained behind all other regions of the world, while half of the continent's 880 million people were obliged to survive on less than $1 per day.

Thus the signs are not propitious. With growing populations and struggling economies, most African states today have little need for foreign labour, and even less capacity to support refugees. According to the UN's Department of Economic and Social Affairs, states like Nigeria and the Democratic Republic of the Congo are projected to grow by 141 and 127 million respectively by the year 2020.[78] While still only 12 per cent of the world's population of 6.3 billion in 2005, the struggle to feed the growing numbers of Africa's poor under current economic and political conditions makes it unlikely that either unskilled voluntary migrants or refugees will find much succour in neighbouring states.

Sadly, in many respects Africa's predicament was worse in 2001 than it was during the first decade of independence. The continent's share of world trade declined to half of the average in 1980, school attendance was down and 50 per cent of all women remained illiterate. Increasing numbers of youths were accustomed to lives of violence, not of study and skill development. According to one recent author, 'Many states no longer even make symbolic efforts to demonstrate concern with the welfare of their populations, and discourses of participatory governance or local entrepreneurship largely become performances deployed to attract donor interest.'[79] By the end of the century more than half of the countries in Africa relied on developed states to fund large portions of their national budgets. Twenty-firstcentury Africa was the only continent where life expectancy was falling, and where the benefits of economic globalization remained unrealized due to the lack of infrastructure and skills.[80] And every effort to reverse these trends, every attempt to inspire hope, was countered by the deadly AIDS pandemic. The cycle of misfortune appeared to be entrenched.

Chapter 4

Migrants in the Islamic World

For what had been one of the world's leading civilizations throughout the medieval and early modern eras, the immediate post-war period for adherents of Islam was marked by a series of political and cultural crises that frustrated efforts to cultivate a unified Islamic community. Indeed, despite a shared linguistic and religious tradition, the Islamic world after 1945 was extraordinary in its diversity. It included some of the world's richest and poorest states. Densely populated and resource-starved countries like Egypt and Pakistan, and sparsely populated but resource-intensive kingdoms like Kuwait, the United Arab Emirates, Libya and Saudi Arabia, each pursued strongly nationalistic agendas that effectively precluded the growth of Muslim – or more narrowly in the Middle East – Arab nationalism or economic integration. For centuries Muslim merchants and conquerors had spread the faith through migration and settlement, but after 1800 a resurgent West began a fateful encounter with the Islamic world that would have important consequences for the movement of peoples across international borders. Most of that movement in the half century after World War II involved the temporary relocation of unskilled men and women from poorer states to oil-exporting countries, the permanent emigration of highly skilled workers to the developed West, and the involuntary movement of refugees fleeing interstate conflict and civil wars. To a very large degree, migration in the post-war Islamic world was symptomatic of a great economic chasm between a fortunate few (and sparsely populated) petrodollar kingdoms and resource-poor, demographically expansive and newly independent Muslim states.

The nineteenth- and early twentieth-century triad of major Islamic powers in the Middle East – the Ottoman Empire, Egypt and Iran – was replaced after World War I by a host of Western-inspired governments in Turkey, Syria, Iraq, Palestine, Transjordan and Lebanon. Each of these governments, with varying degrees of success, adopted a secular profile in politics and law, and each embraced an economic development model that was inspired by the West. Only Saudi Arabia, Turkey, Iran and Yemen could be said to have exercised anything approaching full sovereignty during the interwar years (1918–39), while the domestic and foreign policies of the other states in the region remained under the indirect control of Europeans. The League of Nations had sanctioned the carve-up of the Ottoman Empire after 1918, but the League's goal of preparing the successor states for independence under the guidance of 'advanced nations' was subordinated to the regional power interests of the British and French.[1] Meanwhile the replacement of Ottoman authority with a series of nascent states, each with its own currency, tariff policies and sovereign borders, upset the traditional free flow of migrants across the Middle East, inhibited regional economic integration and frustrated advocates of pan-Arab political solidarity.

European control over the peoples of the Middle East came to an end after World War II, but not before the formation of a small Jewish state in Palestine led to a new flash point in relations between Islam and the West. And the failed military effort by neighbouring Arab states to destroy Israel at the moment of its birth in 1948 created a massive Palestinian refugee problem that would defy solution throughout the second half of the twentieth century and into our own day. By the year 2000, large intra-regional migration flows had become a troubling demographic hallmark of many Arab states. According to a UN Development Report in 2001, 70 per cent of young people in the Arab world, making their choices based on life prospects, planned to emigrate from the country of their birth.

Spectacular population growth (the highest rate, along with sub-Saharan Africa, in the world) and high levels of unemployment at home prompted many to relocate beyond national borders in search of work and personal security. The petrodollar windfall enjoyed by oil-producing states in the Gulf region prompted a dramatic upsurge in labour migration to the region in the 1970s and early 1980s. In Sudan, for example, almost two-thirds of the country's skilled professionals were living abroad in 1985, while unskilled men flocked to Libya and Saudi Arabia in search of work in the oil fields.[2] So great was the volume of labour and refugee migration that remittances from expatriate workers to home countries exceeded the value of regional trade in goods, becoming 'a significant factor in the socio-economic stability of some countries of origin'.[3] Indeed as early as the 1970s the movement of people across borders, not the movement of goods and services, was the principal means by which some of the new-found wealth of Arab oil-producing countries was spread to the poorer states of the region.[4]

Migration across international borders also became a significant fact of life for non-Arab Muslims in South and South-east Asia during the period of post-war de-colonization. As in the Middle East, so too elsewhere Europe's imperial powers were reluctant to surrender their colonial possessions. British control over India, for example, extended back to the eighteenth century, when the East India Company undermined the power of the Muslim Mughal emperors and began a period of indirect rule through surrogates. By the mid-1800s the entire subcontinent had come under the direct control of the crown, with trade and tariff policies that clearly disadvantaged the colonized. The tragic partition of the country at the point of independence in the autumn of 1947 led to the flight of 7 million Muslims from India into the newly formed state of Pakistan, while panicked Hindus abandoned their homes and land in Pakistan.[5] Upwards of a million migrants lost their lives in the paroxysm of Hindu–Muslim sectarian violence that characterized the cross-border relocations in 1947–8. Historic social, economic and linguistic affinities were arbitrarily shattered as the boundaries were drawn, and the bloodletting contributed greatly to the hostility and distrust that marked bilateral relations between the two countries for the remainder of the century.

In Pakistan, the migrations prompted by independence were followed by additional flows outside the country once the promise of democratic governance faltered in the late 1940s and '50s. Thousands of Pakistanis exercised their right as members of the British Commonwealth to relocate to the formal colonial metropolis. Pakistani neighbourhoods emerged in a number of British cities, strengthening ethnic diversity but also triggering larger patterns of discrimination and alienation. By the early twenty-first century, a tiny minority of British-born youth of Pakistani descent had become totally disaffected by their status and turned to radical Islamic fundamentalism for a new badge of identity and ancestral self-worth.

Back in Pakistan, tensions between the politically dominant western portion of the country and its eastern counterpart led ultimately to the formation of independent Bangladesh in 1972. But the struggle for independence led to one of the world's largest refugee crises when East Pakistani Muslims, fearing the wrath of the Pakistani army, fled across the border into India. Bangladeshi independence shattered the image of Pakistan as a homeland for all Muslims in South Asia, and to this day the so-called 'Biharis', those displaced by the 1971 war, are not allowed to enter the Pakistani state.[6]

To the north in mountainous Afghanistan, displacement became a way of life for hundreds of thousands in the wake of failed governments, foreign occupation, theocratic dictatorship and chronic warlordism. In the two decades following the 1979 Soviet invasion, an estimated 6 million Afghans fled their war-torn country and another million were believed to be internally displaced.[7] In Indonesia, the world's most populous Muslim state, considerable outflow occurred during decades of authoritarian rule, endemic government corruption and widespread rural poverty. By 2000 this archipelago nation situated between the Indian and Pacific oceans, home to the world's fourth largest population, had emerged as a major source of unskilled migrant contact labour. Most of the movement was to the Arab Middle East before 1990, but the emphasis then shifted to nations in the South Pacific region such as Singapore and Taiwan.[8] And in the aftermath of the 1979 Islamic revolution in Iran, millions who opposed the hardline theocratic regime in Tehran fled to Western countries. The United States, which became a major target of revolutionary animus in Iran, was host to 280,000 Iranian nationals by the end of the twentieth century, with more than half of this population living in the greater Los Angeles metropolitan area alone.[9] Comparable numbers of Iranian expatriates found new homes in Western Europe.

The geographic range of Muslim migration was not restricted to the oil kingdoms and Western Europe. Other pluralistic and technologically advanced nations have hosted Muslim immigrants in recent decades. In 1996 there were between 200,000 and 400,000 Muslims living in Australia, comprising 1.1 per cent of the population. With the demise of the White Australia Policy in the face of ever-growing demand for labour, in 1967 a bilateral immigration agreement was concluded with the government of Turkey. Settlers from Turkey were followed in the 1980s and '90s by Lebanese, Somalian and Bosnian immigrants.

In South Africa, small Muslim communities have existed since the Dutch colonizers brought slaves from their holdings in the East Indies (Malaysia). During the nineteenth century the British introduced Indian indentured servants into the area, including many Indian Muslims. Although a small minority of less than 1.5 per cent of the population, Muslims suffered greatly under the apartheid regime until its collapse in the early 1990s. Beginning in the 1960s, many urban dwellers were involved in anti-apartheid activities as members of Cape Muslim Youth Movement and similar organizations. Despite harsh crackdowns, these protest organizations continued, with Muslims often working in unison with other, non-Muslim, social justice organizations. With the end of apartheid, Muslim reformers turned their attention (so far unsuccessfully) to ridding democratic South Africa of Muslim Family Law, which allows men an inordinate degree of power over women and children.[10]

Since 1945, then, migration within the Muslim world has been shaped by a wide range of factors: independence movements, demographic pressures, civil wars, interstate conflicts, economic booms and busts and intolerant religious fundamentalism. The process of relocation, be it on a temporary or permanent basis, always entailed adjustments and compromises within a majority national culture. But since most Muslim migrants tended to relocate to other Muslim states, those adjustments were made easier by the fact that the receiving culture shared with the newcomers a common linguistic and religious heritage. Migration to the West, on the other hand, involved special challenges associated with assimilation, the public role of women, the separation of religious and civil spheres and, after 11 September 2001, the association of radical Islam with political terrorism. At least 12 million Muslims lived in Western Europe at the start of the twenty-first century, while another 6 million resided in the US.[11] Migrants from the Maghreb (Tunisia, Morocco, Algeria, Mauritania and Libya) faced these challenges in France and Italy, Turks encountered them in Germany, Indonesians in the Netherlands, Saudis in the US and Afghans, Pakistanis and Bangladeshis in Britain. The culture of surveillance that emerged in Western countries after 9/11 had its greatest impact on the self-perception, and self-representation, of Muslim migrants irrespective of their country of origin, contributing to a climate of distrust and disrespect that belied the core values of liberal democracies everywhere.

LABOUR MIGRANTS IN THE GULF OIL STATES

At the beginning of the twenty-first century, the member states of the Gulf Cooperation Council (Saudi Arabia, Kuwait, United Arab Emirates (UAE), Bahrain, Qatar and Oman) hosted approximately 10 million foreigners, the vast majority of whom were temporary contract workers. It was a remarkable figure in light of the fact that fewer than 750,000 expatriates had lived in this arid and underdeveloped region 30 years earlier.[12] The upsurge of migrants was initially tied to the extraction and export of oil, as each of these countries embarked on large-scale development projects at a frenetic pace during the 'oil boom' decade of the 1970s. As major oil-producing states with sparse and poorly educated populations, all of the GCC countries relied upon both skilled and unskilled expatriates – engineers, scientists, communications specialists, bankers, construction labourers and service workers – to provide the manpower necessary in what were rapidly developing economies. More recently, rising unemployment rates and deteriorating living conditions in many Arab countries, especially among younger workers, played an important role in labour migration across the region, with oil states continuing to serve as receiving zones.

Optimists saw an overarching complementarity of resources across the Arab Middle East beginning in the 1970s, with high-income but sparsely populated oil-producing states tapping the human resources of poorer states like Syria, Lebanon, Egypt and Morocco for low-wage unskilled labour and high-skilled technical expertise. Economic inter-dependence and the transfer of labour, it was thought, would promote a greater sense of Arab nationalism throughout the region. Unfortunately, efforts to create free trade areas and common markets were frustrated by countervailing nationalist and protectionist sensibilities. Sadly, intra-regional trade remained at a fraction of the level of trade with industrialized states outside the region. National rivalries, ideological differences and occasional military conflict inhibited the direct flow of goods and capital, leaving migrant labour remittances as the largest single engine of regional economic integration.

Building Saudi Arabia

Never before had one region of the world developed as rapidly in so short a period of time as the Arabian peninsula. Sparsely populated, largely illiterate and relatively poor in 1945, the peoples of this arid region were of marginal interest to the world's most powerful coun-tries. Within three decades, however, they enjoyed the highest per capita incomes in the world and were eagerly courted by developed countries whose appetite for petroleum products appeared insatiable.[13] An enormous material transformation occurred in the desert as trad-itional monarchs used a significant portion of their new oil wealth to build infrastructure and expand social services. They created a series of 'rentier' states where a single commodity took the place of domestic tax revenues, allowing absolutist rulers to enjoy complete financial independence from their subjects.

The kingdom of Saudi Arabia led the way in these efforts, deftly fusing conservative religious values and authoritarian political culture with dynamic economic modernization under state auspices. Beginning in the 1960s, these modernization efforts involved the recruitment of millions of temporary guest workers, an influx of skilled and unskilled labour from neighbouring Muslim states, from South and South East Asia and (most controversially) from the technologically advanced West. The presence of the latter migrants, most of whom were skilled professionals in the oil industry, was deeply unsettling to Islamist elements within traditional Saudi society who condemned the secularizing influence of the West. Their animus was directed against both the infidel Westerners and their own political leaders, who in their eyes had forfeited the right to rule by virtue of their relationships with the US and Europe. By the 1990s the Saudi state had created a vast security apparatus to identify, expel or jail internal opponents of the regime.

The kingdom was established in 1932, after the elimination of Ottoman influence and decades of internecine struggle amongst tribal groups and rival confederations. King Ibn Saud (r. 1932–53) claimed leadership over a family that first rose to prominence during the eighteenth century. Embracing a puritanical form of Islam championed by Muhammad ibn al-Wahhab, the incipient Saudi state wrested control over the holy cities of Mecca and Medina from the Ottomans, but suffered a series of setbacks at the hands of Muhammad Ali of Egypt during the early nineteenth century. The family maintained its regional power base, however, and under Ibn Saud forged an independent kingdom free from the taint of European influence that marked a number of Arab regimes in the Middle East.

Once in power, the King inaugurated a process of centralization and control over the region's many desert tribes. In addition, he solidified the ruling family's alliance with the kingdom's Wahhabi religious leaders, giving the latter exclusive jurisdiction over education, law and public morality within the kingdom. Ibn Saud portrayed himself as the defender of Islam's holiest sites, carefully managing the annual pilgrimage to Mecca and strongly affirming the religious basis of the state. More controversially, during the 1930s he entered into a number of commercial agreements with Western oil companies, just as the full extent of the kingdom's oil reserves was uncovered by geologists. Since the Saudis had never experienced European colonial domination during the nineteenth century, they were less xenophobic towards the West than other Arab states.[14] Commercial production for export began in 1938, but it was only after World War II, as developed countries switched from coal to oil as their principal industrial fuel, that the enormous significance of oil to Saudi Arabia's economic well-being became apparent to all.

As the demand for oil increased worldwide after 1945, Western companies, led by the California-based Arabian American Oil Company (Aramco), set pricing policies and undertook a series of infrastructure projects in the kingdom. During the 1950s and '60s, the exploitation of Saudi oil reserves provided generous income to the private companies, and to the American government, which collected taxes from US businesses operating overseas. Still, Saudi revenue from oil was significant and grew modestly during these decades.[15] Needing additional unskilled labour resources, Aramco recruited thousands of Arab workers to its expanding Saudi oil fields. Men from Egypt, Yemen, Jordan, Syria, Kuwait, together with Muslims from Pakistan, India and the Philippines, assumed low-paying jobs and lived for the most part in sub-standard accommodation. Muslim migrants from South and South East Asia were especially welcome, since the authorities believed that they would be less interested in permanent settlement. Whatever the point of origin, compliance with workplace protocol was essential for expatriates. When labour unrest occurred at Aramco facilities in 1945, for example, the Saudi government immediately deported the striking workers.[16] In these early years the monarchy refused to permit union activities and took a dim view of workers' rights generally, a position that would not change significantly once oil revenues allowed for accelerated development and the arrival of millions of foreign workers in the 1970s.

As oil revenues increased, Saudi Arabia's monarchs engaged in a delicate balancing act, hoping to marry Western-style economic development with traditional social and religious practices under the framework of an absolutist state. It was a difficult undertaking in a country where some conservative religious leaders criticized even the smallest concession to Western technology as apostasy. A kingdom-wide Central Planning Organization was established in 1965 and, by 1970, the first of a series of five-year plans for economic development was launched. King Faisal (r. 1964–75) instituted free health insurance and education for Saudi citizens, while transportation, communications and agricultural development projects all received significant funding. Food was subsidized, and there were only token charges for basic utilities. Apartment complexes, state-of-the-art hospitals and a variety of public buildings were constructed across the kingdom. Two new industrial cities, Yanbu' on the Red Sea and Jubayl on the Arab Gulf, became destination points for internal migrants.[17]

Urban population grew at breakneck speed. Only 30 per cent of Saudis lived in cities in 1960, but by the end of the century the figure had increased to a remarkable 84 per cent, higher than the world average.[18] Educational change was also rapid and dramatic. From a handful of primary and secondary schools in the 1960s, almost 3 million Saudi students were enrolled in the early 1990s. A number of universities were established during the same period, although wealthy Saudi males were often sent to better-known European and US institutions for specialized training in management, engineering and medicine. Meanwhile the economy's manpower demands continued as the development plans were implemented; by 1970, for example, there were more than 225,000 Yemeni workers in Saudi Arabia, together with 40,000 Syrians and 50,000 Jordanians and Palestinians.[19]

Domestic development, and the parallel need for labour, intensified again after the dramatic fiscal changes following in the wake of the 1973 OPEC oil embargo. Although the Organization of Petroleum Exporting Countries was founded in 1960, major producing countries did not take steps to gain greater control over the industry until the early 1970s. The precipitant was the US decision to provide significant military aid to Israel during the October 1973 Arab–Israeli War. The OPEC partners approved an embargo on oil shipments to supporters of Israel (especially the US) and a sharp cutback on overall production for export. As developed states scrambled to purchase supplies from non-OPEC producers, the cost of oil escalated on global markets. The subsequent OPEC price hikes represented a boon for all of the member states, but the impact on Saudi finances was greatest. In the year before the embargo, the kingdom's oil revenues were $6.4 billion, representing 50 per cent of total earnings as agreed with foreign companies in the kingdom. The following year the revenues shot up to almost $28 billion, and by 1981 – when prices peaked – the total reached $102 billion. By this date the kingdom owned a majority stake in the oil companies' operations and soon enjoyed complete ownership. The stage was set for a historic transformation of the country's infrastructure.[20]

The wealth generated by the expansion of the oil industry, and the ruling family's decision to invest in a wide variety of improvement projects, fostered the emergence of a new middle class of educators, businessmen and government officials. It also pointed up the need for even more sources of skilled and unskilled labour, especially in light of the fact that Saudi women were not allowed to enter the workforce. The potential disruptive impact of foreign workers, especially non-Muslims, on traditional Saudi culture was weighed against the urgent need for labour, and the development imperative triumphed. Between 1973 and 1980 millions of foreign workers poured into the kingdom and, by the latter year, foreign nationals made up an astonishing 31 per cent of the country's population, and 53 per cent of its workforce.[21]

Labourers would normally enter the country on a service visa sponsored by a private company or individual employer. The employer was responsible for supervising their workers and providing accommodation. It is estimated that by 1980 there were approximately 2 million foreign workers, together with 400,000 dependants, in the kingdom amidst a total population of between 5 and 11 million Saudis.[22] The overwhelming majority of the newcomers were engaged in low-skill, low-wage service. In the city of Unayzah, for example, more than half of the labour force consisted of expatriates. Most found work as agricultural labourers, domestic servants and unskilled construction hands, all forms of activities eschewed by the growing number of middle-class Saudis. The expatriates normally divided by nationality, thus their numerical strength rarely translated into better wages or conditions. Easily terminated by contract and deported, most foreign workers remained wary of efforts to organize or protest. Westerners, of whom there were 100,000 in 1980, were restricted in their housing options, with most living in segregated communities adjacent to major oil fields.

The opportunity to work in an oil-producing state was for many poor Muslims a chance to save and remit considerable sums to family members at home. In 2002 the secretariat of the Gulf Cooperation Council indicted that a total of $27 billion had been remitted, with $16 billion of that total coming from workers in Saudi Arabia. But foreign workers in Saudi Arabia paid a steep price for the chance to earn more than what was available at home; they had few if any legal protections and, if poor and unskilled, might find themselves at the mercy of unscrupulous employers, indifferent state officials, and sharia court judges who operated without reference to a fixed rule of law. Exploitative work conditions, lack of overtime pay, wages withheld for long periods of time, restrictions on movement outside the workplace, arbitrary arrests – all combined to foster an environment of fear amongst workers.

A 2004 report by Human Rights Watch recorded stories of female migrants forced to work long hours in hospitals, shops and private homes, confined to locked dormitories and rooms during off hours, and sexually abused by private employers. Stories of arbitrary arrests, secret trials and executions by beheading – all unbeknown to family members or embassy officials – were related by the relatives of victims in a variety of sending countries. In 2002 even the kingdom's highest religious authority, Grand Mufti Sheikh Abdul Aziz al Sheikh, confided that migrants suffered 'exploitation and oppression'.[23] Modest changes occurred in recent years, but the life of the temporary guest worker remained very difficult. In 2004 it was announced that foreigners would be eligible for citizenship if they met a set of strict require-ments, including fluency in written and spoken Arabic, adherence to Islam and a residency requirement of ten years. There were few qualified candidates, a clear signal that the government was not about to sanction the formation of a multicultural society.

Throughout this period of unprecedented economic growth and change, the emergence of a vibrant middle class of Saudi citizens did not inform any significant change in the kingdom's political culture. All Saudi nationals remained clients of a patronage state, while real power remained in the hands of the royal family, whose members hoped to compensate for the absence of political rights with the prom-ise of greater material wealth. The kingdom's constitution consisted of the Quran and sharia law. There were no political parties, and the al Saud family, together with a close circle of advisors, set policy in secret for the entire kingdom.[24] Neighbouring Arab states that had ousted their monarchs in the 1950s and '60s, particularly Egypt, South Yemen and Iraq, represented an ideological threat to the Saudi royal family and in response the government earmarked up to 40 per cent of total annual revenues for national defence.[25] Patronage and largesse allowed the monarchy to win the allegiance of most members of the emerging middle class. Arms agreements with the United States during the 1970s and '80s enabled the regime to secure some of the most sophisticated military hardware available, but even with the additional firepower, the ruling family remained extremely wary of liberation movements elsewhere in the Arab world, and dissidents within. This suspicion had an important influence on immigration policy for, despite the large numbers of expatriates, the government strictly limited most guest workers to temporary status without any hope of permanent residency.

A general downturn in the economy following a worldwide drop in oil prices during the 1980s and '90s, together with the costs incurred during the first Gulf War, strained the state's resources and limited its ability to provide the generous social benefits that Saudis had come to expect. Budget deficits became the norm, even when there were temporary spikes in the price of crude. The slowdown frustrated a subject population that had grown used to economic good times. It also hardened attitudes against the presence of so many foreign workers in the country. The stationing of thousands of American troops on Saudi soil during the 1991 Gulf War only exacerbated this anti-foreigner sentiment. The kingdom's population had expanded rapidly during the final third of the twentieth century, from approximately 6 million in 1970 to 23 million in 2003. By 2004, 50 per cent of the Saudi population was under fifteen years of age. Educational opportunities remained in place for Saudi men and women, but with unemployment hovering at 30 per cent for youth and 10 per cent overall, the pressure to increase domestic job opportunities by reducing the presence of expatriates was strong.

There were approximately 7 million foreigners in the kingdom in 2003, just under one-third of the country's total population. Expatriate workers, skilled and unskilled, made up over two-thirds of the national workforce.[26] In a series of initiatives and regulations known as

'Saudiization', the Ministry of Labour sought to lower dependence on foreign workers across all sectors of the economy. The task was made difficult due to the fact that most Saudis, like citizens of many other developed countries, were unwilling to accept low wage positions in the service and construction industries – the very areas where migrant workers were concentrated.[27] And in a pattern that that was familiar elsewhere, Saudi businesses that were used to hiring low-wage foreign workers were understandably reluctant to spend more to compensate their own nationals.

The long-term stability of the Saudi monarchy rested squarely on its ability to encourage economic growth in areas unrelated to oil production, thereby providing meaningful work to a new generation. The political consequences of burgeoning youth unemployment were recognized by the ruling elite, but 'Saudiization' – the reduction in foreigners living in the kingdom – was not going to solve the deeper structural problems of the oil-dependent economy. Inexpensive foreign labour had become an unofficial subsidy to industry and private employers during the age of petrolization, while little had been done to change the aversion to technical and vocational training that appeared at the heart of Saudi notions of appropriate work.[28] The population that came of age during the boom times was not about to lower its expectations with regard to 'honourable' employment. Unhappily for the monarchy, the culture of affluence inspired by the sale of oil, and the formation of a rentier state that was supposed to serve as a bulwark of the existing political order, had raised expectations to a level that were no longer realistic.

Despite efforts at diversification, the fact remained that one non-renewable commodity accounted for 75 per cent of the public revenues at the end of the twentieth century. Radical opposition to a regime that owned virtually the entire economy was highlighted as early as 1979 when the Great Mosque of Mecca was seized temporarily by rebels. The kingdom's relationship with the US became the target of Islamist elements throughout the Arab world, prompting further government repression of peaceful dissent during the 1990s. Terrorist attacks against government and Western-owned facilities drove many expatriates from the kingdom at the turn of the century, and in the aftermath of 9/11 (and the discovery that most of the hijackers were Saudi nationals), the regime's ability to maintain Western support was deeply compromised. For millions of Saudis, and for additional millions of expatriates who had contributed so much to the development of the modern kingdom, the future remained uncertain.

Persian Gulf Neighbours

With a tiny population of 35,000 at the start of the twentieth century, Kuwait was dominated by a small group of merchant traders, and it was their ancestors who in the mid eighteenth century designated the Al Sabah family to administer local affairs. Although first established in the sixteenth century, Kuwait was under the nominal control of the Ottoman Empire until the end of World War I, when the Al Sabah aligned themselves with the British who had a strong naval presence in the Lower Persian Gulf. An 1899 pact established Kuwait as a virtual British protectorate, an agreement that proved valuable in 1920, when Ibn Saud's forces attacked Kuwait and British military assistance enabled the defenders to turn back the Saudi assault. Although the successful defence of the region fostered a new sense of nationalism that was previously lacking among the emirate's town dwellers and their rural neighbours, the British continued to oversee foreign relations and defence until independence was achieved peacefully in 1961. When oil was discovered in 1938, the small town of Kuwait was suffering economically from a Saudi trade boycott and from the larger effects of the worldwide depression. World War II prevented the British-owned Kuwait Oil Company from exporting petroleum, but immediately after the war oil companies began recruiting a foreign workforce. Most of the initial newcomers were Palestinians who had been made homeless after the creation of the State of Israel in 1948.[29] During those early post-war years foreigners were welcome in the emirate, and little effort was made to formalize the process of entry.

During this period the population of Kuwait grew modestly, reaching just over 200,000 in 1957, but as oil revenues raised the level of infrastructure and basic services, both the native and expatriate populations burgeoned. Home to 10 per cent of the world's known oil reserves, the export of petroleum accounted for nearly 80 per cent of government revenues at the start of the twenty-first century. Even as early as the 1960s, Kuwaitis enjoyed an unparalleled level of 'cradle to grave' benefits, including free housing, education and health care, together with a promise of public-sector employment and exemption from income tax. Foreign workers, while denied citizenship rights, took full advantage of the improved lifestyle that was now available to all residents. By 2006 there were over 2.4 million people living in the emirate, of whom fewer than half were Kuwaiti citizens. During the 1960s most of the foreign workers hailed from other Arab countries in the region, especially Egypt, Lebanon, Iraq and Syria, but after the 1973 spike in oil prices a larger number of workers from South Asia made their appearance. Since independence, Kuwait has held the distinction of being the oil-producing country with the heaviest reliance upon foreign labour. In 2005 the labour force numbered 1.67 million, with expatriates holding 80 per cent of all positions.[30]

The 1990 Iraqi invasion, seven-month occupation and eventual ouster left the country's infrastructure in a shambles. More than 300,000 Kuwaitis, including the emir, fled the country just prior to the invasion. Saddam Hussein ordered a scorched earth policy as his forces retreated before a coalition led by the US, leaving the country's oil fields aflame. The cost of repairs to infrastructure was more than $40 billion, leading to budget deficits for most of the 1990s. During the occupation, the invaders mistreated, tortured and killed thousands, prompting the post-war government to focus greater attention on the role of foreigners in the country. When Palestinian leader Yasser Arafat supported the Iraqi invasion of Kuwait in 1990, for example, the fate of the emirate's largest expatriate community became precarious. Once restored to power, the Kuwaiti government forced most of the 400,000 Palestinians to leave the country. The government then pledged to restrict the number of resident expatriates to half of the pre-war total. Indeed, for a brief period after the liberation in February 1991, Kuwaitis were for the first time in many years the largest ethnic group in the country. But national reconstruction could not have taken place without another influx of foreign workers, and by the mid 1990s non-Kuwaitis again constituted a majority.

Kuwaitis needed foreign workers to build a modern infrastructure in the 1960s and '70s, and to maintain and service that infrastructure in subsequent decades. Both before and after the Iraqi invasion, the emirate was much more Western-orientated than its Saudi, Iraqi and Iranian neighbours, with English serving as a second language, a vast array of imported goods, a strong multi-ethnic service economy and a robust consumer culture. Since citizens dominated the public sector, enjoying good wages and retirement with full benefits after only twenty years of service, it was in the private sector where the greatest need for foreign labour existed. The foreign worker communities were stratified by profession and residency, with Arabs rarely accepting service or menial labour and typically entering the country as individuals with a specified contract. Asians, on the other hand, worked through recruitment companies in the sending country and were obliged to pay high fees for the service. Working in dirtier, low-paying jobs, Asian expatriates were more easily controlled and more likely to return home after a few years.[31]

In the other small kingdoms and emirates of the Persian Gulf, a similar pattern of temporary labour recruitment emerged. The tribal rulers of Bahrain, Qatar and the UAE were able to break free of their historic alliances with the merchant elite of the region. Bureaucratic states were created, urbanization intensified and workers from the Palestinian territories, Egypt, Jordan, Yemen and Pakistan accounted for a large minority, and in some cases a majority, of the population by the early 1980s. The political leadership of these countries has remained remarkably stable since the withdrawal of the British in the 1960s and '70s, but even in Kuwait and Bahrain, where limited political rights were extended to a minority of the male population, the long-term viability of the state relied on the production and sale of oil, and (in the short term) on the continued availability of abundant labour from abroad.[32]

Non-Arabs and the Feminization of Labour

While neither sending nor receiving countries maintain comprehensive migration data, immigrants to Gulf oil states from South and South-east Asia constituted a large percentage of the total expatriate population. In 1975 there were 1.82 million foreign workers in the Gulf states, with Asians accounting for almost 20 per cent of the whole. Five years later the total had reached 2.8 million, with almost 29 per cent coming from countries in South and South-east Asia. By 1985 the member states of the six-nation Gulf Cooperation Council (GCC) hosted 2.2 million South Asians and 1 million South-east Asians, as compared to a total of 1.5 million Arabs. Thus Asians from Pakistan, India, Bangladesh, Sri Lanka, the Philippines, Thailand and South Korea became the dominant immigrant group in the region. For Pakistan, one of the largest sending countries, the remittances from nationals working in the oil states became the single largest source of export earnings, reaching US$2 billion in 1987–8.[33]

In virtually all of the member states of the GCC, a significant shift to the recruitment of female temporary labour took place during the last quarter of the twentieth century. As income levels increased for the citizens of Arab countries in the Middle East, the hiring of single females to carry out a variety of domestic duties became a symbol of social status and middle-class respectability. By 2000 approximately 30 per cent of all migrants to GCC countries were female, up from a mere 8 per cent just twenty years earlier. Major sending areas included Sri Lanka, the Philippines, Bangladesh and Indonesia, where even educated women joined the migrant pool in the expectation of remitting significant sums to family members over the course of their service in the Middle East. Once in the employ of a family, however, domestic workers were susceptible to a wide range of personal and financial challenges, including long hours, non-payment of overtime service, verbal abuse and sexual mistreatment by male employers who were also the victim's visa sponsor. Since domestic workers were not covered by the labour laws of most Arab countries, opportunities for employee abuse abounded.[34]

PALESTINIANS AND ISRAELIS

From the moment of its formation under League of Nations auspices, the tiny British Mandate of Palestine generated friction and conflict both on the ground and in the larger arena of international power relations. Such was not always the case in this resource-poor and deeply contested land. For upwards of four centuries, the Turkish Ottoman Empire had employed a system of governance in the region that allowed for a great deal of local autonomy. Orthodox Christian, Muslim and Jewish populations were responsible for organizing their own religious, cultural and even legal affairs. There was a high degree of religious tolerance during this period and, by 1900, for the most part, Palestine's roughly 700,000 inhabitants (94,000 of whom were Jewish) lived together in peace.[35] Certainly the Jewish minority in Palestine 'generally fared better among Arab populations than in most European states'.[36] Jewish immigrants from Eastern Europe and Russia began settling in the region beginning in the 1880s, but in view of their minority status, few thought in terms of a future Jewish state. During the Mandate period (1920–48) further immigration was spurred by a British promise to facilitate the creation of a national homeland for European Jewry, and by a strong Zionist movement that laid claim to land inhabited by an Arab majority for over a millennium.

Zionism and Western Influence

For most Zionists, Palestine was the ancient Jewish Holy Land, site of the biblical Kingdom of Israel and key to the redemption of the Jewish people. When combined with centuries of discrimination at the hands of European governments, the appeal of a possible return to Zion and the creation of a modern nation state was strong at the start of the twentieth century. This was especially true for East European Jews who faced the worst forms of anti-Semitism, including racial massacres or pogroms in Tsarist Russia. In *The Jewish State* (1896), the Hungarian journalist Theodor Herzl brought together various strands of Zionist thought in making the case for the creation of a sovereign state, although he did not identify Palestine as the only acceptable location. It was not, after all, prime colonial territory flowing with rich natural resources. Visiting in 1867, the American Mark Twain described Palestine as a 'hopeless, dreary, heart-broken land'.[37] Through Herzl's efforts, a well-attended Zionist Congress was held in Basel, Switzerland in 1897, and subsequent annual meetings solidified the goal of forging an autonomous state in the land that Twain disparaged.[38] Not unlike the European settlement of the Americas in the sixteenth and seventeenth centuries, the proposed migration to the Holy Land took little account of the existing indigenous population, their history or traditions. Palestine was *tabula rasa* for those who had never been to the region, and settlers were keen to bring the benefits of Western civilization to an underdeveloped region.

Unhappily for these early Zionists, there was virtually no diplomatic support in Europe for the creation of a national Jewish homeland before 1917. But World War I utterly transformed the diplomatic playing field in the Middle East. In that year the British government, eager to secure Jewish support in the US, and hoping to wield greater influence in the region in the event of an Ottoman defeat, approved a resolution viewing 'with favour the establishment in Palestine of a National Home for the Jewish people' and pledging to 'use their best endeavours to facilitate the achievement of this object'. But the so-called 'Balfour Declaration' also stated that 'nothing shall be done which may prejudice the civil and religious rights of existing non-Jewish communities in Palestine', a statement that was difficult to square with support for a new homeland. Enjoying an eight to one majority in Palestine in the years after the war, Arab residents protested loudly, and sometimes rioted, whenever a new wave of Jewish immigrants arrived. The British attempted to create national institutions that would bring the two sides together, but Arab leaders flatly rejected a proposed 1922 constitution that featured a legislature composed of Jewish, Christian and Muslim members. Indeed most Arabs refused to participate in any Mandate-wide organizations, fearful that such activity would imply an acceptance of the Balfour Declaration.[39]

Hostility between Palestinians and Jewish settlers intensified during the 1920s and '30s. Immigration began to drop in the late 1920s, as the hardships associated with life in the Yishuv (the Jewish community in Palestine) prompted more European Jews to choose the US as a destination country. But movement to Palestine accelerated again after Hitler's 1933 seizure of power in Germany, and as Western countries like the US tightened their immigration regimes. From just over

174,000 settlers in 1931, the Jewish population spiked to 630,000 by 1946, at a time when there were 1.3 million Arabs in the territory.[40] And by the end of the 1930s, Zionist purchasing organizations had bought almost 10 per cent of the cultivable land in the Mandate. As Palestinian peasants were evicted summarily from lands that they had worked for generations, resentment towards British authorities, wealthy Arabs who sold land to Zionists and towards Jewish settlers themselves intensified. A general strike in 1936 was followed by three years of civil disobedience and spontaneous Arab violence against British and Jewish settler interests in the Mandate. Despite an influx of 20,000 British troops and the jailing or exiling of Palestinian leaders, order was not restored until 1939. In the meantime, the growing strategic importance of the region, and German interest in the Arab cause, led to a fundamental shift in British policy.[41]

As war clouds began to gather across Europe in the spring and summer of 1939, Arab governments demonstrated greater interest in the plight of Palestinians. The British government, concerned over future access to oil fields, now claimed that it was not British policy to forward the creation of a Jewish state and that future immigration to the Mandate would be severely restricted – and completely suspended in ten years. However, the experience of total war, and in particular the horrors of the Holocaust, transformed Western – especially American – sentiment and raised international support for Jewish refugees who wished to settle in Palestine.[42] This support grew even as militant Zionist paramilitary groups in Palestine carried out a campaign of terror against key facilities and government personnel. By 1945, as the war ended in Europe, British troops faced an intense – and seemingly intractable – guerrilla conflict in Palestine, and within two years handed the entire matter over to the United Nations.

Victors and Vanquished

In November 1947 the General Assembly of the UN, acting on the advice of a majority of a Special Committee on Palestine, voted for the creation of two states in the former Mandate territory, one Jewish with

56 per cent of the land, and one Arab with the remaining 44 per cent. Under the plan the city of Jerusalem would become a special international district. Bereft of leadership from within, member states of the Arab League assumed the public voice of the Palestinians and unanimously rejected the partition plan, calling instead for a unified state that would be democratic, pluralist and secular. It was a compelling but in the end futile demand in light of Western support for the Jewish people in a post-Holocaust environment. Over the next six months Zionist military forces seized Arab-occupied lands that had been designated as Israel's in the UN partition plan – even though the majority population of these areas was Muslim. Inter-communal warfare, marked by both Jewish and Arab atrocities, was the result, and in the end some 400,000 Palestinians were forced to flee their ancestral homes in the face of superior force. As the last British high commissioner departed the port city of Haifa unceremoniously on 14 May 1948, leaving behind neither a functioning government nor any sense of hope for Palestinian exiles, Zionist leaders declared the independence of the State of Israel. The demographic and political landscape of Palestine had changed fatefully and dramatically in very rapid order.

Thus began what has since evolved into the longest, and most intractable, refugee problem of the post-war era. Not since land-hungry Protestant settlers from Scotland arrived in the north of Ireland in the early seventeenth century had British 'plantation' policy – the great civilizing mission – carried such momentous consequences for the future. Just as Protestant settlement fuelled four centuries of sectarian violence and mutual disdain in England's Irish dependency, so too the Mandate experiment and the creation of the State of Israel in Palestine embittered Arab populations across the Middle East. For displaced Palestinians and their Arab League supporters, the Mandate had been a calculated anti-Arab imperialist exercise, and the State of Israel was little more than another illustration of European colonialism in action.[43] Arabs, it seemed, were now made responsible for centuries of European anti-Semitism; lacking the fiscal, political, military and organizational clout of their unwelcome neighbours, Palestinians entered the post-war world as refugees – homeless, jobless and apparently paying for the sins of others.

When an ill-coordinated assault against the nascent Israeli state by Egyptian, Syrian, Jordanian, Lebanese and Iraqi forces failed miserably in 1948, the armistice agreements with each combatant provided few assurances for Palestinians who remained in Israel. The assassination of a special UN commissioner appointed to resolve the conflict by members of a Zionist paramilitary organization in autumn 1948 signalled the depth of the crisis.[44] Israel was now in control of 78 per cent of the former Mandate territory, as opposed to the 56 per cent agreed by the UN partition resolution. A mass exodus of some 700,000 people ensued, with Israeli military forces taking the opportunity to expel others who were thought to be members of irregular forces. In the coastal cities the depopulation was nearly total. Most of the refugees fled to the West Bank (controlled by the new Kingdom of Jordan), the Gaza Strip (controlled by Egypt), Syria and Lebanon. The UN created a separate bureau for Palestinian refugees, the UN Relief and Works Agency, to address immediate humanitarian needs, but no long-term solution was put forward by the international community. The year 1948 became *al-nakba*, the disaster, for the Palestinian people, and the identifier remains to this day.[45]

Jewish emigration to the new state proceeded apace after independence. Soon after its improbable military victory, the Israeli government made the fateful decision not to allow the return of Arab refugees, and began to level about 350 abandoned Arab towns and villages, replacing many of them with new Jewish settlements.[46] Approximately 700,000 people arrived by 1951, doubling the size of the total Jewish population to 1.3 million. Half of the immigrants came from Eastern European countries, so-called Ashkenazi Jews, many of whom were survivors of the Nazi Holocaust. The Ashkenazim, in general better educated and highly skilled, provided most of the political leadership for the new state. But a significant number of immigrants came from neighbouring Arab states, poorer Sephardic Jews who were forced out of their homes after 1948 and who remained generally less well integrated into mainstream Israeli society.[47] In 1952 the country's unicameral legislature, the Knesset, passed a Nationality Law that awarded automatic citizenship to any Jewish immigrant while also extending the same rights to the country's remaining 160,000 Arab Palestinians. The latter group was subject to a series of irksome measures, however, including the requirement to carry special identity cards when travelling within the country. Most Israeli Arabs were relegated, de facto, to second-class status during the state's formative years, experiencing job and wage discrimination, political powerlessness and arbitrary land expropriation. In the words of two contemporary scholars, Israeli Arabs 'became citizens of a state that celebrated its independence around an event that they considered their biggest catastrophe'.[48]

Refugees and the Right of Return

In spite of the many disabilities associated with minority status, not least of which were the loss of land, economic restrictions, overcrowding in designated towns and villages and the lingering suspicion of disloyalty, the Palestinian population of Israel grew modestly during the second half of the twentieth century. By 2000 Palestinian–Israelis constituted approximately 15 per cent of the total population, or some 1.2 million in a country of 6.5 million. While always on the fringes of Israeli society, many benefited from the emergence of a modern economy in the Jewish state. For the majority refugee population, however, conditions were much harsher. Between 1948 and 1967 neither the Egyptian administration in Gaza nor, more importantly, Jordanian authorities in the West Bank (where more than half of the pre-war Palestinian population was now living) were eager to promote the idea of a future Palestinian state. Indeed Jordan's King Abdallah, while publicly representing Palestinians in their call for repatriation, hoped that his 1950 annexation of the West Bank would eventually lead to the 'Jordanization' of the region and the incorporation of the refugees into his kingdom. Exiled, demoralized and lacking any champions among the leadership of regional Arab states, the Palestinian national movement made little progress during the years 1948–67. In tiny Gaza, where almost 200,000 refugees overwhelmed an indigenous population of 88,000, the rural, non-industrialized economy was utterly inadequate to the task of resettlement.

The controversial Israeli position on the 'right of return' was that Palestinians had voluntarily elected to leave during 1947–8, and had therefore forfeited any rights they might claim within the country. Jewish public opinion, bolstered by waves of new immigrants, was adamantly opposed to an influx of Palestinians, while the Israeli military was wary of a potential fifth column should repatriation occur. By the mid-1960s, Palestinians came to the realization that neither the leading Arab states nor the wider international community as represented by the UN was prepared to press for the right of return or compensation for those who had been expelled from their ancestral lands.

In 1962 the example of the successful, if bloody and protracted, Algerian revolution against France gave some Palestinian activists new hope. Two years later the Palestine Liberation Organization was established as the political and military voice of nationalists, and organized guerrilla attacks against Israel began in an effort to raise awareness of the refugee situation. But three years after the creation of the PLO, and in the aftermath of a six-day pre-emptive war in which Israel handily defeated the combined forces of Syria, Egypt and Jordan, the Jewish state took control over Jerusalem, the West Bank, Gaza, the Sinai and the Golan Heights. Thousands of additional Palestinians fled to crowded refugee camps in Jordan, Lebanon and Syria as all of the former British Mandate of Palestine came under Israeli authority. Those who remained, some 1.5 million Palestinians, now lived under a state that had yet to fully embrace equal rights for its own Arab citizens. Military rule now became the daily reality for these people. Ironically, the stunning 1967 military victory, which was followed by the establishment of Jewish settlements in the captured lands, undercut the Zionist dream of a homogenous Jewish state and turned Israel into an occupying force that refused to acknowledge applicable international conventions.

Intifada

Israeli efforts to quash all expressions of Palestinian nationalist sentiment in the years since the 1967 war included the harassment, detention and even expulsion of journalists, trade unionists, academics and religious and community leaders who were identified as security risks. Although material conditions for Palestinians, especially as measured by income and consumption, improved during the period of occupation, the harsh nature of Israeli tactics finally led to a general uprising in 1987 called the intifada or 'shaking off'. Unorganized street demonstrations were followed by efforts at political and economic disengagement from the Israeli state. The nonviolent resistance continued despite mass arrests, harsh reprisals and military curfews. After more than four decades of occupation, Palestinian nationalist sentiment and the demand for political self-determination had remained strong.[49]

In July 1988 Jordan's King Hussein relinquished Jordan's claims to the West Bank, clearing the way for the PLO and its exiled leaders to emerge as the most important representative of the Palestinians in the occupied territories. In November 1988, PLO leader Yasser Arafat, in a meeting of the Palestinian National Congress held in Algiers, withdrew the traditional call for the destruction of Israel and renounced the use of terrorism. Instead the PLO committed itself to direct negotiation with Israel and a permanent peace based on a two-state solution in the former British Mandate. After two years of multiparty negotiations, in 1993 a comprehensive agreement between the PLO and Israel's new Labour government was signed on the White House lawn. The way forward now had a set of road markers; a Declaration of Principles called for a five-year period during which final status issues, including refugees, would be negotiated.

When little diplomatic progress was made over the next few years, however, rejectionist elements on both sides gained the upper hand. A second, much more lethal, intifada erupted in September 2000, scuttling efforts to reach agreement on multiple fronts and leaving Palestinians in their stateless condition. Israeli settlements in the West Bank continued to grow in number and size, and after 9/11 Israeli Prime Minister Ariel Sharon began to portray Israeli actions against Palestinian militants as but another front in the global war on terror. In 2002 the hard-line Sharon government began construction on what was planned as a 440-mile separation wall to prevent incursions by terrorists. Fittingly, perhaps, construction of the wall would be on Palestinian land confiscated for the purpose.[50]

The United Nations Relief and Works Agency (UNRWA) began its assistance efforts as a temporary entity in 1950 but, due to the failure to resolve the Palestinian refugee issue, its mandate was renewed repeatedly over the following decades. The agency provided food, shelter, education and health services to generations of refugees. By 2006 the number of Palestinian refugees in the occupied territories and neighbouring countries totalled 4.3 million. One-third of the total lived in officially recognized refugee camps, while the majority lived in towns and cities in close proximity to the camps. In Gaza alone, 70 per cent of the population, or 900,000 people, were dependent on emergency food relief provided by UNRWA. A shockingly high 40 per cent of the population remained unemployed at the start of the twenty-first century.

FRAGILE STATES AND REGIONAL LEGACIES: JORDAN, LEBANON AND EGYPT

Before World War I, the small number of emigrants from Ottoman-controlled lands that later became the independent states of Syria, Lebanon and Jordan, commonly referred to themselves as Syrians. Mostly Christian and Jewish merchants and financiers, few of the migrants who left for destinations in Europe or America intended to stay abroad, although in many cases economic success overseas led to permanent residence.[51] A great deal of regional migration within this part of the empire took place as well. Craftsmen, traders and unskilled urban workers travelled throughout the region during the first half of the twentieth century, strengthening the expectation among many that a larger political unity would emerge after the collapse of the Ottoman Empire. The British had encouraged this line of thinking during the course of the war, but expectations were dashed with the erection of French and British Mandate territories. The formation of small, sparsely populated and economically fragile mandates after World War I transformed centuries of normal regional movement into a question of international migration.

Jordan and Its Refugees

In an effort to retain major influence in the Middle East and to check French ambitions, the British in 1921 appointed the Hashemite leader Amir Abdallah as leader of its mandate in Transjordan. An arid region east of the Jordan River, inhabited by Bedouin tribes who cared little for the emerging regime of international borders, it was an unlikely setting for state-building. The British government continued to provide financial, military and political assistance to the new state until May 1946, always reserving the right to intervene to protect imperial interests. A special military force, the so-called Arab Legion, was recruited and deployed to end the long tradition of tribal raiding, while most administrative offices were staffed by Palestinian and British officials. Abdallah attempted to engage with Zionist leaders over the future status of Palestine during the 1920s and '30s, but his meddling only earned him the ire of regional Arab leaders.

During World War II Transjordan offered military support to the British, and in repayment for services rendered an independent kingdom was proclaimed in 1946 with Abdallah as monarch. The new country was disadvantaged by its arid landscape, lack of natural resources and shared borders with regionally more powerful states. Flanked by Syria to the north, Iraq to the east, Saudi Arabia to the east and south and (after 1948) Israel to the west, Jordan's future would be bound up in the discordant relations between Jews and Arabs over land and nationhood. Refugees fleeing civil war in Lebanon during the 1970s, the Iran–Iraq war in the 1980s and civil war in Iraq after the American invasion of 2003 all used Jordan as a transit country – and as a safe haven. So too did Arabs seeking work throughout the greater Gulf region. But it has been relations with Israel that have proved most significant in terms of the flow of displaced people during the second half of the twentieth century.

The most prominent refugees, of course, were Palestinians and their descendants. As we have seen, most came to Transjordan after the creation of the State of Israel in May 1948 and the Israeli triumph in a war with neighbouring Arab states that same year. Although Abdallah's forces took control of the West Bank and East Jerusalem during the fighting, thereby adding 400,000 Palestinians to the kingdom's population, thousands of others were made homeless during and immediately after the conflict. They took up what was hoped to be temporary residence in Syria, Lebanon, Egypt and Saudi Arabia, but the largest number fled east into Jordan where the majority of the population was – and remains – ethnically Palestinian. In the spring of 1949 Abdullah annexed the West Bank and East Jerusalem and announced that his expanded kingdom would be known as Jordan. He awarded Palestinians full Jordanian citizenship and appointed Palestinians to his cabinet, but many considered him to be the tool of the British and thus partly responsible for the debacle in the Palestine Mandate. The idea of a 'Jordanian option' or federation between Palestinians and Hashemite Bedouin Jordanians first emerged after al-nakba but foundered repeatedly due to its implicit renunciation of the historic Palestinian homeland.

Political opposition to the Hashemite monarchy emerged soon after the annexation of the West Bank. The king was assassinated by a Palestinian nationalist in 1951 and, after the brief reign of his unstable son Talal, Abdallah's grandson Hussein became the reigning monarch at the age of eighteen. The monarchy was tested repeatedly during the 1950s and '60s, with the king escaping a number of assassination and coup attempts, while adroitly balancing Western and Arab League interests. By the early 1960s revenues from tourism and US aid allowed the economy to grow at a modest rate. But clashes along the Israeli–Jordanian border reminded both sides that the larger issue of Arab hostility towards the Jewish state, and the fate of refugees who fled in 1948, shaped Middle East politics. The 1967 Israeli humiliation of Egypt, Syria and Jordan in a six-day war ended with the Israeli occupation of the West Bank and East Jerusalem, further exacerbating King Hussein's refugee dilemma as an additional 300,000 Palestinians entered the kingdom.

The resounding military defeat in 1967 fuelled Palestinian militancy in Jordan. Resistance fighters attacked Israel from bases in Egypt, Syria and Jordan, making the Hashemite kingdom their unofficial headquarters. By 1970 the Popular Front for the Liberation of Palestine (with Syrian backing) directly challenged King Hussein's authority and civil war erupted. Although the Jordanian army eventually prevailed in the bloody fighting and successfully expelled the PLO leadership, King Hussein became the nemesis of Palestinian militants throughout the Middle East. The animus directed toward the King did little to alter facts on the ground, however; thirty years after the expulsion of the PLO leadership, Palestinian refugees and their descendants living in Jordan numbered over 1.7 million, the longest-standing refugee population in the world.[52]

With the 1973 spike in oil prices, King Hussein, employing the rhetoric of pan-Arab unity, encouraged more than 400,000 Palestinians living in Jordan to migrate to the regional oil-producing countries in search of employment. Although Palestinians had been granted full citizenship rights in Jordan, job opportunities remained minimal in the resource-poor kingdom. During the 1970s and '80s remittances from these Palestinian workers provided an important boost to the Jordanian domestic economy, peaking at $1.3 billion per year in the mid-1980s (a quarter of total GDP) when as many as 40 per cent of Jordanian workers were expatriated. The remittances – and the job opportunities – evaporated during and after the 1991 Gulf War, when approximately 300,000 workers returned to Jordan, just as the country was facing acute economic hardship and international isolation for its unwillingness to support the effort to oust Iraqi military forces from Kuwait.[53]

The return of so many nationals, especially young second-generation Jordanians who had lived their entire lives abroad, placed enormous strain on the kingdom's public services and housing stock. The Gulf oil states withheld their economic aid to Jordan and rationing was imposed on basic commodities. By 1991 the unemployment rate shot up to 25 per cent, but the crisis had eased somewhat by the end of the decade as more Jordanian professionals found work in other Arab countries. At the turn of the century over 400,000 Jordanian nationals had again exercised their option to relocate abroad. Conversely, the migration of Palestinians and, since 2003, displaced Iraqis into Jordan continued unabated, posing a chronic problem for a government that had limited resources to assist further refugees.

Lebanon and Egypt

Soon after *al-nakbah*, more than 100,000 Palestinian refugees found safe haven in Lebanon, a country that lacked a strong sense of national integration. In 1943 a confessional political system was agreed whereby the president of the republic would be a Christian Maronite, the prime minister would be a Sunni and the speaker a Shia. Achieving independence in 1946, political loyalty tended in the direction of sect, not state. UNRWA built fifteen Palestinian refugee camps on lands that were leased to it by the Lebanese government but, as the numbers expanded and the encampments became permanent, the confessional character of the state was slowly compromised. Most of the refugees lived in ramshackle camps and were denied citizenship rights by a majority Christian Maronite government that wished to see the emergence of Lebanon as a crossroads between East and West. That government initially repressed Palestinian political activity but, in the aftermath of defeat in the 1967 war and Israeli occupation of Golan, Gaza and the West Bank, Lebanese authorities began to allow the refugee camps greater autonomy. As the number of refugees grew to 300,000 after the expulsion of the PLO from Jordan, the character of the camps changed. Soon they were dominated by Palestinian fighters who were intent upon using the country as a base of operations for guerrilla resistance against Israel.[54] By the early 1970s the camps were being targeted by right-wing Christian militias and the Lebanese army, weakening the country's political fabric and setting the stage for widespread civil unrest.

When civil war finally erupted between Lebanon's two main political factions in 1975, the Palestinians were drawn into the fight on the side of the Lebanese National Movement, a loose alliance of Muslim forces. In the summer of 1976, the opposition Lebanese Front, in response to Palestinian partisanship, lay siege to a large refugee camp in East Beirut. Before the fighting ended over 2,500 Palestinians had died. Two years later, Israel invaded southern Lebanon with the goal of rooting out PLO militants, but withdrew under strong international pressure. In 1982 Israel invaded again, this time with overwhelming force. After surrounding Beirut and shelling the city, a US-brokered ceasefire allowed for the overseas evacuation of PLO leaders and their fighting forces. But when the ceasefire broke down in September 1983, Israeli forces took the capital city and their right-wing Christian allies proceeded to massacre upwards of 1,000 Palestinian civilians – mostly women, children and elderly men – in the city's Sabra and Shatilla refugee camps. An estimated 20,000 people were killed during the three months of the Israeli-inspired war. Many of the dead were Palestinian civilians. In 1985, in an effort to prevent Palestinian fighters from regrouping in southern Lebanon, Syrian-backed militiamen attacked the remaining camps, causing further displacement and hardship.[55] Twelve official camps remained in the country in 2005, home to 394,000 people, or about 10 per cent of the total population of Lebanon. Many professions were closed to the Palestinians as they were considered foreign, and social services were not available outside what was offered by UNRWA.[56] As in Jordan, stateless Palestinians were unable to count on regional Arab states for either protection or for leadership in the struggle to regain their homeland.

A population-intensive but resource-poor country throughout the second half of the twentieth century, Egypt had the largest, and most urbanized, citizenry in the Middle East. There were approximately 58 million Egyptians in 1994, with 15 per cent of these under the age of four.[57] As a leading participant in several costly and unsuccessful wars against Israel, the country's economic resources were severely depleted at a time of rapid demographic expansion. And with most of the population concentrated in less than 4 per cent of the total land mass of the country along the Nile and the Delta, the pressure on cultivated land was intense. By the 1990s, almost half of the population lived in overcrowded urban areas. Faced with chronically high levels of unemployment, especially among the better educated, the emigration option remained key to the country's internal political and social stability. Leaving home for better opportunities abroad was a familiar phenomenon with a long pedigree: as early as 1918 over a million Egyptians had emigrated for financial and professional reasons.

After the 1952 revolution, the government sponsored a programme that supplied neighbouring states with trained teachers. But during the 1960s the Nasser regime generally discouraged emigration, especially when it involved skilled professionals who were needed at home. After the 1973 oil boom, and again in 1979, a conscious effort was made to eliminate barriers to free movement, and a Ministry of Migration office was opened to facilitate relocation and to research Arab labour markets. In order to ease a growing unemployment problem at home, the government provided incentives for Egyptians who took jobs in neighbouring Arab states, including the elimination of income taxes on income earned abroad. Saudi Arabia, Kuwait, UAE, Qatar, Iraq and Libya were the main receiving countries, with almost 400,000 workers employed in neighbouring states by 1975.[58] Five years later Egyptians comprised 30 per cent of the workforce in Kuwait, 33 per cent in Saudi Arabia, 20 per cent in UAE and 40 per cent in Jordan. By the 1990s the number of construction and unskilled migrants decreased in response to a regional economic downturn, but more Egyptian scientists, technicians and other skilled professionals accepted appointments elsewhere.[59] Salaries for teachers, professors, doctors, engineers and bankers were much more attractive in a number of regional states. In Egypt, as in so many sending countries, remittances from citizens working in other states became an important component of Gross National Product (GNP) and a source of foreign exchange.

MUSLIM MIGRANTS AND REFUGEES FROM SOUTH ASIA

A South Asian State for Muslims

The argument for the partition of India in 1947 centred on the perceived need for an autonomous state dedicated to Muslim identity on a subcontinent where the overwhelming majority of the population was Hindu. Pakistan would emancipate poor Muslims from their Hindu landlords; it would create new economic opportunities for the urban Muslim classes from Delhi and Mumbai; and it would establish an Islamic state for the devout.[60] It was an unusual polity from the outset: two territorial blocks separated by one thousand miles of Indian territory; home to peoples whose ethnic, tribal and regional loyalties often took precedence over any efforts to achieve a stable national identity.

And while millions of Muslims did cross the border into the new state after independence (by 1951 almost 10 per cent of Pakistanis were migrants from India), India retained its own enormous Muslim population. Indeed there were more than 50 million Indian Muslims after independence, and their numbers had increased to 120 million by the end of the twentieth century. Most of the Urdu-speaking elite of Muslim professionals left for Pakistan, fearful that they would not have access to government employment in India once Hindi was made the official language. Those who remained behind were for the most part poor landless labourers, farmers and shopkeepers. Controversially, India's secular government exempted Muslims from the uniform national civil code, allowing sharia law to set the standard for Muslims with respect to marriage and divorce, the status of women and educational practice. While often embattled as a distinct minority, millions of India's Muslims found little that was compelling about an Islamic form of nationalism and opted instead for the maintenance of their culture within the borders of a secular democracy.[61]

India's Muslims have on occasion been the target of extremists who sought to advance their own Hindu version of communal politics, but in the main Muslims who elected not to emigrate to Pakistan after partition have fared better than co-religionists who did leave. Since independence, three of India's presidents have been Muslim, and a significant middle class has emerged in the entertainment and software industries.[62] Conditions in Pakistan were decidedly less sanguine for the majority of citizens. By 1951 refugees from India were concentrated in a number of Western cities; in Karachi, for example, they accounted for 57 per cent of the population. By the mid-1950s the migrants dominated a number of professions and held a large proportion of higher-level government jobs. The traditional leaders of more rural areas resented the growing political power of the refugees and their descendants and, under the country's second constitution of 1962, the influence of the migrant community was reduced.[63]

Oscillating between military and civilian regimes for the past half century, unsuccessful in a series of military conflicts with its larger neighbour, rent by regional, ethnic and linguistic differences and challenged by skyrocketing fertility rates and religious fundamentalists eager to establish a theocratic state, living conditions in Pakistan fuelled the emigration of skilled professionals and uneducated labourers alike. The population growth rate, at 3 per cent annually, was among the world's highest at the end of the twentieth century, with few couples regularly practising contraception. Low levels of education amongst the female population, combined with deep cultural conservatism and patriarchy, have hindered all family planning efforts undertaken by the government.[64] Urban overcrowding was particularly challenging, with overall urban population quadrupling between 1951 and 1981. By the mid-1990s roughly 32 per cent of Pakistan's citizens lived in urban areas, and half of the population was under fifteen. In cities like Lahore and Karachi, youthful Pakistanis, most of whom were male, found it difficult to secure meaningful work, or the educational training that would qualify them for jobs in the professions.[65]

During the 1970s the government encouraged migration to the oil kingdoms, establishing a Ministry of Labour, Manpower and Overseas Pakistanis to regulate the flow and to assist expatriate communities. At its peak in the 1980s, between 2.5 and 3 million Pakistani workers were located in the Gulf states, or some 10 per cent of the total Pakistani workforce. These migrants remitted over $3 billion annually to approximately 12 million dependants in Pakistan, a figure that represented fully half of the country's foreign exchange earnings.[66] By 1981 almost 3 million Pakistanis were living in India, together with almost 8 million migrants from Bangladesh (former East Pakistan).[67] There were approximately 34 million citizens at the time of the country's first census in 1951, and close to 140 million at the beginning of the twenty-first century. Recent projections of 219 million by 2015 would make Pakistan the world's fifth most populous country, insuring that migration would continue to be viewed as the only option for a meaningful life. Without this option the prospect of social unrest or, even worse, thousands of young men ripe for extremist solutions to the country's ills, was a sobering possibility. Recognizing the potential for destabilization, the government issued over a million clearances for overseas work during the 1980s and another 715,000 permits were issued during the period 1990–94. The remittances of these workers were larger than the total of official development aid delivered to Pakistan.[68]

By 2006 remittances totalled $5 billion per year. Gulf states facing their own population explosions were unwilling to accept more labourers from Pakistan and began to expel illegal residents from South Asia.[69]

Migration to Britain began in the early 1950s, with a large influx occurring just before new restrictive legislation was adopted in 1962. The financial attraction was considerable, even before the oil boom of the 1970s. Pakistani men living in Britain typically earned 30 times the wages that were available at home. By 1981 they represented the third largest ethnic minority in Britain behind Indians and Afro-Caribbeans.[70] Settling in urban areas, especially Birmingham, Bradford and east London, the migrant communities quickly established their own retail and residential enclaves, while also building religious schools and mosques. Government support for Afghan resistance fighters during the decade-long Soviet occupation of Afghanistan in the 1980s led to the movement of millions of Afghan refugees into the north of Pakistan. The mountainous frontier between the two states became a haven for Islamic radicals, many of whom formed the backbone of the Taliban regime during the 1990s.

Afghanistan's Travail

In a mountainous country composed of nomadic, tribal and ethnically diverse peoples, major powers – from the British in the nineteenth century to the Soviets in the twentieth – have attempted to gain a strategic foothold. When, in the spring of 1979, the communist People's Democratic Party of Afghanistan overthrew the family that had ruled since the eighteenth century, the new rulers inaugurated a series of reforms that included land redistribution, secular education and the emancipation of females. These steps alienated conservative religious and tribal leaders, precipitating clashes around the country. Concerned that Afghanistan was descending into civil war and that the fallout would extend into the neighbouring Central Asian Soviet republics, Soviet troops intervened in late December 1979. But resistance to foreign intervention emerged almost immediately, as Afghan politicians continued to feud amongst themselves and as the poorly trained Afghan army ceded the initiative to the Red Army. The conflict was brutal, with more than a million people killed in a decade-long struggle. Within three years of the start of hostilities, one-fifth of the country's population, terrified by native guerrilla fighters and Soviet troops alike, had fled across the border into Pakistan.[71]

The US administration under Ronald Reagan supplied the Afghan mujahideen rebels with ample military equipment through Pakistan. The operation was covert but annual aid reached as high as $280 million per year in the mid 1980s. For many of these guerrilla fighters, the battle against the Soviets was a *jihad* against infidels who had forced so many of their kinfolk into refugee camps. And the camps grew exponentially as the Soviets employed a scorched-earth policy in populated rural areas of the country. At its peak in 1990, the camps in Pakistan were home to 3.2 million Afghans, while those in Iran held an additional 2.9 million.[72] Most of the refugees returned home in the early 1990s with assistance from UNHCR, and after the withdrawal of Soviet troops and the fall of the communist regime. But the exodus would begin again when the fundamentalist Taliban regime fought its way into power. Composed of young and rootless religious zealots who had been born in refugee camps and known nothing but war during their lifetime, the Taliban first emerged as a decisive military and polit-ical force in 1994, ultimately seizing power two years later. Their gender policies had the effect of decimating the schools and the health services, where women traditionally had played a strong leadership role, while their depredations against the remaining bureaucracies led to the flight of most of the country's educated class. UN agencies and NGOs found it impossible to do their work in the face of ever more bizarre Taliban edicts and began withdrawing from the country.

They were soon followed by millions of Afghans. The Taliban cared little for the essential work of government; meeting the material needs of a desperately poor population interfered with the repressive Islamicist project. Decades of war, economic collapse, repression, human rights abuses, malnutrition and, in the late 1990s, prolonged drought drove a new wave of refugees, more than 2 million by 1999, back across the borders into Iran and Pakistan. There various UN and NGO agencies struggled to provide basic living needs. Only with the overthrow of the

Taliban in the autumn of 2001 did a major repatriation effort begin, with the overwhelming majority of displaced persons back in the country by the end of 2005. The formation of an internationally recognized government, together with extensive international aid, has eased the process of return, but serious security, infrastructure, economic and environmental challenges pose new dangers for the returnees. Without ongoing reconstruction and reconciliation efforts, the fate of Muslims in one of the world's poorest countries remains precarious.

THE FATE OF PAN-ARABISM AND MUSLIM MIGRATION AFTER 9/11

At the end of World War II, the call to end European control over the Arab Middle East echoed broadly across the political spectrum. The centuries-old goal of uniting the Arab peoples took a new turn in 1948 as the destruction of the 'neo-colonial' state of Israel became the rallying point for nationalists in the region. Avenging the defeat of 1948 served as the focus of organization for the next two decades, with Nasser of Egypt and the Ba'th parties of Syria and Iraq claiming the mantle of leadership in the Arab community. The long-awaited unity of Arab peoples would strengthen the role of Islam in the global community and allow for the free movement of Muslims throughout the region as economic opportunities emerged. Failure in the 1967 war with Israel discredited aspirant pan-Arabist leaders like Nasser, and in the 1970s what leadership remained shifted to the conservative oil states of the Gulf. But while they were willing to offer much-needed financial assistance to the beleaguered Palestinian cause, the post-war Arab states began to follow their own, more narrowly nationalistic, course of development.

In the late 1980s Iraq's Ba'thist ruler Saddam Hussein tried to assume the mantle of leadership within the Arab world, but his instigation and prosecution of a bloodly decade-long war with Iran, followed by the invasion of Kuwait, revealed the true depth of his commitment to Islamic fellowship. Egypt, Syria, Saudi Arabia and the Gulf states all allied themselves with the US and the UN in the effort to oust Saddam's forces from Kuwait. By the early 1990s the original pan-Arab vision was in a shambles. The region was characterized by extended royal families, authoritarian governments and military regimes, each opposed to the unrestricted movement of peoples across international boundaries. That is, of course, unless carefully controlled migration advantaged the local economy. In the United Arab Emirates, 80 per cent of the population was made up of temporary foreign workers. The figures for Qatar and Bahrain were 66 per cent and 33 per cent respectively. Yet none of the guest workers could aspire to permanent residency, much less citizenship. Trans-national Arab identity counted for very little in a region of competitive nation states.

If migration within the Muslim world had become more difficult at the turn of the century, relocation outside the Arab Middle East, or the wider Muslim lands, was especially challenging. The attacks against the United States by nineteen members of the al-Qaeda terrorist network in September 2001 immensely complicated the lives of all Muslims living and travelling in the developed countries of the West. Once it was revealed that all of the 9/11 hijackers had entered the US on temporary visas, and that three of them had overstayed their legal limit in the country, the stigmatization of Muslims as potential security threats began.

In the US, admissions policies were hastily revamped; the federal government's powers of detention were expanded; established migrant communities were subject to greater surveillance; financial transactions were closely monitored; and universities were required to provide detailed personal information about their Middle Eastern and Muslim students.[73] As it became clearer that the non-state al-Qaeda network exercised a global reach thanks to the support of failed and 'rogue' states, that operatives could successfully penetrate traditional screening networks and that asymmetrical warfare and 'soft targets' were the focus of terrorists, an unconventional form of global combat involving both international military and domestic police components was inaugurated. The latter involved strategies and practices that placed an enormous strain on civil liberties in a number of Western countries, no more so than in the US. The 'securitization of migration' had begun, and Muslims of all ages and backgrounds found themselves placed on an ever-expanding 'persons of interest' list.[74]

Although the 9/11 terrorists were non-state actors, the government of the US and its partners responded to the mass murder in traditional statist terms. Simply put, those states that were believed to harbour or support terrorists were to be held responsible for acts of violence organized and carried out from safe havens. The Taliban regime in Afghanistan was quickly overthrown, and a US-led pre-emptive attack against Saddam Hussein's Iraq was carried out on the grounds (inaccurate in the end) that the regime held weapons of mass destruction that might be made available to terrorist groups like al-Qaeda. In the US some 1,200 citizens and non-citizens, most of whom were Muslim, were arrested and detained in the immediate aftermath of the 9/11 attacks, while hundreds of others were deported for visa violations.

With more than 12 million Muslims living in Europe, and another 6 million in the US, the events of 9/11 clearly added to the difficulties faced by Muslims who had relocated to the West. Public debate intensified over the compatibility of Islamic values with Western liberalism and secular political values. When, in the summer of 2005, a small group of British-born men of Pakistani descent blew themselves up in crowded underground trains and a London bus, killing 55 and injuring 100 others, new questions arose regarding the vulnerability of the public to unconventional warfare. How had the suicide bombers, all of whom had been born and raised as British citizens, come under the influence of Islamist radicals? Should the state begin a more vigorous campaign of ethnic profiling in order to pre-empt future attacks?

The latter question seemed to have been answered in the affirmative one year later when British authorities arrested sixteen ethnic Pakistanis for plotting to blow up US-registered passenger aircraft over the Atlantic. It was revealed that the suspects, including one woman, had been under surveillance for the better part of a year, and that Pakistani security services had partnered with British investigators during the course of the probe. Irrespective of how often authorities in Britain and the US insisted that the war on terror was not targeting mainstream Islam, the fact that acts of terror against civilian populations were being carried out under the banner of an Islamic holy war strained relations between communities. In a new and disturbing era of unconventional warfare where, to use the American president's language, 'Islamo-fascists' targeted innocent civilians and threatened free institutions and freedom of thought, the job of identifying and defeating the enemy inevitably meant that immigrant communities – even long-established ones – would be disrupted and unsettled. Muslim migration had become a matter of national security.

Chapter 5

Global Workers from South and East Asia

Perhaps the central feature of international migration in the decades after World War II was its global reach. The first great era of transcontinental and transoceanic migration, made possible by the advent of cheap rail and steamship transport during the half-century beginning in 1870, was very much a European-dominated affair. European migrants – women, men and entire family units – fanned out across the globe to myriad colonial destinations, and in particular to countries like the US, Canada and Australia, in anticipation of economic betterment and social mobility. In many cases these migrants left densely populated and politically troubled regions in Europe to settle in emerging countries and colonies that were eager to attract additional labour. Underpopulated and richly endowed with land and natural resources, these destination countries had virtually no immigration protocols and welcomed the free flow of newcomers. As we have seen, more than 50 million Europeans emigrated during these decades, with the overwhelming majority determined to settle on a permanent basis in their adopted states.

The environment after World War II was markedly different. Sending and receiving areas proliferated, with Europeans constituting but a small (and still shrinking) minority of international migrants. In large measure the new migration flows were from the less developed 'South' to more affluent regions in the post-industrial 'North'. The immediate post-war years witnessed the movement of peoples from the colonial periphery to the metropole, but during the final quarter of the century and beyond ever greater numbers emigrated from recently independent states in South and East Asia to destinations around the globe, irrespective of earlier colonial connections. In 2002 the United Nations estimated that out of the 175 million people who resided outside their country of birth, 50 million were Asians.[1] Some countries of origin in developing regions actively encouraged temporary labour migration and came to rely upon expatriate remittances as an important source of national income. Rapidly growing economies meant that Asia and the Middle East served as preferred destinations for unskilled manual and domestic workers, while highly educated citizens departed in record numbers to pursue broader and more lucrative professional opportunities in the mature economies of the Western hemisphere.

South and East Asian communities established roots in a number of European and North American urban centres, but the highly skilled and increasingly affluent members of these communities soon relocated to the suburbs and adopted many of the values of Western commercial culture. Still, most of these new migrant communities retained close connections with the land of their birth, with air travel between sending and destination countries becoming commonplace for members of the middle classes. More than any other sending area, South and East Asia provided the affluent North with a new type of immigrant phenomenon. Referred to as the 'brain drain' by sending countries in the 1960s, by the beginning of the twenty-first century some of these highly skilled emigrants, having made their fortunes and professional mark in the West, opted for a return home to countries that in the interval had embraced market-based economic reforms and offered the expatriate investor the attraction of lower labour costs.

In East Asia, recent regional migration has featured two distinct trends: the prominence of 'professional' labour brokers, and the centrality of sending governments in organizing and promoting overseas opportunities. Since the 1970s states like Indonesia, the Philippines and China have facilitated the relocation of citizens as part of a larger national economic strategy. Labour export agencies emerged within the national bureaucracy to work with receiving countries and to offer training to prospective migrants. State-to-state relationships were formalized through quota controls, with the understanding on both sides that the foreign workers could not apply for permanent residency, naturalization or family reunification. Private brokers and larger recruitment agencies offered services ranging from the preparation of travel documents, transportation to and from the receiving country and housing accommodation during the term of the labour contract. Recruitment services became a lucrative industry during the final quarter of the twentieth century, especially since the overwhelming majority of migrants were destined to return home after the completion of a labour contract. Although licensed and regulated by the sending state, the opportunities for abuse in a climate of deregulation were enormous. Individuals and agencies emerged offering counterfeit travel documents, clandestine transportation to receiving countries and guarantees of employment despite the migrant's illegal status. Even under the auspices of official state-to-state agreements, migrants were denied political rights and faced the constant threat of deportation from the host country, while conditions for those who entered illegally were especially precarious.[2]

The burst of international migration from heavily populated countries like India, China and Indonesia in recent decades reflected both the adoption of market-based models of development by previously closed command economies, and new approaches to the deployment of labour resources in response to fluid market demands. Rising affluence in some countries propelled the outflow of domestic and other unskilled workers from states where opportunities were few and compensation minimal. In some instances even skilled workers from a country where professional opportunities were scarce were willing to assume unskilled posts overseas if the remuneration met certain standards. The majority of international migrants from South and East Asia during the past quarter of a century were relocating voluntarily in search of economic betterment.

For millions of women and men in the south-east Asian states of Vietnam, Cambodia and Laos, however, international relocation was the product of war and dislocation. As political refugees from victorious communist governments in the mid- to late 1970s, most were accommodated in Western countries, like the US and France, that had been deeply involved in the region's military conflicts. But as the departures continued into the 1980s, 'compassion fatigue' set in and countries adjacent to the sending zones began to reject the newcomers as economic migrants. It would not be until the 1990s, when the Vietnamese government began to adopt market reforms and re-establish relations with the capitalist West, that the outflow came to an end.

GENDERED EMIGRATION: THE PHILIPPINES, INDONESIA AND SRI LANKA

Prior to the 1970s, international migration was primarily a male phenomenon in the countries of South, South-east and East Asia. A large percentage of these men were university students and skilled professionals studying and working in the developed West. Even during the heyday of temporary labour migration to the oil-producing states of the Middle East, the vast majority of those who were recruited to work on infrastructure projects were male. By the early 1980s, however, a greater demand for female domestic, child care and health care workers emerged. The shift took place first in the rapidly developing oil kingdoms, followed by a similar demand during the late 1980s and early 1990s in the so-called 'Tiger' economies of Singapore, Hong Kong, Japan, Malaysia, Taiwan and South Korea.

The transition from a male-dominated international labour experience to a female-centred paradigm had its greatest impact on women in the Philippines, Indonesia and Sri Lanka. In each of these countries 'women comprise some 60 to 80 per cent of migrants legally deployed every year'.[3] Many of the migrants found themselves working in vulnerable sectors of the host country's economy, especially in domestic service and the entertainment industry, which were not protected under most labour legislation. Unscrupulous brokers and agents were more likely to exploit female migrants, while private employers enjoyed wide discretion with respect to wages and working conditions.

The growth of domestic service in countries where females entered the professional ranks created stark differences and inequalities for all working women. Rather than a progressive movement of empower-ment for all women, new forms of exploitation resulted in an environment shaped by physical intimacy and social difference. Professional women in receiving countries freed themselves from housework and childcare as they pursued new levels of job satisfaction and upward mobility. Not unlike their Western counterparts, they adopted the language of equality, career achievement and public engagement as they redefined gender boundaries. But these goals could only be achieved through the outsourcing of housework and childcare to foreign domestics who sacrificed family and friends at home for low wages and limited autonomy abroad.

The greatest proportion of overseas domestics were young and single, but a significant number of married women left behind spouses and children to become breadwinners. Service as a transnational mother placed additional strains on households already struggling to meet basic needs in an increasingly globalized economy. Ironically, the advancement of middle-class women in global cities like Taipei, Hong Kong, Kuala Lumpur and Singapore came about less through the trans-formation of gender roles but instead within the context of expanding low-wage opportunities for women from less developed countries. The gender conventions remained in place – women were carers and housekeepers – only the occupants changed. Amidst the surge in female labour migration throughout the region, gendered divi-sion of work was never challenged, only reassigned along racial and national lines.[4]

THE FILIPINO LABOUR DIASPORA

During nearly half a century of American control (1901–46), the modest number of migrants from the Philippines who sought work overseas typically found employment in the sugar and pineapple plan-tations of Hawaii, in the agricultural economy of West Coast states like California and Oregon and in Alaska's fishing industry. Numbering approximately 150,000 in 1930, the workers – most of whom were males – were treated as internal migrants, since the Philippines remained a US colony. After independence in 1946, however, Filipino migrants seeking permanent relocation fanned out across the globe, with the majority settling in Australia and New Zealand.

Only in the 1970s, under the authoritarian government of Ferdinand Marcos, did the phenomenon of temporary labour migration grip this archipelago state of 7,000 islands. The outflow continued after the establishment of a democratic government in 1986, with an astonishing 9 per cent of the Filipino population, or 8.1 million individuals, living and working abroad in late 2004. This translated into an average of 2,500 departures per day, with a significant minority of the emigrants coming from the ranks of professionals in the field of medicine, especially nurses and other carers. Since 1992 women have outnumbered men in the labour migrant category, filling domestic, service and professional positions from Hong Kong to Kuwait. In addition to their residence in almost 200 countries worldwide, Filipinos constituted approximately a quarter of the world's merchant marine population, with over a quarter of a million sea-based workers contracted by a number of different national carriers.

The strong culture of migration that developed in the Philippines after independence spread to school-age children during the final decades of the twentieth century, with one poll of pre-teens reporting that almost 50 per cent planned to work abroad some day.[5] The revenues from overseas workers became a cornerstone of the post-war Philippines' economy, prompting the government to set a target of deploying a million workers overseas each year. Over 1,000 government-licensed recruitment agencies were in business at the turn of the twenty-first century, organizing travel and agreeing contract terms for millions of workers. From a modest level of $103 million in 1975, annual remittances reached a total of $7 billion in 2002. During the final quarter of the twentieth century, between 34 and 54 per cent of Filipino families came to rely on foreign remittances as a key source of household consumer income. For its part, the government encouraged expatriate investment in struggling domestic enterprises. During the 1990s, official government estimates placed remittances at over 5.2 per cent of the GNP. With a population that continued to grow at twice the rate of the Asian region as a whole, and with domestic economic development lagging, the migration option, despite its enormously disruptive impact on family life, remained a major economic strategy for millions of skilled and unskilled Filipinos.[6]

Perhaps more than any other sending country, gender mattered when it came to Filipino migration trends. Men generally relocated and accepted employment in states where construction and manufacturing needs were greatest, while women tended to take up residence where the demand for service and entertainment workers was most acute. Males predominated in the Middle East, for example, while women workers constituted a majority in more developed states. The two most popular Western destination countries, the US and Italy, never created the type of formal recruitment policies that were characteristic of the Gulf oil states. Filipino emigration flows to the US remained strong due to the former colonial relationship and the active recruitment of female nurses beginning as early as the 1960s, while strong cultural ties with the Roman Catholic Church solidified the movement of female domestic workers into Italy.[7] Not only single women but mothers too chose emigration for economic advancement, leading to what one scholar has called a 'care crisis' in the Philippines as children from transnational households were cared for increasingly by members of extended families. By the early twenty-first century, an estimated 9 million Filipino children under the age of eighteen were growing up without at least one parent.[8]

Female carers, especially nurses, typically found greater professional opportunities in highly developed states. In 1989, Filipino nurses 'comprised the overwhelming majority (73 per cent) of foreign nurse graduates in the United States'.[9] They were concentrated in large metropolitan areas like New York and Chicago, where the demand for skilled nurses was most pronounced. In an effort to retain many of these temporary professionals, in December 1989 the US Congress passed the Immigration Nursing Relief Act, designed to facilitate the transition to permanent residency status. Because of their English language abilities, both the UK and the US recruited heavily in the Philippines. In 2001 the Philippines sent three times the number of nurses abroad as in 1996, exacerbating the care crisis in rural and poor areas of the country.[10]

Religion and Ethnicity in Indonesia and Sri Lanka

During the post-war decades, the Netherlands hosted a large community of expatriates from Indonesia, a Dutch colony until 1949. Most desired permanent resettlement, and generous family reunification policies guaranteed that the transition to a new culture would not be traumatic. Beginning in the 1970s, however, as select Middle Eastern and subsequently Asian economies reached maturity, the Muslim world's most populous country (and the world's fourth most populous overall), emerged as a major source of overseas contract labour. At the start of the twenty-first century an estimated 2.5 million Indonesians, or 3 per cent of the national workforce, found temporary employment outside the country. And most of the growth was attributed largely to the feminization of the migrant workforce. In response to unprecedented demand, agents and recruiters were especially interested in female domestic labourers for postings in Saudi Arabia, Malaysia, Singapore and Hong Kong.

The majority of unskilled female Indonesians who travelled abroad in the 1980s were situated in the Saudi Kingdom (where the added attraction of the Haj was key to recruitment). Later Singapore, Hong Kong and Taiwan became choice destinations for women who were employed as household maids and servants. There were, for example, only 10,000 Indonesians in Taiwan as recently as 1991, but ten years later the total had exploded to over 90,000. The vast majority of these temporary residents were female domestics. Similarly in Singapore in 2002, 70 per cent of all newly hired domestic workers were from Indonesia. By the early twenty-first century, Indonesia had become the leading source of housemaids across Asia. Undocumented flows, especially between Indonesia and Malaysia, represented an additional 'shadow' labour pool that was highly susceptible to mistreatment and abuse. A 1993 amnesty in Malaysia revealed that there were almost half a million undocumented Indonesians working in the country.[11]

The emergence of an overseas labour market for women, and the popularity of this option for younger, single females, created difficult tensions within this majority Muslim state where the propriety of patriarchal power had long been assumed. In the early 1980s, just as the phenomenon of female contract labour was expanding, the Indonesian government's 'Guideline for State Policy' defined women as 'reproducers of the next generation of workers'. It was not until the early 1990s that women were officially recognized as a 'human resource' whose contributions to society extended beyond the confines of fertility. Still, as late as 1997 the Minister of Women's Affairs requested that the government ban the further export of women domestics. The request was not met, but Indonesian women who wished to work overseas had to be at least 22 years old and needed written permission to leave the country from their fathers or husbands.[12]

While still under British control, the island colony of Ceylon set a precedent in South Asia by adopting universal adult suffrage in 1931. After independence in 1948, a democratic parliamentary form of government was adopted, and it remained in place until rising ethnic tensions between the Sinhalese majority and the Tamil minority fractured the unity of the state in the early 1980s. Tamil immigrants had first arrived on the island in the third century BCE, but during the nineteenth century the British recruited large numbers of South Indian Tamils to work in the export-orientated coffee and tea plantation economy. Concentrated in the northern region of the country and constituting approximately 12 per cent of a total population of almost 19 million, Tamil politicians began to call for greater religious, linguistic and political autonomy in the 1960s, fearful that the majority would turn Sri Lanka into a Sinhalese-speaking Buddhist state.

In fact, despite high voter turnout and the relative success of Sri Lankan democracy during the first few decades after independence, tensions between the Sinhalese and Tamil communities had deep roots. Soon after independence, the government passed legislation that made it difficult for Tamil immigrants from India to gain citizenship. A move to deport non-citizens was championed by Sinhalese politicians, and in 1964 an agreement between India and Sri Lanka led to the deportation of approximately 525,000 of the 900,000 Indian Tamils living in the island country.[13] The Official Language Act of 1956 further alienated the Tamil-speaking minority, as Sinhala was declared the official language of the country. Government employment opportunities, the main source of high-status jobs, were also limited as Sinhala became a more important language at the national level. The long-smouldering conflict erupted into open civil war in 1984, leading to numerous bloody exchanges, the intervention of Indian troops between 1987 and 1990 and the eventual exodus or internal displacement of hundreds of thousands of Tamil citizens. By the close of the century the war had reached a stalemate, with the death toll reaching over 75,000. Almost a third of Sri Lanka's total Tamil population (over 700,000 people) lived abroad, while another third of the total had at some point experienced internal displacement. The majority of overseas Tamils were resident in England, Germany, Switzerland and Canada, but additional communities were present in a large number of countries around the world.[14]

INDIA FROM INDENTURE TO INTERNET

Large-scale, organized emigration from India began under British imperial control during the 1830s and '40s. The main port of embarkation was Calcutta in the north-east, with early recruits coming from the immediate hinterland. Eventually additional port cities like Madras in the south-east and Bombay in the west became key points of departure. Prompted by the end of slavery and the ongoing need for a cheap plantation workforce, Indians – Hindus and Muslims alike – departed under terms of indenture contracts for locations across the breadth of the empire. Mauritius, Malaya, Burma, Celyon, Jamaica, Trinidad, British Guiana – all became destination colonies for impoverished Indians seeking a modicum of economic betterment.[15] Few found it, however, with most workers spending years abroad under harsh conditions with colonial authorities offering little protection from the abuses of unscrupulous employers. Five-year contracts became the norm in the 1860s and, while most indenture agreements included return passage after the contract expired, conditions on ships returning to India were consistently unhealthy and dangerous, with resulting high mortality rates. Between 1842 and 1870, an estimated half a million Indians emigrated under indenture, serving in both British and French colonies.[16]

There was always a conflicted view of expatriates within majority Hindu culture. Despite the fact that migrants were typically in search of a better life, the overseas Indian was thought to have 'lost his caste and with it his place in society'.[17] Even so, during the colonial period Indian authorities were deeply concerned about the expatriate population and voiced those concerns strongly at the imperial conferences that took place before World War II. Demanding that overseas Indians be accorded equal rights with other populations in the Dominions, delegates lobbied against enormous odds to protect their vulnerable countrymen. This posture changed dramatically after independence in 1947, however, as Nehru's government disregarded the status of overseas Indians in its formulation of foreign policy. Those living abroad now were advised to integrate into the majority culture of their host countries; in essence they were viewed as having forfeited their rights as Indians and were denied any opportunity to secure dual citizenship. In addition, Prime Minister Nehru's fixation with economic autarchy and protectionism for domestic producers meant that the potential contributions of Indians living abroad to internal economic development were ignored.[18] Those ties that remained between the diaspora communities and India were based exclusively on family relationships, not government or private sector initiatives.

Nehru's anti-imperial position did not prevent the movement of his fellow countrymen to the seat of empire after independence. The Labour government's 1948 Nationality Act facilitated voluntary relocation between colonies, Commonwealth states and the United Kingdom. Indians, especially those from Punjab and Gujarat, began to take advantage of the remarkable post-war expansion of industry in Britain, with the peak immigration period occurring during the decade 1955–65. Most of the newcomers concentrated in urban centres of the English midlands, although Greater London also provided opportunities for unskilled workers. Community associations like the Indian Society of Great Britain, centred in Birmingham, and the Indian Association of Bradford organized a vibrant cultural life around familiar festivals and holidays. In addition to entry-level careers in industry, Indian entrepreneurs opened small shops and restaurants to service not only fellow immigrants, but also the changing culinary tastes of the majority population. By the decade of the 1980s Indians in the UK 'had achieved the highest per capita incomes of all ethnic groups in England, had almost fully moved into non-manual labour, and had produced professionals at double the rate of white British citizens'.[19]

Across the Atlantic a different pattern of Indian resettlement was unfolding. There were fewer than 4,000 Indians living in the US at the end of World War II and, while these residents were granted rights of naturalization in 1946 under the Luce-Celler bill, restrictions on the entry of new immigrants from South Asia were rigorously enforced. Indeed fewer than 6,400 Indians were admitted to the US during the period 1946–64.[20] The civil rights-inspired 1965 Immigration and Naturalization Act, which allowed 20,000 new immigrants per country per year, transformed the Indian presence in the US, but only for members of India's tiny middle class. While fewer than 600 Indian nationals were permitted entry in 1965, by 1974 the figure reached just under 13,000.

The emigrants to the US were unlike the post-war newcomers to Britain or the 1960s temporary labour migrants to the oil-producing kingdoms of the Gulf. Most of those who entered the US were well educated, almost immediately entered into the professions, and within short order relocated from the city centre to the neighbouring suburbs. As instantly successful middle-class newcomers, they complemented the dominant American immigration myth of hard work leading to material success. Left behind, of course, were tens of millions of Indians who lived well below the poverty line as established by India's national Planning Commission.[21] The amelioration of material conditions for the majority depended at least in part on the availability of highly skilled professionals and business people in India, and increasing numbers of these citizens were leaving. By 1978, the number of annual emigrants from India to the US had reached 190,000, exceeding the totals for both China and Japan.[22] It was no surprise, then, that the government in the post-Nehru era became alarmed at what it perceived to be the flight of highly trained physicians, engineers and business people to the US. Unable to stop the outward flow, beginning in the 1970s the authorities in Delhi began cultivating overseas Indian associations as a means of securing crucial investment funds for

Indian industries. Skilled emigrants were now referred to as non-resident Indians (NRI) implying that the evolving overseas communities were made up largely of sojourners who might someday return.

During the 1990s, the Indian-born population in the US nearly doubled, from 500,000 to 1 million, making Indians the third largest immigrant group in the country after Mexicans and Filipinos. If one includes all people in the US who claimed Indian descent, the total approached nearly 1.7 million. By 2003, the 71,000 Indians who entered the US legally represented the second largest national cohort after Mexicans. Not surprisingly, virtually all of the newcomers were highly skilled professionals seeking better economic opportunities in the world's largest economy. Indeed some 75 per cent of working Indians in the US at the turn of the century were college educated. Three states – California, New York and New Jersey – hosted just under half of the total immigrant population from South Asia's largest country.[23] In California's Silicon Valley, for example, Indians educated at one of their home country's highly competitive Institutes of Technology made up a large minority of employees at some of the biggest and most successful firms. The same phenomenon emerged on the east coast, with highly educated 'techies' from India enjoying levels of opportunity that were only becoming available for a tiny minority at home by the late 1990s. Indian entrepreneurs purchased and managed motel and convenience store chains across the US; newly minted Indian PhDs entered the faculty ranks at colleges across the country; and the American Association of Physicians of Indian Origin estimated that between 10 and 12 per cent of all medical school students in the US were Indian.[24]

At the start of the 1990s, India's political leaders recognized that without a new economic strategy to address its balance of payments crisis, the country was headed for bankruptcy. Nehru's pursuit of economic self-sufficiency and planned development, embraced by the state for nearly half a century, had at its core a strong suspicion of foreign investment and outside control over Indian industries. Critics complained that state control and large bureaucracies hampered development in a wide variety of sectors, while high tariffs, ostensibly protecting domestic enterprises from outside competition, resulted in shabby products and poor-quality services. Faced with impending fiscal disaster, in 1991 the government recognized the value of establishing closer ties with the overseas community.[25] It decided to permit foreign investment in select areas of the economy while slashing tariffs on most imported goods. The NRI community pressed for even greater openings during the second half of the decade and in particular called for dual citizenship in order to smooth the investing process. This concession was finally secured in 2002. As a result return migration quickened at the start of the twenty-first century, but a good deal of mistrust remained. India's internet industries matured and expanded rapidly to serve a global client base during the final years of the twentieth century, and in some instances start-up companies were headed by NRI who elected to return home. By 2003 India was generating almost $10 billion in revenues from the export of computer-related products and services. But in general overseas Indians from the professional ranks established permanent residency in the West, where they enjoyed higher than average incomes, and in 2005 alone sent an estimated $23 billion back to their natal land.[26]

India's Sikhs: Conflicted Migrants

The Sikh community, whose historic homeland was located in the Punjab region of north-west India and south-east Pakistan, numbered some 16 million worldwide at the close of the twentieth century. A million of these men and women lived in diasporic communities around the globe, with the majority concentrated in Britain, Canada and the US. For much of the post-war period, Indian Sikhs, who represent a mere 2 per cent of India's overall population, have been involved in nationalistic calls for greater autonomy and, failing that, an independent homeland in Indian-controlled Punjab referred to as Khalistan. The latter call intensified dramatically in 1984 after the government of Prime Minister Indira Gandhi sent in troops to the Golden Temple at Amritsar, holy site and symbolic centre of Sikhism, to root out suspected secessionists. This assault, combined with simultaneous attacks against 37 additional Sikh shrines in Punjab, galvanized support for a sovereign state amongst expatriate Sikhs worldwide and instantly turned India's Sikh community into a persecuted religious minority.

First emerging in the late fifteenth century under the leadership of Guru Nanak, the Sikh community of Punjab suffered intermittent persecution under India's Mogul emperors over the next two centuries. Almost always in a defensive posture, Sikhs developed a martial tradition in response to Mogul intolerance and belligerence. Drawn mainly from the lower social classes of Punjab's Jat peasantry, the Sikhs had a value system that emphasized equality in a caste-conscious society, the rejection of ritual and renunciation and the propriety of just struggle against oppressors. Under British colonial rule, the condition of the Sikh community improved significantly, with Sikh military prowess translating into employment opportunities and even preferential treatment within the colonial system. Britain imposed its rule over Punjab in 1849, and by the start of World War I Sikhs made up a third of the colonial armed forces in the subcontinent. Economic development in the form of canal and rail construction in Punjab, and the protection of peasants against unscrupulous money-lenders, facilitated a British 'divide and rule' policy that clearly benefited Sikhs.[27] Although they represented only 14 per cent of the population of Punjab (Muslims were in the majority), Sikhs founded schools, cultivated the Punjabi language and in general developed a strong sense of separate identity during the late colonial period.

This favouritism carried over into the realm of migration opportunities. Unlike the majority of Indians abroad, Sikhs were never involved in the harsh indenture system that characterized so much of late nineteenth-century overseas travel from the subcontinent. By the time that Sikhs began leaving Punjab in the 1860s, over 2 million Indian indentured servants had departed for destinations as varied as Fiji, Kenya and the West Indies. The typical Sikh overseas experiences almost always related to service in the British colonial state, typically as soldiers and security personnel, but also as commercial middlemen, peddlers and caretakers.[28] Beginning with service in Burma in the early 1860s, Sikh regiments subsequently took up posts in colonial Malaya, East Asia and East Africa, demonstrating a high level of martial ability, discipline and loyalty.

Many of the soldiers stayed on after their military service came to an end. In Malaya, for example, there were over 15,000 Sikhs engaged in civilian professions in 1931. Hong Kong was another preferred posting and by 1939 more than a third of the city's police force was Sikh.[29] Some Sikh civilians worked overseas as railway workers and commercial traders. This was the case in East Africa, where work on the Uganda railroad began in 1895.[30] In British Columbia, where the first migrants arrived in 1903 or 1904, a small community of Sikhs worked as farm labourers and in the nascent lumber industry. Before the US imposed discriminatory immigration laws in 1923, approximately 10,000 Sikhs settled in California, with additional communities forming in Oregon and Washington State.[31] Not unlike the overseas Irish, who also were subject to British colonial rule, Sikhs abroad retained a strong sense of community with the homeland that was closely tied to religion. They exhibited a strong interest in their non-state 'homeland' and lent material support whenever that homeland seemed under threat.

In 1947 the Punjab was partitioned as part of the overall division of the subcontinent between Pakistan and India. There was a total evacuation of the Sikh community from the western, Pakistani controlled portion of the Punjab, birthplace of Guru Nanak and the shrines associated with early Sikhism. Millions were displaced and subject to the myriad hardships of refugee relocation.[32] As Commonwealth citizens who did not require an internal sponsor, thousands of these Punjabi Sikhs sailed for new homes in Britain, while others arrived in the UK from Hong Kong and, in the 1970s, from Kenya and Uganda as twice-removed exiles. By the 1990s there were over half a million Sikhs living in Britain, with the majority concentrated in London and in the industrial cities of the Midlands. Many of the exiles from Kenya and from Idi Amin's Uganda entered Britain as complete family units, sometimes multi-generational. Those with financial resources were able to find employment in the professions while affording their children access to higher education.

With the lifting of restrictions against South Asians in Canada and the US during the 1940s, thousands more Sikhs ventured even further from their troubled homeland. In Canada, a generous family reunification policy starting in the 1960s enabled sponsored relatives to join wage earners. By 1991 the country's Sikh population was just under 200,000 with chain migration continuing at high levels.[33] In general the Sikh communities of Britain, Canada and the US have prospered economically and served as advocates for the protection and advancement of Sikh culture within the larger Indian polity. Remittances became an important link with the homeland, especially as migrant communities achieved middle-class status. Gurdwaras were built in the Sikh-populated neighbourhoods of large cities and served as key social and religious centres.

It was not until the army assault on Amritsar in 1984 that Sikh loyalty to the Indian state was put to the test. Protest marches were organized in overseas receiving countries and strident calls for independence were heard. Indian Independence celebrations in New York, Toronto and Vancouver in August 1984 were disrupted by demonstrators. The subsequent assassination of Prime Minister Indira Gandhi by two of her Sikh bodyguards in October 1984 led to a killing spree in major cities of north India, with innocent Sikh civilians fleeing for their lives. Thousands of Sikhs became internal exiles while others applied for political asylum overseas. In the aftermath of the Mrs Gandhi's assassination, the Indian government became deeply suspicious of expatriate Sikh organizations and began surveillance operations through overseas embassies. When Prime Minister Rajiv Gandhi visited England in October 1985, a plot to assassinate him was uncovered and two Sikhs were convicted the following year.[34] And when an Air India flight en route from Montreal to India was bombed in the summer of 1985, resulting in the deaths of all aboard, two Canadian Sikhs were arrested and charged with the terrorist act.

Threats against Indian politicians and calls for a Sikh national homeland continued over the next few years. But as tensions eased during the 1990s and economic conditions in India improved, the focus on independence was replaced by a drive for greater power within the Indian polity. The election of Dr Manmohan Singh as prime minister of India in 2004 contributed significantly to the decline of separatist sentiment in Pubjab and reassured many expatriate communities that the Indian state would respect the unique culture of the Sikh minority. Still, the memory of Amritsar remained uppermost in the collective conscience of Sikhs abroad, and their efforts to preserve and transmit their culture to those born abroad testified to the depth of the relationship with the historic homeland.

India's Neighbour to the North

In the mountainous, landlocked country of Nepal, chronic rural poverty and, more recently, a Marxist military insurgency against the monarchy have led to the relocation of some 1.5 million citizens. With a total population of approximately 27 million, the export of labour has become an important feature of national policy. As early as 1985 the government established a labour policy that facilitated the movement of Nepalese nationals to more than a dozen countries. About half of the total found work in India, where a large percentage were recruited into public sector employment, and in particular the Indian military. By the 1990s there were over 50,000 Nepalese serving in the Indian armed forces, while another 200,000 were employed in civilian public sector services.

The remainder of the migrant pool travelled as far afield as the oil states of the Middle East to select countries in South East Asia. A 2002 estimate placed the number of Nepalese in the Gulf at just under half a million while Hong Kong, Singapore and Brunei were the most popular destination points in South East Asia. The vast majority of Nepalese expatriates were male, but by the turn of the century an increasing number of unskilled females joined the search for greater economic and physical security. The government's heavy-handed efforts to quash the Marxist insurgency has led in recent years to much abuse of innocent civilians caught up in the conflict, further propelling internal and external migration. For the latter group, the government's failure to lift the country out of its subsistence and service-orientated economy has only exacerbated migration flows and provided support for the insurgency.[35]

CHINA FROM MARX TO MARKETS

Chinese emigration outside the expansive 'Middle Kingdom' was exceptional prior to the nineteenth century and the age of European imperialism. As the world's leader in technology, commerce, urbanization and political sophistication during long centuries when much of the rest of the world – Europe included – was struggling to maintain a subsistence lifestyle, there was little incentive for the Chinese to relocate. The Confucian tradition had always emphasized the importance of remaining close to home in order to serve one's parents in their declining years, making loyalty to village and homeland powerful constants of Chinese agrarian culture.[36] Traders, sojourners and military personnel occasionally travelled abroad, but in general China's leaders discouraged migration and eschewed official contact with distant regimes.

The famous maritime expeditions of the early fourteenth-century Ming navigator Zheng He, which took place between 1405 and 1433, introduced thousands of Chinese seamen to South Asia, the Arabian Gulf and East Africa. But the commercial fruits of these voyages were limited, and the Ming emperor brought the exploits to an abrupt end in the 1430s, partially on the grounds that there was little to be gained from continued contact with lesser kingdoms to the south and west. Chinese ethnocentrism therefore was solidified by contact with other regions of the world, and despite the very real hardships faced by China's peasantry over the centuries – especially during periods of dynastic transition – life outside the Middle Kingdom seemed even worse. In 1717 a government that was already deeply suspicious of overseas commercial trade placed a ban on all emigration, and by 1759 European trade had been restricted to the one port of Canton. Although a dead letter by the early nineteenth century, the ban on emigration was not lifted until 1860 and not officially revoked until 1893.[37]

Demographic pressures, rebellions against the Qing dynasty, chronic warlordism, recurring famine and foreign (especially British) incursions during the nineteenth century undermined China's sovereignty and in the process changed this sedentary pattern forever. From a population of 100 million at the start of the seventeenth century (a figure greater than all of Europe's kingdoms combined), China's population had burgeoned to over 430 million by 1850. Pressure on arable land was enormous and the government's ability to provide domestic security was crumbling. In the wake of the protracted and brutal Taiping Rebellion of 1850-64, in which as many as 20 million Chinese died, refugees fled to Vietnam, Singapore and as far away as California.[38] Europe's imperial powers took advantage of the internal unrest to meet the growing labour needs in a number of their colonial holdings. With the advent of steamship transport in the mid-1860s, the cost of relocation plummeted and the out-migration accelerated. It is estimated that over 6.3 million Chinese moved overseas between 1868 and 1939, with the majority taking up residence and employment in South East Asian colonies. With few exceptions, they departed as indentured labourers or 'coolies', and the vast majority – at least 5 million – were younger males who hoped someday to return to their home districts after securing enough wealth to purchase land and settle down.[39]

In general these Chinese migrants and their descendants traced their roots to the three southern coastal provinces of Guangdong, Fujian and Zhejiang, areas that experienced the most extensive contact and interaction with Europe's colonial powers during the nineteenth century. Once overseas, the newcomers were assigned the most menial of unskilled jobs, often in crowded urban settings, and found great difficulty assimilating in the destination colonies. Part of the hostility directed at the Chinese migrant communities was the product of resentment against a small minority who over time became successful shopkeepers and businessmen. This was especially true in the colonies that later became independent Indonesia, Malaysia, Thailand, the Philippines, Singapore and Vietnam. By the time of independence after World War II the Chinese had emerged as influential figures in the urban economies of these new states. Even greater hostility towards Chinese migrants was exhibited in the West and in Europe's settler colonies. Beginning in the 1880s, the US, Canada, Australia and New Zealand adopted exclusionary laws that prohibited the immigration of any Chinese, and these racist policies remained in place into the 1960s and '70s.

The Communist Regime and Emigration

China experienced enormous internal dislocations between the fall of the Qing dynasty in 1911 and the defeat of Japan in 1945. The high hopes of Western-style republican revolution descended into warlordism and, beginning in the 1920s, military clashes between the forces of the nationalist Guomindang and a small but committed communist insurgency. The unrest kept the number of migrants high, affecting even the professional ranks of teachers and journalists. Both sides in the civil conflict appealed to the overseas Chinese for material support, with the Guomindang government establishing an Overseas Chinese Affairs Department that was charged with affording diplomatic protection to expatriates. A new research institute was created at Jinan University to study the sojourning phenomenon, and repeated appeals were made to expatriate communities for financial support.[40]

World War II began in 1937 for the Chinese, as Japanese forces – already in control of Manchuria since 1931 – began a series of brutal and merciless assaults that resulted in the occupation of much of the north and east of the country. In the wake of Japanese aggression, internal displacement became normative for millions of Chinese civilians. The ranks of the Chinese communists, led by Mao Zedong, swelled as the struggle against Japan intensified, with CCP armies alone growing from 90,000 men in 1937 to over 900,000 by 1945. Unlike the nationalists, the Chinese communists engaged in an aggressive guerrilla campaign against the Japanese occupiers, winning the support of millions of peasants in the process. Although both the Soviets and the Americans recognized the nationalist Kuomintang as the legitimate government of liberated China in 1945, Mao's communist forces defeated the more numerous nationalist armies in a civil war and took control of the country in 1949. Over a million nationalists fled from the mainland to Taiwan after the communist victory in the post-war struggle for power, while hundreds of thousands more headed south to the tiny British colony of Hong Kong.

The existence of two Chinas after 1949 complicated allegiances for the expatriate communities around the world. Millions of overseas Chinese continued to think of themselves as sojourners, even if they had established roots and prospered in new countries. Repatriation was lost as an option for most after the seizure of power by communists on the mainland. Most foreigners living in China were expelled by 1950, and the People's Republic, reverting to an earlier imperial position, strongly opposed both internal relocation and the out-migration of

Chinese nationals. The Sino-Soviet split and the economic failures associated with the Great Leap Forward (1958) and the Cultural Revolution (1966–76) exacerbated the official xenophobia that was always couched in the language of 'self-reliance'.[41] The government's penchant for confiscating remittances from expatriates who had made their fortunes in one of the Western capitalist states deeply discouraged further links between members of these communities and the homeland. And after Mao's government cracked down on private land ownership, there was little incentive for overseas Chinese to think about returning home during their retirement years. There was a modest flow of ethnic Chinese from British-controlled Hong Kong and from Taiwan to the West in the post-war years, but with the independence of Europe's colonies in South-east Asia, the new nationalist governments stopped the colonial practice of recruiting Chinese labour.

During the first decades of the Cold War destinations in the West became more attractive to those in Hong Kong and Taiwan who could relocate. The old racist immigration restrictions were lifted in countries like the US and Australia, and larger numbers of ethnic Chinese and their families, some re-migrants from South-east Asian countries, took the opportunity to relocate in the West. On the mainland, it was not until the death of Mao and the opening of China's economy to the global market in the late 1970s that a resurgence of overseas emigration occurred. Students – male and female – began travelling abroad for specialized university training, new businesses leaders entered into relationships with Western firms and sent managers abroad and highly skilled professionals began to exercise the newly permitted option of work overseas. Sending areas in China became somewhat more diverse, and a greater gender balance was achieved. Chinese communities abroad increased from 12.7 million people in 1963 to over 32 million in 1997.

The vast majority of overseas Chinese continued to reside in South-east Asia, but Asia's global share shrank from 99.6 per cent to 77.7 per cent during this period. Destinations in North America, Europe and Oceania now became more popular, and China's opening to world trade and foreign investment allowed for easier relocation and entry.[42] There were, for example, just 170,000 Chinese-born immigrants in the

US in 1970 but by 2000 that figure had expanded to just over 1.5 million. In Canada, the Chinese had become the largest immigrant group by the start of the twenty-first century, accounting for 16.1 per cent of all newcomers in 2001.[43] Similarly, travel to and settlement in Western Europe became more commonplace during the 1990s, and migrant communities were more heterogeneous, divided by language, class and political persuasion.[44]

One of the more significant features of recent Chinese migration to the developed West was the overall affluence of the newcomers. Historically the Chinese overseas have settled and built communities in and around major cities, and the new migrants continued this pattern, contributing to the formation of 'global cities' like Toronto, New York, Hong Kong and Singapore where transnational companies, people and capital from diverse origins interacted and conducted business. Since the 1980s the tradition of sending remittances was renewed, with affluent overseas Chinese once again contributing to community projects in native towns and villages. Another feature was the economic predominance of expatriate Chinese in some South-east Asian destination countries.

In Indonesia, for example, the world's most populous Muslim country, ethnic Chinese controlled 70 per cent of the country's capital and operated three-quarters of the 200 largest businesses by the early 1990s. A similar pattern of economic influence by a small, urbanized Chinese population emerged in Thailand. Between 1882 and 1917 almost 1.5 million (mostly male) Chinese lived and worked in Thailand, and while most eventually returned home, some of those who stayed rose from the status of small shopkeepers and traders to emerge in a generation or two as leading figures in domestic commerce and industry.[45]

The Canadian Example

In terms of the growth in numbers, occupational grouping and spatial relations, the story of Chinese migration to Canada illustrates the dramatic changes that have occurred since the end of Chinese insularity under Mao Zedong. The gold rush of the late 1850s and '60s in British

Columbia provided the occasion for the earliest arrival of approximately 2,000 Chinese as prospectors, many re-migrants from San Francisco but mostly from Hong Kong. This was followed by the introduction of contract labourers who were recruited by Canadian Pacific Railroad in the 1880s, an undertaking that required thousands of workers prepared to endure harsh conditions at very low pay. In the first national census of 1881, the total Chinese population of British Columbia was a modest 4,350. Three years later the total had grown to over 10,000, with the increase due almost entirely to railroad construction. Not surprisingly given the nature of the work environment, the immigrants were almost exclusively male. When an economic downturn struck the West in 1885, a vocal anti-Chinese movement in British Columbia prompted the national government to restrict the entry of additional immigrants. A series of laws were passed over the next two decades raising the head tax on Chinese immigrants, but slow growth continued until by 1911 there were just under 28,000 Chinese in Canada. The overwhelming majority of the settlers were resident in poor Chinatown communities in the western cities of Vancouver, Victoria, New Westminster and Nanaimo.[46]

Following the precedent set by the US in 1882, the Canadian federal government enacted its own Chinese Exclusion Act in 1923, prohibiting entry to all but consular officials, merchants and students. The ban was only lifted in 1947, but restrictions continued to be applied against Asian immigrants until 1962 when a new entry protocol was adopted that prohibited discrimination on the basis of country of origin. Younger Canadian-born Chinese began to move out of the urban Chinatowns during the 1960s and '70s; smaller Chinatowns began to disappear as older residents and proprietors died and as urban redevelopment projects were begun. After 1967 immigration authorities adopted a new points system that favoured education, professional skills and knowledge of English and/or French. The 1967 Immigration Act also included a generous family reunification provision. Ethnic Chinese immigrants now came from a wider variety of sending areas, including the US, Taiwan, Hong Kong, Britain and South-east Asia. Highly skilled professionals tended to dominate, taking up residence in and around major cities like Toronto and Vancouver. In the early 1980s Ontario overtook British Columbia as the primary residential province for Chinese immigrants. In an effort to attract new businesses and investment to Canada, the federal government offered incentives to prospective immigrants whose business experience and job-creation potential augured well for the domestic economy. Many of the newcomers were Chinese, transforming the typical immigrant profile in just under a century from that of cheap labourer who huddled in impoverished urban Chinatowns to seasoned entrepreneur or skilled professional who lived in the suburbs and commuted to the major urban centres.[47]

Ambivalent Communities: Chinese in Malaysia, Thailand and Vietnam

Chinese settlement in the Malay Peninsula and Western Borneo contributed greatly to the formation of both colonial society and later independent Malaysia. The Portuguese and later the Dutch established a colonial presence in the peninsula, but it was the British who, gaining control during the second half of the eighteenth century, recruited the first Chinese indentured labourers. Early migrants worked in tin mines, cleared forests for agriculture and participated in the colonial retail economy. Over time these sojourners formed social organizations, temples and schools in an effort to maintain a link with their homeland. Over 150,000 Chinese immigrants were arriving each year at the start of the twentieth century, with the total doubling by the 1930s. Men were the first to arrive, but in the 1930s large numbers of female migrants arrived to work in domestic service, the rubber and tin industries and as prostitutes. So strong was the Chinese role in the economy at independence in 1957 that the government adopted an affirmative action policy for education and employment targeted at native Malays. By 1990 the Chinese population represented over 28 per cent of the country's total population, or 4.9 million in a population of 18.4 million. But as job opportunities in the public sector began to decrease for Chinese residents, greater numbers of skilled workers re-migrated to Australia, the US, Canada and the UK. A recession in 1985, for example, led to the outflow of 40,000 Malaysians of Chinese heritage over the subsequent five years.[48]

The Chinese presence in the land that became modern Thailand reached back to the early fourteenth century, when the latter was already a tributary state to the larger empire to the north. By the sixteenth century there was a large Chinese commercial quarter in the capital city of Ayudhya, where the Portuguese recorded the business acumen of their Chinese rivals. In the seventeenth century, the Thai monarchy entrusted the Chinese as managers of royal trade monopolies. By the early twentieth century estimates placed the Chinese community in Bangkok at 50 per cent of the total. But it was also at this time that Thai nationalism became a part of official court discourse, and one result was a growing anti-Chinese tide that included strongly racist overtones. Beginning in the 1930s and continuing to the end of World War II, the Thai government attempted to restrict the entry of Chinese migrants and to promote native businesses. Chinese were excluded from 27 different professions, and the fee for resident permits was raised dramatically. Conditions improved somewhat after 1945, with the assimilation and social integration of ethnic Chinese progressing further than in any other country in the region. Many Chinese adopted Thai names, attended government schools and, in the end, continued their domination of the Thai urban economy. By the close of the twentieth century there were an estimated 4.5 to 6 million ethnic Chinese in a total population of almost 60 million.[49]

In Vietnam the experience was very different. Here the size of the ethnic Chinese population declined during the final quarter of the twentieth century. The earliest Chinese to settle in Vietnam were merchants who established their base in the main southern port city of Saigon (Ho Chi Minh City). A colonial census conducted by the French in 1911 reported just under 300,000 Chinese in Vietnam. Most were situated in and around Saigon in the south, but there was also a considerable rural population just across the border from China in the north. After the communist victory in 1975, many Chinese-owned businesses were expropriated by the state, and Chinese residents were obliged to register as Vietnamese citizens. After the Red Army attacked Vietnam in 1979, many Chinese living in the north of the country were forced to leave. Only in the 1980s, when the authorities in Hanoi began to experiment with modest market-based economic reforms, did the situation of the Chinese mercantile population begin to ease.[50]

VIETNAM'S SORROW AND RECOVERY

French colonial rule in Vietnam began in 1858 when an expedition of fourteen ships and 2,500 men attacked Danang and Saigon. The assault, ostensibly in defence of French Catholic missionaries who were being harassed by royal authorities, expanded over the next few years to include Cambodia and Laos, what the colonizers called *Indochine française*. Vietnam's Nguyen dynasty was obliged to sign treaties that opened the country to additional missionaries, increased French access to key ports and forfeited the right to cede territory to third countries without French approval. The dynasty was also expected to suppress all forms of indigenous resistance to French exploitations but local uprisings, often led by common people, continued into the 1890s. Colonial authorities imposed heavy taxes on the native peasantry, created state monopolies over the production of alcohol and opium, and focused on rice production for export using *corvee*, or unpaid labour. A small minority of educated Vietnamese were permitted to hold lower-level posts in the colonial administration, and it was from the ranks of this elite that the first stirrings of nationalist sentiment emerged.[51]

The swift defeat and occupation of France by the Nazis in 1940 had immediate political repercussions in Vietnam. The Japanese established a military presence in the colony in 1941, and in 1944, recognizing that they might lose the war and fearful that the European powers would return, they granted independence to the Vietnamese. The communist guerrilla leader Ho Chi Minh, who had led a Vietnam Independence League, the Vietminh, since 1941, declared the establishment of the Democratic Republic of Vietnam in September 1945. But the French, under leadership of Charles de Gaulle and with British backing, announced their determination to reassert control over South East Asia. A terrible famine in the first months of 1945, exacerbated by a Japanese decision to redirect the rice harvest for its own use, claimed the lives of approximately a million Vietnamese. In this dire situation,

French military forces succeeded in retaking the south of the country, but the communists, borrowing from the Chinese example, won the support of rural peasants who had suffered massive economic exploitation under the Europeans. The communists established political and military control over the north and in 1946 began combat operations against the French in what became known as the first Indochina War (1946–54).

Cold War and Colonialism

The Vietminh strategy combined the rhetoric of national liberation with the economic appeal of rural revolution and equality. By 1953 the US was absorbing a large portion of the military costs of French operations, while Ho Chi Minh's forces were supplied by China and the Soviet Union. When Vietminh fighters prevailed over a French force of 16,000 men at Dienbienphu in the spring of 1954, hopes for an all-out defeat of the communists evaporated. In the treaty ending hostilities that was signed in Geneva that year, the country was temporarily partitioned at the seventeenth parallel.[52] Although there had been major internal dislocations during the conflict, there had been few international refugees. Approximately 55,000 people, the majority of whom were sympathizers with the Vietminh, sought refuge in neighbouring Thailand, but most were repatriated. Free elections scheduled for 1956 were designed to reunite the country under a popularly elected government.

Under the terms of the 1954 Geneva Accords, civilians were allowed to choose between the communist-led Democratic Republic of Vietnam and the American-backed Republic of Vietnam. A mass exodus of people from soon-to-be communist-controlled areas in the north of the country began, sometimes accompanied by withdrawing French troops. Over the next year close to a million Vietnamese, the majority of whom were Roman Catholic small landowners, relocated to the south aboard French and American aircraft and ships. They represented one tenth of the population of the north, and they left behind homes, possessions and associations in this permanent exodus. During the same period approximately 130,000 armed soldiers and communist political cadres left the south for the Marxist state in the north.[53]

Neither the US nor the Republic of Vietnam had signed the Geneva Accords, and with US support the new leader in the south, Ngo Dinh Diem, began a crackdown against communist dissidents who had remained behind after 1954. Both the Eisenhower and Kennedy administrations steadfastly supported the regime in the south despite Diem's penchant for repression and his government's failure to address the acute social and economic inequalities facing the country's 15 million peasants. When South Vietnamese military officers, with covert support from the Americans, assassinated Diem in November 1963, the unpopularity of the anti-communist state translated into growing support for the guerrilla insurgency that was funded and supplied from the north.

The Second Indochina War lasted from 1964 until 1975, claiming the lives of millions of Vietnamese, devastating much of the land, crippling industry and transport and subjecting almost half of the country's inhabitants to some form of temporary internal dislocation.[54] But even with the massive fiscal and military support of the US, South Vietnam's corrupt military government was unable to prevail over its northern opponents. The US military withdrew in 1973, and as the victorious communist forces made their final push towards Saigon in April 1975, a second exodus, this time out of a country, began in earnest. Hundreds of thousands who had served in the South Vietnamese armed forces, together with thousands of officials, feared for their lives under a communist authority.[55] Before the last American helicopter departed from the US embassy, tens of thousands of South Vietnamese had clogged roads across the country in a desperate attempt to flee. Only a tiny fraction succeeded. Fixed wing aircraft were used to evacuate people from the capital until the runways were damaged beyond repair by enemy shelling, and giant helicopters were then employed in a final, chaotic attempt to rescue more than 7,000 people.

Approximately 132,000 Vietnamese managed to escape the country before the communist takeover on 30 April 1975, with 73,000 of this total evacuating by sea. Most of the latter were rescued by US ships stationed off the Vietnamese coastline, while others made their way to neighbouring countries in small craft. By the end of 1975, the majority of these early Vietnamese refugees had been resettled in the US, with France and Canada accepting an additional 15,000.[56] In general, this first wave of post-war refugees tended to be skilled and better educated than subsequent migrants. Almost two-thirds had at least minimal training in English, having worked in some capacity for the American-backed regime in the south, and the majority were able to find work – albeit not always at the same skill level – once they were settled in the US. These initial refugees were welcomed as friends and fellow soldiers in the war, and their asylum and resettlement were embraced as a moral obligation by a superpower that had failed in its efforts to defeat the communist North Vietnamese.

Boat People

The largest and, in terms of the international community, most challenging exodus from Vietnam had yet to begin. Relatively few South Vietnamese civilians sought to escape the new regime in the first years after the fall of Saigon. As the triumphant communist government took control over the whole of the country, however, communist re-education camps were established in remote rural areas. Many fallen regime politicians, civil servants, military personnel, religious leaders, educators and artists – those most likely to flee – were obliged to attend what was thought would be brief courses in communist indoctrination. In fact, many of the detainees spent years subjected to hard labour under brutal living conditions. Owners of large businesses and farms were similarly re-educated and their property confiscated by the state. In 1976 small groups of disaffected Vietnamese began paying boat owners for clandestine passage to Thailand, Malaysia and Singapore. The following year these involuntary countries of first asylum began rejecting these 'boat people' and forcing them back out to sea. Soon the Vietnamese government became complicit in the exodus, with corrupt officials and contractors acting with impunity. Fewer than 6,000 Vietnamese had fled the country in 1976, but by 1979 the total had grown to over 100,000, creating a humanitarian dilemma for neighbouring states and blurring the distinction between political refugees and economic migrants.[57]

By 1978 large ships carrying thousands of passengers began transporting refugees, only to be refused the right to dock in destination countries. As the crisis escalated, member states of the Association of South East Asian Nations (ASEAN) appealed to the international community for assistance. In response the US, Canada and France expanded their entry policies to accommodate thousands of additional refugees not only from Vietnam but also from Cambodia and Laos. By the end of 1980 some 40 nations had resettled 300,000 boat people. The US, still locked in a decades-old ideological struggle with communism, accepted the largest number as a gesture of solidarity with those who claimed to be oppressed by Vietnam's Marxist government.

In addition to the early flight of boat people, ethnic Chinese living in Vietnam joined the refugee phenomenon. In 1979 a crackdown on ethnic Chinese business people, combined with a brief war between China and Vietnam, prompted the exodus of almost 250,000 people across the northern border into the People's Republic. Simultaneously, tens of thousands of refugees from Cambodia fleeing the genocidal policies of the Khmer Rouge regime flooded into Vietnam. Communist Vietnam had become both a receiving and a sending country in the midst of two military conflicts, one in neighbouring Cambodia and another against Cambodia's powerful ally in Beijing.

Refugees or Economic Migrants?

Those who fled Vietnam, Cambodia and Laos during the 1980s have been labelled 'second-wave refugees'. They were generally poorer, younger and members of ethnic minorities such as the Cham, Montagnard and Khmer peoples, and they were treated in a less sympathetic manner as economic migrants by countries of first asylum.[58] Between 1980 and 1984 over 250,000 Vietnamese sought shelter in temporary camps across South East Asia. In 1987 Thailand, Malaysia and Hong Kong reported sharply increased levels of refugee arrivals from Vietnam, and in 1989 an international conference was held in Geneva with the goal of discouraging further migration from Vietnam and repatriating non-political refugees. The US opposed involuntary repatriation and in 1990 signed an agreement with Vietnam accepting an additional 400,000 refugees spread over a number of years. Adjustment to a new culture was difficult for older Vietnamese, with many regretting a profound loss of traditions and familiar surroundings. But for the generation born in the US, the so-called '1.5 generation', enormous strides were taken in terms of levels of educational and professional attainment during the 1990s.[59]

Jobs and Lives

The Vietnamese experience of lives shattered by war and the 'push' factor of political repression was not unique in South and East Asia in the decades after World War II. Certainly millions of Hindus and Muslims felt compelled to migrate across international borders in the wake of the break-up of the Indian subcontinent in 1947. And there were ample numbers of refugees from the Cambodia's genocidal Khmer Rouge regime, from Tamil-majority areas of Sri Lanka, and from mainland China after the triumph of communist forces in 1949, to confirm that the tragedy of forced relocation was the monopoly of no one civilization. Doubtless that phenomenon would have been extended had North Koreans, who suffered – and starved – under the Stalinist regime of Kim Il Sung, been allowed to exit their homeland after partition in the 1950s.

But, on the whole, the more recent experience of international migration in the wider Asian context has involved the voluntary search for better lives at home through the sacrifice of temporary or extended labour in another country. As select countries experienced significant economic growth, the demand for labour intensified. Heavily populated and labour-rich states, or states with an abundance of well-educated but poorly compensated professionals, emerged as principal source countries. Government sponsorship, affordable air fares and the ability to communicate instantly with loved ones at home through advances in telecommunications all made the strain of lives apart from loved ones more bearable – at least in the short term. Whether current patterns in the outsourcing of labour would continue into the twenty-first century remained very much an open question. Recent developments in a now booming Indian economy suggest that economic reform and market solutions point the way towards greater global convergence where indigenous labour talent can find meaning-ful work at home. But economic convergence is by no means guaran-teed across the wide spectrum of Asian countries – or elsewhere. Jobs may continue to complicate lives by separating families in search of material betterment in a global culture that defines happiness with consumption, where personal well-being is synonymous with getting and spending.

Conclusion: States, Immigrants and Global Rift

The sovereign nation state in its current form has been part of the Western experience since the mid-seventeenth century. Allegiance to hereditary monarchs who governed kingdoms by divine right, and to religious rulers who occupied the chair of St Peter in Rome, was forcefully repudiated. The solvent of medieval certainties involved a potent combination of religious reformation, Renaissance individualism and a new sense of cultural unity shaped by language, religion and geography. In the late eighteenth century the American and French revolutionaries jettisoned the concept of subject and introduced in its place the idea of the rights-bearing citizen. Allegiance was now connected to a set of political values, social practices and personal freedoms, and was best secured within the context of the sovereign territorial state. Europe's dynastic families fought a rearguard action against emerging republicanism throughout the nineteenth century, but personal monarchy lost its remaining relevancy in the trenches of World War I. By the conclusion of World War II there was a strong international consensus that nation states 'were the most important membership organizations for human flourishing'.[1] Even in the midst of the Cold War, this consensus transcended political ideology and included capitalist, socialist and post-colonial developing countries.

We have seen how global migrants in the post-war period, like those during the great age of emigration in the late nineteenth and early twentieth centuries, crossed international borders for a better life, for human flourishing. Prior to the early 1800s, the costs involved in long-distance migration were such that only persons of means, together with slaves and indentured servants, left their native lands. The first significant waves of free migration began after the end of the Napoleonic wars on the European continent. Responding to the opportunities presented by labour-scarce economies in the Americas, entire families left for new lives across the Atlantic. Transportation costs plummeted with the advent of steam transport and after 1850 large numbers of working-class Europeans were able to join the move to a widening array of destinations around the globe, but chiefly in North America and Australia. By the late nineteenth century a new regime of indentured servitude, this time featuring migrants from South and East Asia, joined the larger Atlantic economy. Mass migration peaked just before the outbreak of World War I in 1914 and for the next 30 years, through war and depression, a new pattern of immigration restriction took hold in receiving countries.[2]

In the post-war period from 1945 to 1973, Europe, which since the eighteenth century had been the world's leading source of emigrants, became a net receiving zone. Destination countries in Western Europe established bilateral agreements with developing source countries whereby temporary guest workers were admitted for discreet assignments over a defined period of time. Migrants from former colonies were also permitted to settle in European states that were once leaders in the imperial project. By the mid 1960s Western countries, including the US and Australia, dropped the racist national origins quotas that had been adopted in the early decades of the twentieth century, thereby making it easier for migrants from developing regions to gain entry into countries with fully mature economies. Sending areas became more diverse as uniform admissions standards were put in place.

When the West's post-war economic boom ended abruptly in 1973, the guest worker phenomenon shifted to include newly affluent oil-producing states in the Persian Gulf and emerging manufacturing economies in Southeast and East Asia. New migration to Europe became skill-selective, but resident guest workers were permitted to settle on a permanent basis, and their families were allowed to join them. Such was definitely not the case for guest workers in the Gulf oil kingdoms, where all foreign workers – including fellow Muslims – were closely monitored, where their work contracts were limited and where citizenship was forbidden.

With the collapse of the Soviet system in 1991 and the subsequent retreat of command-style economies around the world, there began a period of hope – brief as it turned out – that a new global order was in formation. This new order would maintain the system of territorial nation states, but relations between these states would be altered fundamentally. For the first time in the human experience, it seemed, a genuine opportunity had arisen to establish for the world's burgeoning population a level of personal security, nutrition, health, housing, education and employment that made life truly meaningful. The fiscal resources were at hand, and success was assured if only governments would act together and embrace market-orientated models of economic development. In the brightest scenario, the need to migrate across international borders might be greatly reduced; human flourishing, it was hoped, could occur at home.

By the closing decade of the twentieth century, a set of discreet shifts in world migration patterns was clearly under way. The post-war drive by wealthy receiving states to manage inflow resulted in the adoption of greater skill-selection protocols. Thus it was no surprise that more than half of the 10 million people annually who crossed international borders during the 1990s began their journey from another fully developed country. Clearly, a very large aspect of international migration involved women and men from professional backgrounds and comparatively affluent lifestyles. Their mobility mirrored the growth of multinational business and the relocation of manufacturing capacity to low wage, labour rich and politically stable countries outside the developed North.

But alongside this demographic trend another, more controversial pattern of relocation was taking shape in response to global economic realities. According to the International Labour Organization, the US had become the destination country of 81 per cent of migrants from developing countries. Canada and Australia accounted for an additional 11 per cent. Although the Canadian and US populations represented less than 5 per cent of the world's total, these two countries alone received more than half of the world's immigrants, and many of them were unskilled and poor.[3] Taxpayers in these affluent states began to raise concerns over the admission of unskilled newcomers, even when the immigrants worked almost exclusively in sectors of the economy that were eschewed by citizens. Europe continued its role as a net receiving zone, but restrictions became more comprehensive. Refugee claims were viewed with increasing scepticism across the EU as the line began to blur between asylum seekers and economic migrants. Central and South America, for almost two centuries a receiving zone, now won dubious distinction as a major sending zone to the much more affluent North, in particular to the US. As we have seen, the reception was less than cordial. A robust demand for unskilled, low-wage labour existed in the US, but Americans remained deeply conflicted over the surge in numbers of legal and illegal immigrants from Latin America and elsewhere.[4]

At home the new migrants may have faced unemployment, underemployment, persecution at the hands of state authorities, internal displacement as a result of civil war or religious-ethnic conflict, or nothing more complicated than dissatisfaction at the absence of opportunities to expand professional skills. Given the level of organized and state-sponsored violence around the globe during the second half of the twentieth century, the deep poverty and the burden of overpopulation in developing and failed states, it was remarkable that the level of international migration remained so modest. By the end of the century many international migrants headed towards global cities in wealthy states where demand was high for 'low wage service workers, as well as high salary professional, managerial, technical and professional recruits'.[5] Not all succeeded in reaching their preferred destination, with many living and toiling in neighbouring developing states. But while people resident outside the country of their birth remained no more than a tiny minority of the world's population at the century's end, they increasingly appeared to residents of highly developed destination countries, and to many policy makers in those countries, as a threat to national security, identity and social wellbeing. Sadly, border security became increasingly conflated with national security and the effectiveness of states to maintain a distinct national identity. Even before the events of 9/11, leading scholars in the US like Arthur M. Schlesinger, Samuel Huntington and Myron Weiner warned about the destabilizing effects of large-scale immigration.[6]

THE PROMISE OF CONVERGENCE?

The integration of the world economy that was – and remains – at the centre of the phenomenon known as globalization involved the regular transfer of goods, services, money and ideas across international borders. The process began in earnest with large national firms hoping to sell their products and services in world markets, and rapidly progressed to the manufacture of goods and the establishment of branch offices in foreign countries. In the 1990s capital markets were liberalized, labour markets were deregulated and public services shifted piecemeal to the private sector. Borrowing and investment seamlessly transcended frontiers, as did the recruitment of key, highly skilled personnel. Global production, finance and distribution processes fostered unprecedented economies of scale and enabled the world economy to function as an integrated whole.[7] The developed states reaped the greatest benefits, but it was assumed that liberalization would eventually lift all boats. Beginning in the early 1980s and continuing into the new century, powerful institutions like the World Bank, the International Monetary Fund and the World Trade Organization all championed market-orientated liberalization, deregulation and privatization.

In the midst of this great cross-border integration, people moved as well but, as we have seen, their movement was more rigorously monitored and controlled. Business people, students and tourists were generally welcomed because they generated income for the destination country without placing any burden upon public services. Temporary workers, asylum seekers and economic migrants faced much more scrutiny and raised widespread suspicion. Indeed in most countries, the contents of container ships were less strictly monitored than arriving passengers at major airports. This fact too had dire consequences, for one of the more disturbing by-products of economic liberalization was the growth of clandestine overseas transport organizations in many of the developing world's major port cities. The growing disparity in income between rural and urban dwellers led to a massive country–city migration in the 1980s and '90s. Peasants flocked to urban areas in search of work and some of these vulnerable people fell victim to unscrupulous recruiters, document forgers and ship owners. Prospective emigrants paid sums as high as US $70,000 to traffickers who promised safe passage and employment in the destination country. Those heading for the US often landed first in Central America, where they were subsequently taken across Mexico and then the US–Mexico border by smugglers. Tragic episodes involving migrants who drowned or died in cargo containers aboard ships headed for the US and Europe made news headlines repeatedly during the late 1990s. Even with such tragedies, the liberalization of immigration regimes never became a priority for transnational financial institutions or for the member states of the United Nations. Indeed the restrictions that were applied by sovereign states on the migration of humans constituted a controversial exception to the draw down of boundaries at the core of recent globalization.

Why wasn't the liberalization of trade policy over the past quarter of a century matched by a comparable opening up of international migration? Why has migration remained such a glaring exception to globalizing trends, particularly in light of the fact that the movement of humans across international borders has direct implications for human rights and social justice in the twenty-first century? According to one team of economists, much of the explanation has to do with lack of reciprocity. Theoretically, open trade benefits both partners since each side desires the other's goods and services. Open migration, on the other hand, involves an inherently unequal relationship. Sending countries typically do not attract migrants to their shores, for all of the obvious reasons.[8] Unhappily the gap between rich and poor states, what economists refer to as divergence, has continued apace. In the early 1960s the per capita GDP in the richest twenty states was eighteen times that in the world's poorest countries. Thirty-five years later the gap had expanded to 37 times.[9] By the first decade of the twenty-first century, globalization had done little to address the problem of economic divergence. One result was the continued movement of economic migrants, both legal and undocumented, across international borders.

Some studies have suggested that the elimination of immigration barriers worldwide would lead to aggregate economic gains for all. World output and income would increase and, while some unskilled workers in developed states would experience greater competition for jobs, wage convergence between source and destination countries would accelerate. Estimates indicated that unhindered migration would provide overall gains to world GDP in the range of 15 and 67 per cent.[10] Open borders, it was argued, would afford countries with low birth rates and ageing populations the opportunity to engage the new workers and taxpayers who would be essential to the maintenance of existing social benefits programmes. Finally, reducing barriers to immigration would eliminate the cost of addressing illegal residency and put an end to trafficking in humans.[11]

If these studies are correct, then how do we explain continued – and perhaps intensifying – opposition to a generous expansion of voluntary migration, at the same time that citizens of wealthy countries strongly support free trade? There is no single overriding answer but a number of factors contributed to anti-immigrant sentiment at the start of the new century. Perhaps most compelling was the widespread belief, referred to repeatedly in this book, that open immigration would overburden publicly funded benefits systems. As long as poor migrants are viewed as taking more from the state than they contribute through taxes, native opposition to more generous admissions policies, even where labour needs are acute, will remain strong. In addition, the varied geography of recent migration, its truly global dimension, makes it harder for citizens of destination countries to establish cultural and linguistic bridges to new migrant communities. Finally, a residual fear that the immigrant represents a possible threat to the nation, a fear brought to the foreground by the 9/11 attacks, militates against greater inclusion. As a result, at the beginning of the twenty-first century there was no international movement in favour of relaxing national immigration restrictions. Indeed the supporters of strong border controls and restrictive admissions policies have successfully emphasized the function of states as guarantors of the material well-being of their own populations. Without strict border controls, it is argued, irresponsible governments might expel their unwanted minorities, impoverished citizens and criminals, leaving more stable and prosperous countries to assume responsibility for the dispossessed. Unregulated inward migration might overwhelm the collective resources of the host country, degrade the environment, compromise cultural formations and advantage potential terrorists.

Obviously, in a world where economic inequalities between nations were minimal, the major incentive to emigration would be eliminated. The conviction of free trade advocates is that wage convergence will develop as production and service activities spread into previously closed or mismanaged economies. The belief that trade will eventually obviate the need for economic migration was central to the approval of the North American Free Trade Agreement, and it informs multinational entities like the WTO. Unfortunately, significant and growing differences between the resources and technology available to wealthy countries, not to mention the very real costs involved in conducting trade, make it unlikely that any significant wage convergence will take place irrespective of the elimination of trade barriers. Poor countries simply enter the free trade environment with too many handicaps. No better illustration of this fact can be found than in the ongoing subsidies that wealthy countries provide to domestic agricultural producers, the very area of the economy where the majority of labourers from poorer states are employed.

When developed countries did welcome newcomers according to skill sets, sending countries fell further behind in terms of development. The source country may have invested considerable public resources in training native professionals, and return on investment disappeared when income earned (and taxes paid) occurred in a developed state where economic incentives were greater. Typically, the source country's precarious fall-back position became the hope that successful expatriates would remit money and invest in their natal land. In a troubling development, remittances became essential tools in the economic planning of many poorer sending states. In 2001 total international remittances exceeded US$72 billion, a figure greater than official international development assistance. Large developing countries like India, the Philippines and Mexico received the biggest totals, but the overall economic impact of remittances was greater for smaller countries. Only direct foreign investment provided a larger total of funding for developing countries.[12]

In December 2003 UN Secretary General Kofi Annan called for the formation of a Global Commission on International Migration. Commission members were charged with raising the profile of international migration issues, with examining the gaps in existing policy approaches to the subject and with presenting recommendations to the UN and other stakeholders regarding ways to better coordinate governance of transnational migration. After two years of work and information-gathering meetings in the Americas, Africa, the Mediterranean, the Middle East and in Asia, members of the Commission issued their final report. At its centre was a call for greater international cooperation and policy coherence, together with the formation of a multilateral agency under the aegis of the UN to facilitate international dialogue. As perhaps the most complex – and controversial – aspect of contemporary globalization, international migration affects the entire spectrum of national policy, from health and environment to trade and human rights. Creating a coordinating body that would focus the work of national and international institutions dedicated to the issue of human migration is an enormous task, but without it the prospect of coming to consensus on the major challenges confronting receiving and sending states in the new century is very poor indeed. In the meantime the inequities grow, the hurt intensifies and, in some quarters, the resentment builds.

References

Introduction: Dimensions of Recent International Migration

1 Anthony Pagden, *Peoples and Empires* (New York, 2003), p. xix, writes that most humans are perennial movers and that 'there have been few peoples for whom a state of permanent immobility is the norm'. This may be true for peoples over the long centuries, but the lives of most modern people do not involve relocation.
2 A. McKeown, 'Global Migration, 1846–1940', *Journal of World History*, 15 (2004), pp. 155–89.
3 Robert J. Flanagan, *Globalization and Labor Conditions: Working Conditions and Worker Rights in a Global Economy* (Oxford, 2006), makes this case and advocates a return to open borders.
4 Peter Stalker, *The No-Nonsense Guide to International Migration* (London, 2001), pp. 42–3.
5 Philip Martin, Susan Martin and Patrick Weil, *Managing Migration: The Promise of Cooperation* (Lanham, MD, 2006), p. 11.
6 Ibid., p. 12.
7 Douglas S. Massey et al., *Worlds in Motion: Understanding International Migration at the End of the Millennium* (Oxford, 1998), p. 2.
8 Bill Jordan and Franck Duvell, *Migration: The Boundaries of Equality and Justice* (Cambridge, 2003), pp. 56–7.
9 Report of the Global Commission on International Migration (New York, 2005), http://www.gcim.org/en/finalreport.html, p. 2.
10 See the conclusions in Martin, Martin and Weil, *Managing Migration*.

Chapter 1: The Changing Face of Europe

1 Helpful surveys include Bernard Bailyn, *The Peopling of British North America* (New York, 1988); Helen I. Cohen, *British Emigration to British North America: the First Hundred Years* (Toronto, 1961); Francis Jennings, *The Invasion of America: Indians, Colonialism, and the Cant of Conquest* (Chapel Hill, NC, 1975); James Axtell, *Natives and Newcomers: The Cultural Origins of North America* (Oxford, 2001).

2 See, for example, Walter T. K. Nugent, *Crossings: The Great Transatlantic Migration, 1870–1914* (Bloomington, IN, 1992); Ronald Skeldon, *Migrational Development: A Global Perspective* (London, 1997); Roger Daniels, *Coming to America: A History of Immigration and Ethnicity in American Life* (New York, 1990); Brian Murphy, *The Other Australia: Experiences of Migration* (Cambridge, 1992).

3 Leslie Page Moch, *Moving Europeans: Migration in Western Europe since 1650* (Bloomington, IN, 2003), p. 170.

4 Klaus F. Zimmerman, 'What We Know About European Migration' in Zimmerman, ed., *European Migration* (Oxford, 2005), p. 4.

5 Douglas S. Massey et al., *Worlds in Motion: Understanding International Migration at the End of the Millennium* (Oxford, 1998), pp. 4–5.

6 Moch, *Moving Europeans*, p. 177; Stephen Castles, *Here for Good: Western Europe's New Ethnic Minorities* (London, 1984), p. 1.

7 Patrick Ireland, *Becoming Europe: Immigration, Integration, and the Welfare State* (Pittsburgh, 2004), p. 3.

8 The introduction to Joshua Cole's *The Power of Large Numbers: Population, Politics, and Gender in Nineteenth-Century France* (London, 2000) offers a good overview.

9 Philip E. Ogden, 'International Migration in the Nineteenth and Twentieth Centuries' in Philip E. Ogden and Paul E. White, eds, *Migrants in Modern France*, (Boston, MA, 1989), p. 39.

10 Gary P. Freeman, 'Immigrant Labour and Racial Conflict' in Ogden and White, *Migrants in Modern France*, pp. 162–3.

11 James F. Hollifield, *Immigrants, Markets, and States: The Political Economy of Postwar Europe* (Cambridge, MA, 1992), p. 55.

12 Stephen Castles, *Ethnicity and Globalization: From Migrant Worker to Transnational Citizen* (London, 2000), p. 65; Castles, *Here for Good*, p. 50.

13 Hollifield, *Immigrants*, p. 61.

14 Amelie Constant, 'Immigrant Adjustment in France and Impacts on the Natives' in Zimmerman, *European Migration*, p. 274.

15 Castles, *Ethnicity and Globalization*, pp. 64–5.

16 Ibid., p. 67.

17 Jan Rath, 'The Netherlands: A Dutch Treat for Anti-Social Families and Immigrant Ethnic Minorities' in Gareth Dale and Mike Cole, eds, *The European Union and Migrant Labour* (Oxford, 1999), p. 160.

18 Hans-Joachim Haffmann-Nowotny, 'Switzerland: A Non-Immigration Immigration Country' in Robin Cohen, ed., *The Cambridge Survey of World Migration* (Cambridge, 1995), p. 303. All future references to this text will be abbreviated to cswm.

19 Tommy Bengtsson, Christer Lundh and Kirk Scott, 'From Boom to Bust: The Economic Integration of Immigrants in Postwar Sweden' in Zimmerman, *European Migration*, pp. 23–5.

20 Gareth Dale, 'Germany: Nation and Immigration' in Dale and Cole, *The European Union and Migrant Labour*, p. 117.

21 Hans Heinrich Blotevogel, Ursula Muller-ter Jund and Gerald Wood, 'From Itinerant Worker to Immigrant? The Geography of Guest Workers in Germany' in Russell King, ed., *Mass Migration in Europe: The Legacy and the Future* (London, 1993), p. 83.

22 Dale, 'Germany', pp. 124–5.

23 Russell King, 'European International Migration 1945–9: A Statistical and

Geographical Overview' in King, *Mass Migration in Europe*, p. 22.

24 Dale, 'Germany', p.129; Ireland, *Becoming Europe*, p. 29.

25 Ireland, *Becoming Europe*, p. 29.

26 Castles, *Here for Good*, p. 75; Ted Robert Gurr, 'Turks in Germany: From Guest Workers to Ethnoclass' in Ted Robert Gurr, ed., *People Versus States: Minorities at Risk in the New Century* (Washington, DC, 2000), p. 22.

27 Nermin Abadan-Unat, 'Identity Crisis of Turkish Migrants' in Ilhan Basgoz and Norman Furniss, eds, *Turkish Workers in Europe: An Interdisciplinary Study* (Bloomington, IN, 1985), p. 6.

28 Dale, 'Germany', p. 132; Blotevogel et al., 'From Itinerant Worker' p. 86; Castles, *Ethnicity and Globalization*, p. 70.

29 Panikos Panayi, ed., *The Impact of Immigration: A Documentary History of the Effects and Experiences of Immigrants in Britain since 1945* (Manchester, 1999), pp. 2–3.

30 N.L. Tranter, *Population and Society, 1750–1940* (London, 1985), offers a comprehensive overview.

31 Castles, *Ethnicity and Globalization*, p. 64.

32 Roxanne Lynn Doty, *Anti-Immigrantism in Western Democracies: Statecraft, Desire, and the Politics of Exclusion* (New York, 2003), p. 45.

33 Kenneth O. Morgan, *Britain since 1945: The People's Peace* (Oxford, 2001), p. 203.

34 Peter Clarke, *Hope and Glory: Britain, 1900–1990* (London, 1996), p. 324.

35 Enoch Powell, 'Rivers of Blood Speech' in http://theoccidentalquarterly.com/vol1no1/ep-rivers.html

36 Panayi, *Impact of Immigration*, p. 28.

37 Thatcher quoted in Doty, *Anti-Immigrantism*, p. 4.

38 John Gubbay, 'The European Union in the Formation, Legitimation and Implementation of Migration Policy' in Dale and Cole, *The European Union and Migrant Labour*, pp. 47–8.

39 Jan Eliansson, 'Immigration in Europe: Promise or Peril?' in Kevin M. Cahill, ed., *Traditions, Values, and Humanitarian Action* (New York, 2003), p. 167.

40 Doty, *Anti-Immigrantism*, p. 4.

41 Krishan Kumar, 'The Idea of Europe: Cultural Legacies, Transnational Imaginings, and the Nation State' in Mabel Berezin and Martin Schain, eds, *Europe without Borders: Remapping Territory, Citizenship, and Identity in a Transnational Age* (Baltimore, MD, 2003), p. 38; Bernard Lewis, *What Went Wrong? The Clash Between Islam and Modernity in the Middle East* (New York, 2002), pp. 6–7.

42 Freeman, 'Immigrant Labour', p. 168.

43 Castles, *Here for Good*, p. 54; Freeman, 'Immigrant Labour', p. 168; Ogden, 'International Migration', p. 51.

44 Patrick Geary, *The Myth of Nations: The Medieval Origins of Europe* (Princeton, NJ, 2002), p. 6.

45 Blotevogel et al., 'From Itinerant Worker', p. 88.

46 Franz-Josef Kemper, 'New Trends in Mass Migration in Germany' in King, *Mass Migration in Europe*, p. 261.

47 Paul A. Silverstein, *Algeria in France: Transpolitics, Race, and Nation* (Bloomington, IN, 2004), p. 28; Gurr, 'Turks in Germany', p. 23.

48 Stephen Castles and Mark J. Miller, *The Age of Migration: International Population Movements in the Modern World* (New York, 1993), p. 91.

49 Peter Stalker, *The No-Nonsense Guide to International Migration* (London, 2001).

50 Desmond Dinan, *Ever Closer Union: An Introduction to European Integration*, 3rd

edn (London, 2005), p. 575–6.

51 Ireland, *Becoming Europe*, p. 132.
52 Castles and Miller, *Age of Migration*, p. 93.
53 Rey Koslowski, *Migrants and Citizens: Demographic Change in the European State System* (Ithaca, NY, 2004), p. 160; Castles and Miller, *Age of Migration*, p. 93.
54 Dinan, *Ever Closer Union*, pp. 589–2.
55 Koslowski, *Migrants and Citizens*, pp. 176–7.
56 Ibid., p. 69; Desmond Dinan, *Europe Recast: A History of the European Union* (London, 2004), pp. 256–7, 314–15.
57 Geary, *Myth of Nations*, offers a comprehensive survey of the polemical misuse of the medieval past for recent political ends. An excellent recent survey is Adrian Hastings, *The Construction of Nationhood: Ethnicity, Religion and Nationalism* (Cambridge, 1997).
58 Panikos Panayi, *An Ethnic History of Europe since 1945* (Harlow, 2000), p. 10.
59 Geary, *Myth of Nations*, p. 10; Krishan Kumar, 'The Idea of Europe: Cultural Legacies, Transnational Imaginings, and the Nation State' in Berezin and Schain, *Europe without Borders*, pp. 33–4.
60 Kant quoted in Koslowski, *Migrants and Citizens*, p. 3.
61 Ibid., pp. 5, 157.
62 The quote from Bouyeri and the Dutch background are from Zachary Shore, *Breeding Bin Ladens: America, Islam, and the Future of Europe* (Baltimore, MD, 2006), pp. 1–6.
63 Ray Hall and Paul White, 'Population Change on the Eve of the Twenty-first Century' in Hall and White, eds, *Europe's Population: Towards the Next Century* (London, 1995), p. 15.

Chapter 2: North–South Divide in the Americas

1 An excellent recent survey is John Charles Chasteen, *Born in Blood and Fire: A Concise History of Latin America*, 2nd edn (New York, 2006). See also Thomas E. Skidmore and Peter H. Smith, *Modern Latin America*, 6th edn (New York, 2005) and Peter Winn, *Americas: The Changing Face of Latin America and the Caribbean* (Berkeley, CA, 1999).
2 B. Lindsay Lowell, 'Skilled Migration Abroad or Human Capital Flight' in *Migration Information Source* (June 2003), http://www.migrationinformation.org/feature/display.cfm?id=135
3 Estimating the pre-Columbian population of the Americas is extremely difficult. See the discussions in Alfred Crosby, *Germs, Seeds, and Animals: Studies in Ecological History* (London, 1994), pp. 21–5; William McNeill, *Plagues and Peoples* (New York, 1998), pp. 212–13; and Sheldon J. Watts, *Epidemics and History: Disease, Power and Imperialism* (New Haven, CT, 1998), pp. 84–8.
4 Aristide R. Zolberg, *A Nation by Design: Immigration Policy in the Fashioning of America* (Cambridge, MA, 2006), p. 26.
5 On Franklin see George Borjas, *Heaven's Door: Immigration Policy and the American Economy* (Princeton, NJ, 1999), p. 3.
6 David G. Gutiérrez, 'Demography and the Shifting Boundaries of "Community": Reflections on US Latinos and the Evolution of Latino Studies' in Gutiérrez, ed., *The Columbia History of Latinos in the United States since 1960* (New York, 2004), p. 3.
7 Skidmore and Smith, *Modern Latin America*, p. 443.

8 Roger Daniels, *Guarding the Golden Door: American Immigration Policy and Immigrants since 1882* (New York, 2004), p. 176; Nilda Chong and Francia Baez, *Latino Culture* (Boston, MA, 2005), p. 1.

9 Gary P. Freeman and Frank D. Bean, 'Mexico and US Worldwide Immigration Policy' in Frank D. Bean, Rodolfo O. de la Garza, eds, *At the Crossroads: Mexico and US Immigration Policy* (Lanham, MD, 1997), p. 23.

10 Gregory Rodriquez, 'Mexican-Americans and the Mestizo Melting Pot' in Tamar Jacoby, ed., *Reinventing the Melting Pot: The New Immigrants and What it Means to be American* (New York, 2004), p. 128.

11 Mark Reisler, 'Always the Laborer, Never the Citizen: Anglo Perceptions of the Mexican Immigrant during the 1920s' in David G. Gutiérrez, ed., *Between Two Worlds: Mexican Immigrants in the United States* (Wilmington, DE, 1996), p. 23.

12 Patricia Zamudio, 'Mexican International Migration' in Maura I. Toro-Morn and Alicea Marixsa, eds, *Migration and Immigration: A Global View* (Westport, CT, 2004), pp. 129–35; Gutiérrez, 'Ethnic Mexicans in the Late Twentieth Century' in Gutiérrez, *Columbia History of Latinos*, pp. 44–5; Zolberg, *A Nation by Design*, pp. 308–11.

13 Brian Hamnett, *A Concise History of Mexico* (Cambridge, 1999), pp. 258–62; John W. Sherman, 'The Mexican Miracle and Its Collapse' in Michael C. Meyer and William H. Beezley, eds, *The Oxford History of Mexico* (New York, 2000), pp. 575–607; Gutiérrez, *Between Two Worlds*, pp. 62–3.

14 Skidmore and Smith, *Modern Latin America*, p. 284.

15 Chisato Yoshida and Alan D. Woodland, *The Economics of Illegal Immigration* (Houndmills, 2005), p. 4.

16 Craig Arceneaux and David Pion-Berlin, *Transforming Latin America: The International and Domestic Origins of Change* (Pittsburgh, PA, 2005), p. 193.

17 Zamudio, 'Mexican International Migration', pp. 133–5. Case studies of recent Mexican emigration to Nebraska, North Carolina, Louisiana and Iowa are contained in Victor Zuniga and Rubin Hernandez-Leon, eds, *New Destinations: Mexican Immigration to the United States* (New York, 2005).

18 Daniels, *Guarding the Golden Door*, p. 177.

19 Lisandro Perez, 'The End of Exile? A New Era in US Immigration Policy Toward Cuba' in Max Castro, ed., *Free Markets, Open Societies, Closed Borders?: Trends in International Migration and Immigration Policy in the Americas* (Miami, FL, 1999), p. 198. A helpful survey of twentieth-century Cuba is Louis A. Perez, Jr, *Cuba: Between Reform and Revolution* (New York, 2006).

20 Maria Cristina Garcia, 'Exiles, Immigrants, and Transnationals: The Cuban Communities in the United States' in Gutiérrez, *Columbia History of Latinos*, pp. 147–51; Zolberg, *Nation by Design*, p. 326.

21 Sharon Ann Navarro and Armando Xavier Mejia, eds, *Latino Americans and Political Participation* (Santa Barbara, CA, 2004), pp. 31–2; Kim Geron, *Latino Political Power* (Boulder, CO, 2005), p. 54.

22 Thomas M. Leonard, *Castro and the Cuban Revolution* (Westport, CT, 1999), pp. 71–4.

23 Garcia, 'Exiles, Immigrants, and Transnationals', pp. 158–66.

24 Perez, *Cuba*, pp. 293–7.

25 Daniels, *Guarding the Golden Door*, p. 181.

26 Marilyn Espitia, 'The Other "Other Hispanics": South American-Origin Latinos in the United States' in Gutiérrez, *Columbia History of Latinos*, pp. 266, 268.

27 Skidmore and Smith, *Modern Latin America*, pp. 72–3. A good survey is David Rock, *Argentina, 1516–1987: From Spanish Colonization to Alfonsín* (Berkeley, CA,

1987), especially chapters 4 and 5.

28 Maia Jachimowicz, 'Argentina: A New Era of Migration and Migration Policy' in *Migration Information Source*, http://www.migrationinformation.org/profiles/display.cfm?id=374. On Argentina's military government after World War II, see Paul Lewis, 'The Right and Military Rule, 1955–1983' in Sandra McGee Deutsch and Ronald H. Dolkart, eds, *The Argentine Right: Its History and Intellectual Origins, 1910 to the Present* (Wilmington, DE, 1993), pp. 147–87.

29 Robert M. Levine, *The History of Brazil* (Westport, CT, 1999), pp. 74–5; Boris Fausto, *A Concise History of Brazil* (Cambridge, 1999), pp. 118–99; Herbert S. Klein, 'European and Asian Migration to Brazil' in *cswm*, pp. 208–13.

30 Thomas Skidmore, *Brazil: Five Centuries of Change* (Oxford, 1999), pp. 140–41.

31 Ernesto Friedrich Amaral and Wilson Fusco, 'Shaping Brazil: The Role of International Migration' in *Migration Information Source* (June 2005), http://www.migrationinformation.org/profiles/display.cfm?id=311

32 Luz Marina Díaz, 'The Migration of Labour in Columbia' in *cswm*, p. 224.

33 Luz Marina Díaz, 'Globalization and Transnationalization between Columbia and Venezuela: New Migratory Trends' in Castro, *Free Markets*, p. 102.

34 Myriam Berube, 'Columbia: In the Crossfire' in *Migration Information Source* (November 2005), http://www.migrationinformation.org/profiles/display.cfm?id=344. On the violence associated with the drugs trade, see Christopher Abel and Marco Palacios, 'Columbia since 1958' in *The Cambridge History of Latin America*, vol. 8 (Cambridge, 1996), pp. 680–81.

35 James Smith, 'Guatemala: Economic Migrants Replace Political Refugees' in *Migration Information Source* (April 2006), http://www.migrationinformation.org/profiles/display.cfm?id=392

36 Arceneaux and Pion-Berlin, *Transforming Latin America*, p. 158; Carlos B. Cordova, *The Salvadoran Americans* (Westport, CT, 2005), pp. 11–18.

37 Susan Gzesh, 'Central Americans and Asylum Policy in the Reagan Era' in *Migration Information Source* (April 2006), http://www.migrationinformation.org/usfocus/display.cfm?id=384

38 Norma Stoltz Chinchilla and Nora Hamilton, 'Central American Immigrants: Diverse Populations, Changing Communities' in Gutiérrez, *Columbia History of Latinos*, pp. 187, 193.

39 Sarah Mahler and Dusan Ugrina, 'Central America: Crossroads of the Americas' in *Migration Information Source* (April 2006), http://www.migrationinformation.org/feature/display.cfm?id=386

40 Dovelyn Agunias, 'Remittance Trends in Central America' in *Migration Information Source* (April 2006), http://www.migrationinformation.org/feature/display.cfm?id=393

41 Katherine Andrade-Eekhoff, 'Migration and Development in El Salvador: Ideals Versus Reality' in *Migration Information Source* (April 2006), http://www.migrationinformation.org/feature/display.cfm?id=387. The best recent survey is Cordova, *The Salvadoran Americans*.

42 Skidmore and Smith, *Modern Latin America*, pp. 47–51.

43 David Reynolds, *One World Divisible* (New York, 2000), p. 462.

44 Skidmore and Smith, *Modern Latin America*, pp. 58–61.

45 Reynolds, *One World Divisible*, p. 471.

46 Maria Cristina Garcia, 'Canada: A Northern Refuge for Central Americans' in *Migration Information Source* (April 2006), http://www.migrationinformation.org/

feature/display.cfm?id=390

47 Alan B. Simons, 'Economic Integration and Designer Immigrants: Canadian Policy in the 1990s' in Castro, *Free Markets*, pp. 53–67.

Chapter 3: Africa: The Displacement Continent

1 Yntiso D. Gebre and Itaru Ohta, 'Displacement in Africa: Conceptual and Practical Concerns' in Yntiso D. Gebre and Itaru Ohta, eds, *Displacement Risks in Africa* (Melbourne, 2005), p. 3.

2 Jeff Crisp, 'No Solution in Sight: The Problem of Protracted Refugee Situations in Africa' in Gebre and Ohta, *Displacement Risks in Africa*, p. 18.

3 International Organization for Migration, *World Migration 2005: Costs and Benefits of International Migration* (Geneva, 2005), p. 34.

4 Adebayo Adedeji, 'Comprehending African Conflicts' in Adebayo Adedeji, ed., *Comprehending and Mastering African Conflicts* (New York, 1999), p. 3.

5 Anthony Clayton, *Frontiersmen: Warfare in Africa since 1950* (London, 1999), p. 2.

6 Martin Meredith, *The Fate of Africa: From the Hopes of Freedom to the Heart of Despair* (New York, 2005), p. 1.

7 Crawford Young, 'The Heritage of Colonialism' in John W. Harbeson and Donald Rothchild, eds, *Africa in World Politics: The African State System in Flux* (Boulder, CO, 2000), p. 36; J. Clyde Mitchell, 'The Causes of Labour Migration' in Abebe Zegeye and Shubi Ishemo, eds, *Forced Labour and Migration: Patterns of Movement in Africa* (London, 1989), pp. 28–30.

8 Martin Meredith, *Fate of Africa* (New York, 2005), p. 4.

9 Aderanti Adepoju, 'Migration in Africa: An Overview' in Jonathan Baker and Tade Akin Aina, *The Migration Experience in Africa* (Stockholm, 1995), p. 90.

10 Bill Freund, *The Making of Contemporary Africa*, 2nd edn (Boulder, CO, 1998), pp. 169–70.

11 Kenneth Swindell, 'People on the Move in West Africa: From Pre-Colonial Polities to Post-Independence States' in cswm, p. 198. See also Philip D. Curtin, 'Africa and Global Patterns of Migration' in Wang Gungwu, ed., *Global History and Migrations* (Boulder, CO, 1997), p. 84.

12 Hania Zlotnik, 'International Migration in Africa: An Analysis Based on Estimates of the Migrant Stock' in *Migration Information Source*, (September 2004), www.migrationinformation.org/profiles/display.cfm?id=252

13 Quoted in Harbeson and Rothchild, *Africa in World Politics*, p. 27.

14 Aderanti Adepoju, 'The Politics of International Migration in Post-Colonial Africa' in cswm, p. 167.

15 David Reynolds, *One World Divisible* (New York, 2000), p. 98.

16 Meredith, *Fate of Africa*, p. 151.

17 Dirk Hoerder, *Cultures in Contact: World Migrations in the Second Millennium* (Durham, NC, 2002), p. 551.

18 J. D. Fage, *A History of Africa*, 3rd edn (New York, 1995), p. 491.

19 Ibid., p. 498.

20 Christopher J. Bakwesegha, 'The OAU and African Refugees' in Yassin El-Ayouty, ed., *The Organization of African Unity after Thirty Years* (Westport, CT, 1994), p. 77.

21 John Sorenson, 'An Overview: Refugees and Development' in Howard Adelman and John Sorenson, eds, *African Refugees: Development Aid and Repatriation* (Boulder, CO, 1994), p. 177.

22 Adepoju, 'Politics of International Migration', p. 43.
23 Andreas Danevad and Oliver Wates, eds, *Internally Displaced People: A Global Survey*, 2nd edn (London, 2002), p. 25. The characteristics of state power reflect the views of Max Weber as contained in Harbeson and Rothchild, *Africa in World Politics*, p. 7.
24 Fage, *History of Africa*, pp. 462–6.
25 Paul Nugent, *Africa Since Independence: A Comparative History* (Houndmills, 2004), pp. 83–4.
26 Jok Madut Jok, 'Sudan: Civil War: 1990s' in Kevin Shillington, ed., *Encyclopedia of African History*, 3 vols (New York, 2005), vol. III, p. 1504.
27 Nugent, *Africa Since Independence*, p. 446.
28 Fage, *History of Africa*, p. 468.
29 Mark Cutts, ed., *The State of the World's Refugees 2000: Fifty Years of Humanitarian Action* (Oxford, 2006), pp. 42–3.
30 Ismail Ahmed, 'Understanding Conflict in Somalia and Somaliland' in Adedeji, *Comprehending and Mastering African Conflicts*, pp. 240–41.
31 Hussein M. Adam, 'Somali Civil Wars' in Taisier M. Ali and Robert O. Matthews, eds, *Civil Wars in Africa: Roots and Resolution* (Montreal, 1999), p. 178.
32 Adepoju, 'Politics of International Migration', p. 170.
33 Adam, 'Somali Civil Wars', p. 181.
34 Ahmed, 'Understanding Conflict', p. 246.
35 Fage, *History of Africa*, p. 501.
36 *World Migration 2005*, p. 36.
37 Adepoju, 'Politics of International Migration', pp. 169–70.
38 Jeff Drumtra, 'West Africa's Refugee Crisis Spills Across Many Borders' in *Migration Information Source* (August 2003), http://www.migrationinformation.org/feature/display.cfm?id=148
39 Awolowo quoted in Meredith, *Fate of Africa*, p. 8.
40 Meredith, *Fate of Africa*, p.194.
41 Quoted in A. A. Afolayan, 'Emigration Dynamics in Nigeria: Landlessness, Poverty, Ethnicity and Differential Responses' in Reginald Appleyard, ed., *Emigration Dynamics in Developing Countries*, 4 vols (Aldershot, 1998), vol. I, p. 44.
42 Achebe quoted in Meredith, *Fate of Africa*, p. 221.
43 Micah Bump, 'Ghana: Searching for Opportunities at Home and Abroad' in *Migration Information Source* (March 2006), http://www.migrationinformation.org/profiles/display.cfm?id=381
44 Meredith, *Fate of Africa*, pp. 96–7.
45 Ibid., p. 98.
46 Ibid., p. 101.
47 Sarah Kenyon Lischer, *Dangerous Sanctuaries: Refugee Camps, Civil War, and the Dilemmas of Humanitarian Aid* (Ithaca, NY, 2005), pp. 73–6.
48 Sadako Ogata, *The Turbulent Decade: Confronting the Refugee Crisis of the 1990s* (New York, 2005), pp. 174, 176.
49 Cutts, *State of the World's Refugees*, p. 246; Lischer, *Dangerous Sanctuaries*, p. 81.
50 Cutts, *State of the World's Refugees*, pp. 254–8, 263.
51 Ibid., p. 272.
52 Nugent, *Africa Since Independence*, pp. 150–53.
53 Joseph Hanlon, 'Mozambique: Renamo, Destabilization' in Shillington, *The Encyclopedia of African History*, vol. II, p. 1042.
54 Shubi L. Ishemo, 'Forced Labour and Migration in Portugal's African Colonies' in cswm, pp. 162–3.

55 Augusto Eduardo Kambwa et al., 'Angola' in Adedeji, *Comprehending and Mastering African Conflicts*, p. 59.

56 Stacey White, Andreas Danevad and Oliver Watts, eds, *Internally Displaced People: A Global Survey* (London, 2002), pp. 32–3.

57 Reynolds, *One World Divisible*, p. 473.

58 Ibid., p. 91.

59 Curtin, 'Africa and Global Patterns of Migration', p. 86.

60 John D. Hargreaves, *Decolonization in Africa*, 2nd edn (London, 1996), pp. 236–7.

61 Fage, *History of Africa*, pp. 488–90; Reynolds, *One World Divisible*, p. 472; Meredith, *Fate of Africa*, pp. 327–8, 627.

62 Meredith, *Fate of Africa*, pp. 644–5.

63 *World Migration 2005*, p. 43.

64 Nugent, *Africa Since Independence*, pp. 358–61.

65 *World Migration, 2005*, p. 43.

66 Carole Rakodi, 'Global Forces, Urban Change, and Urban Management in Africa' in Carole Rakodi, ed., *The Urban Challenge in Africa: Growth and Management of Its Large Cities* (Tokyo, 1997), pp. 24–5.

67 Rakodi, 'Global Forces', p. 34; Abdou Maliq Simone, *For the City Yet to Come: Changing African Life in Four Cities* (Durham, NC, 2004), p. 140.

68 Quoting Adepoju, 'Politics of International Migration', p. 93.

69 Simone, *City Yet to Come*, p. 6.

70 *World Migration 2005*, p. 35; Rakodi, 'Global Forces', p. 52.

71 Josef Gugler and Gudrun Ludwar-Ene, 'Gender and Migration in Africa South of the Sahara' in Baker and Aina, *The Migration Experience in Africa*, pp. 260–61.

72 Zlotnik, 'International Migration in Africa', *Migration Information Source*, (September 2004) http://www.migrationinformation.org/feature/display.cfm?ID=252

73 Gugler and Ludwar-Ene, 'Gender and Migration', p. 264.

74 Hoerder, *Cultures in Contact*, p. 552.

75 David Dixon, 'Characteristics of the African Born in the United States' in *Migration Information Source* (January 2006) http://www.migrationinformation.org/feature/display.cfm?id=366

76 Aderanti Adepoju, 'Linking Population Policies to International Migration in Sub-Saharan Africa' in Appleyard, *Emigration Dynamics*, vol. I, p. 302.

77 Meredith, *Fate of Africa*, p. 686.

78 United Nations, 'Population Challenges and Development Goals' (New York, 2005), pp. 16, 19, http://www.un.org/esa/population/publications/pop_challenges/population_challenges.pdf

79 Simone, *City Yet to Come*, p. 8.

80 Meredith, *Fate of Africa*, pp. 682, 683.

Chapter 4: Migrants in the Islamic World

1 William L. Cleveland, *A History of the Modern Middle East*, 3rd edn (Boulder, CO, 2004), p. 172.

2 Heather J. Sharkey, 'Globalization, Migration, and Identity: Sudan, 1800–2000' in Birgit Schaebler and Leif Stenberg, eds, *Globalization and the Muslim World* (Syracuse, NY, 2004), pp. 130–31.

3 Abbas Mehdi, 'Globalization, Migration and the Arab World' in International Organization for Migration, *Arab Migration in a Globalized World* (Geneva,

2004), pp. 13, 16.

4 Nemat Shafik, 'Has Labor Migration Promoted Economic Integration in the Middle East?' in Ismail Sirageldin and Eqbal Al-Rahmani, eds, *Research in Human Capital and Development: Population and Development Transformations in the Arab World* (Greenwich, CT, 1996), pp. 163–4.

5 Karen Leonard, 'Hyderabadis in Pakistan: Changing Nations' in Crispin Bates, ed., *Community, Empire and Migration: South Asians in Diaspora* (Houndmills, 2001), p. 226.

6 Ibid, p. 228.

7 Erin Patrick, 'Reconstructing Afghanistan: Lessons for Post-War Iraq?' in *Migration Information Source*, (April 2003) http://www.migrationinformation.org/feature/display.cfm?id=117

8 Graeme Hugo, 'Indonesia's Labour Looks Abroad' in *Migration Information Source*, (September 2002) http://www.migrationinformation.org/profiles/display.cfm?id=53

9 Shirin Hakimzadeh and David Dixon, 'Spotlight on the Iranian Foreign Born' in *Migration Information Source*, http://www.migrationinformation.org/usfocus/display.cfm?id=404

10 Anthony H. Johns and Abdullah Saeed, 'Muslims in Australia: The Building of a Community' and Tamara Sonn, 'Muslims in South Africa: A Very Visible Minority' both in Yvonne Yazbeck Haddad and Janet I. Smith, eds, *Muslim Minorities in the West* (Lanham, MD, 2002), pp. 200, 256, 257.

11 Jocelyne Cesari, 'Islam in the West: Mobility and Globalization Revisited' in Schaebler and Stenberg, *Globalization and the Muslim World*, p. 82.

12 Nader Fergany, 'Arab Labour Migration and the Gulf Crisis' in Dan Tschirgi, ed., *The Arab World Today* (Boulder, CO, 1994), p. 92.

13 Cleveland, *Modern Middle East*, p. 451.

14 David E. Long, *The Kingdom of Saudi Arabia* (Gainesville, FL, 1997), p. 108.

15 Soraya Altorki and Donald P. Cole, 'Change in Saudi Arabia: A View from "Paris of Najd"' in Nicholas S. Hopkins and Saad Eddin Ibrahim, eds, *Arab Society: Class, Gender, Power, and Development* (Cairo, 1997), p. 35.

16 James Wynbrandt, *A Brief History of Saudi Arabia* (New York, 2004), p. 200.

17 Altorki and Cole, 'Change in Saudi Arabia', p. 38.

18 Daryl Champion, *The Paradoxical Kingdom: Saudi Arabia and the Momentum of Reform* (New York, 2003), p. 111.

19 Reinhard Schulze, *A Modern History of the Islamic World* (New York, 2000), pp. 200–201.

20 Cleveland, *Modern Middle East*, p. 458.

21 Altorki and Cole, 'Change in Saudi Arabia', p. 38.

22 Cleveland, *Modern Middle East*, p. 459.

23 Virginia N. Sherry, *Saudi Arabia: Bad Dreams, Exploitation and Abuse of Migrant Workers in Saudi Arabia* (New York, 2004), p. 8.

24 Champion, *Paradoxical Kingdom*, p. 60.

25 Wynbrandt, *Brief History of Saudi Arabia*, p. 226.

26 Divya Pakkiasamy, 'Saudi Arabia's Plan for Changing Its Workforce' in *Migration Information Source*, (2004), http://www.migrationinformation.org/feature/display.cfm?id=264

27 Champion, *Paradoxical Kingdom*, p. 200.

28 Ibid., p. 200.

29 Anh Nga Longva, *Walls Built on Sand: Migration, Exclusion, and Society in Kuwait*

(Boulder, CO, 1997), pp. 22–5.

30 CIA Factbook, http://www.cia.gov/cia/publications/factbook/geos/ku.html

31 Longva, *Walls Built on Sand*, pp. 31, 36–7.

32 Ira M. Lapidus, *A History of Islamic Societies* (Cambridge, 2002), pp. 579–80.

33 Hassan N. Gardezi, 'Asian Workers in the Gulf States of the Middle East' in B. Singh Bolaria and Rosmary von Elling Bolaria, eds, *International Labour Migrations* (Delhi, 1997), pp. 115, 117.

34 Gloria Moreno-Fontes Chammartin, 'Domestic Workers: Little Protection for the Underpaid' in *Migration Information Source* (April 2005), http://www.migrationinformation.org/feature/display.cfm?id=300

35 Deborah J. Gerner, *One Land, Two Peoples: The Conflict over Palestine* (Boulder, CO, 1991), p. 11.

36 Quoting Alan Dowty, *Israel/Palestine* (Cambridge, 2005), p. 3.

37 Twain quoted in Dowty, *Israel/Palestine*, p. 12.

38 Gerner, *One Land, Two Peoples*, p. 15.

39 Cleveland, *Modern Middle East*, pp. 247, 254.

40 Dowty, *Israel/Palestine*, p. 73.

41 Ritchie Ovendale, *The Origins of the Arab-Israeli Wars*, 3rd edn (New York, 1999), pp. 75–7.

42 Cleveland, *Modern Middle East*, p. 261.

43 Julie Peteet, *Landscape of Hope and Despair: Palestinian Refugee Camps* (Philadephia, PA, 2005), p. 3.

44 Gerner, *One Land, Two Peoples*, pp. 44–5.

45 Dowty, *Israel/Palestine*, p. 91.

46 Baruch Kimmerling and Joel S. Migdal, *The Palestinian People: A History* (Cambridge, 2003), p. 165.

47 Cleveland, *Modern Middle East*, p. 349.

48 Quoting Kimmerling and Migdal, *The Palestinian People*, p. 169.

49 As'ad Abu Khalil, 'Arab-Israeli Conflict' in Congressional Quarterly, *The Middle East*, 10th edn (Washington, 2005), pp. 61–3.

50 Ibid., p. 75.

51 Seteney Shami, 'Emigration Dynamics in Jordan, Palestine, and Lebanon' in Reginald Appleyard, ed., *Emigration Dynamics in Developing Countries*, 4 vols (Aldershot, 1999) vol. IV, pp. 128–30.

52 Geraldine Chatelard, 'Jordan: A Refugee Haven' in *Migration Information Source* (July 2004), http://www.migrationinformation.org/profiles/display.cfm?id=236

53 Andre Bank, 'Jordan' in Congressional Quarterly, *The Middle East*, p. 307;Robert G. Rabil, *Embattled Neighbors: Syria, Israel, and Lebanon* (Boulder, CO, 2003), p. 46.

54 Peteet, *Landscape of Hope and Despair*, pp. 6–7.

55 Gerner, *One Land, Two Peoples*, pp. 85–8.

56 United Nations Relief and Works Agency, http://www.un.org/unrwa/refugees/lebanon.html

57 Mayar Farrag, 'Emigration Dynamics in Egypt' in Appleyard, *Emigration Dynamics*, vol. IV, p. 44.

58 Magda Kandil, 'Toward a Theory of International Labor Migration: Evidence from Egypt' in Mark Tessler, ed., *Area Studies and Social Science: Strategies for Understanding Middle East Politics* (Bloomington, IN, 1999), p. 85.

59 Farrag, 'Emigration Dynamics in Egypt', vol. IV, pp. 44–51.

60 Stephen Philip Cohen, *The Idea of Pakistan* (Washington, DC, 2004), p. 33.

61 Lapidus, *History of Islamic Societies*, pp. 640–43.
62 Cohen, *Idea of Pakistan*, p. 48.
63 Shahid Javed Burki, 'Migration from Pakistan to the Middle East' in Demetrios G. Papademetriou and Philip L. Martin, eds, *The Unsettled Relationship: Labor Migration and Economic Development* (New York, 1991), p. 140.
64 Ian Talbot, *Pakistan: A Modern History* (New York, 1998), p. 40.
65 Peter Blood, ed., *Pakistan: a country study* (Washington, DC, 1995), pp. 95–7.
66 Blood, *Pakistan*, p. 98. See also Talbot, *Pakistan: A Modern History*, p. 42 and Burki, 'Migration from Pakistan', p. 141.
67 Michael S. Teitelbaum, 'International Migration as a Pivotal Issue' in Robert Chase, Emily Hill and Paul Kennedy, eds, *The Pivotal States* (New York, 1999), p. 282.
68 Ibid., p. 283.
69 Cohen, *Idea of Pakistan*, pp. 231–2, 235.
70 Alison Shaw, *A Pakistani Community in Britain* (Oxford, 1988), p. 11.
71 David Reynolds, *One World Divisible* (New York, 2000), p. 363–5; Schulze, *Modern History of the Islamic World*, p. 232.
72 Angelo Rasanayagam, *Afghanistan: A Modern History* (London, 2003), p. 111.
73 Gary Gerstle, 'The Immigrant as Threat to American Security: A Historical Perspective' in John Tirman, ed., *The Maze of Fear: Security and Migration after 9/11* (New York, 2004), p. 107.
74 Tirman, *Maze of Fear*, p. 3. See also Louise Cainkar, 'The Impact of the September 11 Attacks on Arab and Muslim Communities in the United States' in ibid., p. 215.

Chapter 5: Global Workers from South and East Asia

1 Pei-Chia Lan, *Global Cinderellas: Migrant Domestics and Newly Rich Employers in Taiwan* (Durham, NC, 2006), p. 2.
2 Ibid., pp. 30–33.
3 Maruja M.B. Asis, 'Asian Women Migrants: Going the Distance, But Not Far Enough' in *Migration Information Source* (March 2003), http://www.migrationinformation.org/feature/display.cfm?id=103
4 Lan, *Global Cinderellas*, pp. 4–5, 14.
5 Philip Martin, Susan Martin and Patrick Weill, *Managing Migration: The Promise of Cooperation* (Lanham, MD, 2006), p. 30; Maruja M.B. Asis, 'The Philippines' Culture of Migration' in *Migration Information Source* (January 2006), http://www.migrationinformation.org/profiles/display.cfm?id=364
6 I.F. Bagasao, 'Migration and Development: The Philippine Experience' in Samuel Munzele Maimbo and Dilip Ratha, eds, *Remittances: Development Impact and Future Prospects* (Washington, DC, 2005), pp. 134, 138–9; Kevin O'Neil, 'Labour Export as Government Policy: The Case of the Philippines' in *Migration Information Source* (January 2004), http://www.migrationinformation.org/feature/display.cfm?id=191
7 Rhacel Salazar Parreñas, *Servants of Globalization: Women, Migration and Domestic Work* (Stanford, CA, 2001), pp. 3, 38–9.
8 Rhacel Salazar Parreñas, *Children of Global Migration: Transnational Families and Gendered Woes* (Stanford, CA, 2005), p. 12.
9 Quoting Catherine Ceniza Choy, *Empire of Care: Nursing and Migration in Filipino-American History* (Durham, NC, 2003), p. 2.

10 Kimberly Hamilton and Jennifer Yau, 'The Global Tug of War for Health Care Workers' in *Migration Information Source* (December 2004), http://www.migrationinformation.org/feature/display.cfm?id=271

11 Lan, *Global Cinderellas*, pp. 48, 49–50; Graeme Hugo, 'Indonesia's Labor Looks Abroad' in *Migration Information Source* (September 2002), http://www.migrationinformation.org/profiles/display.cfm?id=53

12 Lan, *Global Cinderellas*, p. 52.

13 Alan T. Wood, *Asian Democracy in World History* (New York, 2004), pp. 99–101; Craig Baxter, Yogendra K. Malik, Charles H. Kennedy and Robert C. Oberst, *Government and Politics in South Asia*, 5th edn (Boulder, CO, 2002), p. 333.

14 Oivind Fuglerud, *Life on the Outside: The Tamil Diaspora and Long Distance Nationalism* (London, 1999), pp. 1–2.

15 Hugh Tinker, *A New System of Slavery: The Export of Indian Labour Overseas, 1830–1920* (Oxford, 1974), pp. 61–115, offers the best overview of these early years. See also Joan M. Jensen, *Passage from India: Asian Indian Immigrants in North America* (New Haven, CT, 1988).

16 Tinker, *New System*, p. 113.

17 Marie Lall, 'Mother India's Forgotten Children' in Eva Ostergaard-Nielsen, ed., *International Migration and Sending Countries* (Houndmills, 2003), p. 133.

18 Ibid., p. 122.

19 Sandhya Shukla, *India Abroad: Diasporic Cultures of Postwar America and England* (Princeton, NJ, 2003), p. 69.

20 Shukla, *India Abroad*, pp. 43, 46.

21 Robert Stern, *Changing India: Bourgeois Revolution on the Subcontinent*, 2nd edn (Cambridge, 2003), p. 6.

22 Shukla, *India Abroad*, p. 58–9, 65.

23 Ibid., p. 3; Elizabeth Grieco, 'The Foreign Born from India in the United States' in *Migration Information Source* (December 2003), http://www.migrationinformation.org/usfocus/display.cfm?id=185; *IndiaTimes* (16 July 2003), http://timesofindia.indiatimes.com/cms.dll/html/uncomp/articleshow?msid=78451; William Dowell and Tony Karon, 'A Passage from India' *Time.Com* http://www.time.com/time/daily/special/india

24 Erin Texeira, 'Indian Immigrants Swarm to America' in *Courier Post Online* (22 October 2006), http://www.courierpostonline.com/apps/pbcs.dll/article?aid=/20061022/news01/61022006/1004/living

25 Arthur W. Helweg, *Strangers in a Not-So-Strange Land: Indian American Immigrants in the Global Age* (Belmont, CA, 2004), p. 13.

26 Martin, Martin and Weil, *Managing Migration*, p. 28.

27 Darshan Singh Tatla, *The Sikh Diaspora: The Search for Statehood* (Seattle, WA, 1999), pp. 14–16.

28 W.H. McLeod, 'The First Forty Years of Sikh Migration' in N. Gerald Barrier and Verne A. Dusenbery, eds, *The Sikh Diaspora: Migration and the Experience Beyond Punjab* (Delhi, 1989), pp. 36–7.

29 Tatla, *Sikh Diaspora*, p. 49.

30 N. Gerald Barrier, 'Sikh Emigrants and their Homeland' in Barrier and Dusenbery, *Sikh Diaspora*, p. 67.

31 McLeod, 'First Forty Years', p. 106.

32 W.H. McLeod, *The Sikhs: History, Religion, and Society* (New York, 1989), p. 102.

33 Parminder Bhachu, 'The East African Sikh Diaspora' in Barrier and Dusenberry, *Sikh Diaspora*, p. 240; Tatla, *Sikh Diaspora*, pp. 56–7.

34 Arthur W. Helwig, 'Sikh Politics in India' in Barrier and Dusenberry, *Sikh Diaspora*, p. 320.

35 David Seddon, 'Nepal's Dependence on Exporting Labour' in *Migration Information Source* (January 2005), http://www.migrationinformation.org/profiles/display.cfm?id=277

36 Yu Zhou, 'Chinese Immigrants in the Global Economy' in Maura I. Toro-Morn and Marixsa Alicea, eds, *Migration and Immigration: A Global View* (Westport, CT, 2004), p. 35.

37 Lynn Pan, 'Emigration from China' in Lynn Pan, ed., *The Encyclopedia of the Chinese Overseas* (Cambridge, MA, 1999), p. 49.

38 Ibid., p. 56.

39 Ronald Skeldon, 'China: From Exceptional Case to Global Participant' in *Migration Information Source* (April 2004), http://www.migrationinformation.org/profiles/display.cfm?id=219

40 Wang Gungwu, *The Chinese Overseas: From Earthbound China to the Quest for Autonomy* (Cambridge, MA, 2000), pp. 72–3.

41 Pan, *Encyclopedia of the Chinese Overseas*, p. 58.

42 Laurence J.C. Ma, 'Space, Place, and Transnationalism in the Chinese Diaspora' in Laurence J.C. Ma and Carolyn Cartier, eds, *The Chinese Diaspora: Space, Place, Mobility, and Identity* (Lanham, MD, 2003), p. 19.

43 Skeldon, 'China: From Exceptional Case' in *Migration Information Source* (April 2004), http://www.migrationinformation.org/profiles/display.cfm?id=219

44 Skeldon, 'The Chinese Diaspora or the Migration of Chinese Peoples?' in Ma and Cartier, *The Chinese Diaspora*, p. 62.

45 Thomas Sowell, *Migrations and Culture* (New York, 1996), pp. 176, 183.

46 David Chuenyan Lai, 'From Downtown Slums to Suburban Malls: Chinese Migration and Settlement in Canada' in Ma and Cartier, eds, *The Chinese Diaspora*, pp. 312–15.

47 Ibid., pp. 319–25.

48 Carolyn Cartier, 'Diaspora and Social Restructuring in Postcolonial Malaysia' in Ma and Cartier, *The Chinese Diaspora*, pp. 70, 73, 80.

49 Pan, *Encyclopedia of the Chinese Overseas*, p. 221.

50 Jonathan Rigg, 'Exclusion and Embeddedness: The Chinese in Thailand and Vietnam' in Ma and Cartier, *The Chinese Diaspora*, pp. 103–4, 106–8.

51 Sucheng Chan, ed, *The Vietnamese American 1.5 Generation* (Philadelphia, 2006), pp. 14–16.

52 Nghai M. Vo, *The Vietnamese Boat People, 1954 and 1975–1992* (Jefferson, NC, 2006), pp. 13–16.

53 Louis A. Wiesner, *Victims and Survivors: Displaced Persons and Other War Victims in Vietnam, 1954–1975* (Westport, CT, 1988), pp. 5–7; Chan, *Vietnamese American*, p. 45.

54 Wiesner, *Victims and Survivors*, p. 345.

55 Paul James Rutledge, *The Vietnamese Experience in America* ((Bloomington, IN, 1992), p. 1.

56 Chan, *Vietnamese American*, pp. 64–5.

57 Vo, *Vietnamese Boat People*, p. 83; Chan, *Vietnamese American*, p. 67.

58 Rutledge, *Vietnamese Experience*, p. 6.

59 D.R. SarDesai, *Vietnam: Past and Present*, 3rd edn, (Boulder, CO, 1998), pp. 177–8; James M. Freeman, *Changing Identities: Vietnamese Americans, 1975–1995* (Boston, 1995), p. 7.

Conclusion: States, Immigrants and Global Rift

1 Bill Jordan and Franck Duvell, *Migration: The Boundaries of Equality and Justice* (Cambridge, 2003), p. 5.
2 Timothy J. Hatton and Jeffrey G. Williamson, *Global Migration and the World Economy: Two Centuries of Policy and Performance* (Cambridge, MA, 2006), pp. 394–5.
3 Robert J. Flanagan, *Globalization and Labor Conditions: Working Conditions and Worker Rights in a Global Economy* (Oxford, 2006), pp. 93–4.
4 Roxanne Lynn Doty, *Anti-Immigrantism in Western Democracies* (London, 2003), p. 3.
5 Jordan and Duvell, *Migration*, p. 63.
6 See Myron Weiner, *The Global Migration Crisis: Challenge to States and Human Rights* (New York, 1995); Arthur Schlesinger, Jr, *The Disuniting of America: Reflections on a Multi-Cultural Society* (New York, 1992); Samuel P. Huntington, 'The West: Unique, Not Universal' in *Foreign Affairs* vol. 75, no. 6, pp. 28–46.
7 Jordan and Duvell, *Migration*, p. 9.
8 Hatton and Williamson, *Global Migration*, p. 400.
9 Jordan and Duvell, *Migration*, p. 57.
10 Flanagan, *Globalization*, pp. 108–9.
11 Ibid., p. 116.
12 Ibid., p. 106.

Select Bibliography

Abel, Christopher and Marco Palacios, 'Columbia since 1958', in *The Cambridge History of Latin America*, vol. VIII (Cambridge, 1996), pp. 680–81.

Adedeji, Adebayo, ed., *Comprehending and Mastering African Conflicts* (New York, 1999)

Adelman, Howard and John Sorenson, eds, *African Refugees: Development Aid and Repatriation* (Boulder, CO, 1994)

Ali, Taisier M. and Robert O. Matthews, eds, *Civil Wars in Africa: Roots and Resolution* (Montreal, 1999)

Appleyard, Reginald, ed., *Emigration Dynamics in Developing Countries*, 4 vols (Aldershot, 1998)

Arceneaux, Craig and David Pion-Berlin, *Transforming Latin America: The International and Domestic Origins of Change* (Pittsburgh, PA, 2005)

Axtell, James, *Natives and Newcomers: The Cultural Origins of North America* (Oxford, 2001)

Bailyn, Bernard, *The Peopling of British North America* (New York, 1988)

Baker, Jonathan and Tade Akin Aina, *The Migration Experience in Africa* (Stockholm, 1995)

Barrier, N. Gerald and Verne A. Dusenbery, eds, *The Sikh Diaspora: Migration and the Experience Beyond Punjab* (Delhi, 1989)

Basgoz, Ilhan and Norman Furniss, eds, *Turkish Workers in Europe: An Interdisciplinary Study* (Bloomington, IN, 1985)

Bates, Crispin, ed., *Community, Empire and Migration: South Asians in Diaspora* (Houndmills, 2001)

Baxter, Craig, Yogendra K. Malik, Charles H. Kennedy and Robert C. Oberst, *Government and Politics in South Asia*, 5th edn (Boulder, CO, 2002)

Bean, Frank D. and Rodolfo O. de la Garza, eds, *At the Crossroads: Mexico and US Immigration Policy* (Lanham, MD, 1997)

Berezin, Mabel and Martin Schain, eds, *Europe without Borders: Remapping Territory, Citizenship, and Identity in a Transnational Age* (Baltimore, MD, 2003)

Blood, Peter, ed., *Pakistan: a country study* (Washington, DC, 1995)

Bolaria, B. Singh and Rosmary von Elling Bolaria, eds, *International Labour Migrations* (Delhi, 1997)

Borjas, George, *Heaven's Door: Immigration Policy and the American Economy* (Princeton, NJ, 1999)

Cahill, Kevin M., ed., *Traditions, Values, and Humanitarian Action* (New York, 2003)

Castles, Stephen and Mark J. Miller, *The Age of Migration: International Population Movements in the Modern World* (New York, 1993)

Castles, Stephen, *Here for Good: Western Europe's New Ethnic Minorities* (London, 1984)

—, *Ethnicity and Globalization: From Migrant Worker to Transnational Citizen* (London, 2000)

Castro, Max, ed., *Free Markets, Open Societies, Closed Borders?: Trends in International Migration and Immigration Policy in the Americas* (Miami, FL, 1999)

Champion, Daryl, *The Paradoxical Kingdom: Saudi Arabia and the Momentum of Reform* (New York, 2003)

Chan, Sucheng, ed., *The Vietnamese American 1.5 Generation* (Philadelphia, PA, 2006)

Chase, Robert, Emily Hill and Paul Kennedy, eds, *The Pivotal States* (New York, 1999)

Chasteen, John Charles, *Born in Blood and Fire: A Concise History of Latin America*, 2nd edn (New York, 2006)

Chong, Nilda and Francia Baez, *Latino Culture* (Boston, MA, 2005)

Choy, Catherine Ceniza, *Empire of Care: Nursing and Migration in Filipino-American History* (Durham, NC, 2003)

Clarke, Peter, *Hope and Glory: Britain, 1900–1990* (London, 1996)

Clayton, Anthony, *Frontiersmen: Warfare in Africa since 1950* (London, 1999)

Cleveland, William L., *A History of the Modern Middle East*, 3rd edn (Boulder, CO, 2004)

Cohen, Helen I., *British Emigration to British North America: the First Hundred Years* (Toronto, 1961)

Cohen, Robin, ed., *The Cambridge Survey of World Migration* (Cambridge, 1995)

Cohen, Stephen Philip, *The Idea of Pakistan* (Washington, DC, 2004)

Cole, Joshua, *The Power of Large Numbers: Population, Politics, and Gender in Nineteenth-Century France* (London, 2000)

Cordova, Carlos B., *The Salvadoran Americans* (Westport, CT, 2005)

Crosby, Alfred, *Germs, Seeds, and Animals: Studies in Ecological History* (London, 1994)

Cutts, Mark, ed., *The State of the World's Refugees 2000: Fifty Years of Humanitarian Action* (Oxford, 2000)

Dale, Gareth and Mike Cole, eds, *The European Union and Migrant Labour* (Oxford, 1999)

Danevad, Andreas and Oliver Wates, eds, *Internally Displaced People: A Global Survey*, 2nd edn (London, 2002)

Daniels, Roger, *Coming to America: A History of Immigration and Ethnicity in American Life* (New York, 1990)

—, *Guarding the Golden Door: American Immigration Policy and Immigrants since 1882* (New York, 2004)

Deutsch, Sandra McGee and Ronald H. Dolkart, eds, *The Argentine Right: Its History and Intellectual Origins, 1910 to the Present* (Wilmington, DE, 1993)

Dinan, Desmond, *Ever Closer Union: An Introduction to European Integration*, 3rd edn (London, 2005)

—, *Europe Recast: A History of the European Union* (London, 2004)

Doty, Roxanne Lynn, *Anti-Immigrantism in Western Democracies: Statecraft, Desire, and the Politics of Exclusion* (New York, 2003)

Dowty, Alan, *Israel/Palestine* (Cambridge, 2005)

El-Ayouty, Yassin, ed., *The Organization of African Unity after Thirty Years* (Westport, CT, 1994)

Fage, J. D., *A History of Africa*, 3rd edn (New York, 1995)

Fausto, Boris, *A Concise History of Brazil* (Cambridge, 1999)

Flanagan, Robert J., *Globalization and Labor Conditions: Working Conditions and Worker Rights in a Global Economy* (Oxford, 2006)

Freeman, James M., *Changing Identities: Vietnamese Americans, 1975–1995* (Boston, MA, 1995)

Freund, Bill, *The Making of Contemporary Africa*, 2nd edn (Boulder, CO, 1998)

Fuglerud, Oivind, *Life on the Outside: The Tamil Diaspora and Long Distance Nationalism* (London, 1999)

Geary, Patrick, *The Myth of Nations: The Medieval Origins of Europe* (Princeton, 2002)

Gebre, Yntiso D. and Itaru Ohta, eds, *Displacement Risks in Africa* (Melbourne, 2005)

Gerner, Deborah J., *One Land, Two Peoples: The Conflict over Palestine* (Boulder, CO, 1991)

Geron, Kim, *Latino Political Power* (Boulder, CO, 2005)

Gurr, Ted Robert, ed., *People Versus States: Minorities at Risk in the New Century* (Washington, DC, 2000)

Gutiérrez , David G., ed., *The Columbia History of Latinos in the United States since 1960* (New York, 2004)

—, ed., *Between Two Worlds: Mexican Immigrants in the United States* (Wilmington, DE, 1996)

Haddad, Yvonne Yazbeck and Janet I. Smith, eds, *Muslim Minorities in the West* (Lanham, MD, 2002)

Hall, Ray and Paul White, eds, *Europe's Population: Towards the Next Century* (London, 1995)

Hamnett, Brian, *A Concise History of Mexico* (Cambridge, 1999)

Harbeson, John W. and Donald Rothchild, eds, *Africa in World Politics: The African State System in Flux* (Boulder, CO, 2000)

Hargreaves, John D., *Decolonization in Africa*, 2nd edn (London, 1996)

Hastings, Adrian, *The Construction of Nationhood: Ethnicity, Religion and Nationalism* (Cambridge, 1997)

Hatton, Timothy J. and Jeffrey G. Williamson, *Global Migration and the World Economy: Two Centuries of Policy and Performance* (Cambridge, MA, 2006)

Helweg, Arthur W., *Strangers in a Not-So-Strange Land: Indian American Immigrants in the Global Age* (Belmont, CA, 2004)

Hoerder, Dirk, *Cultures in Contact: World Migrations in the Second Millennium* (Durham, NC, 2002)

Hollifield, James F., *Immigrants, Markets, and States: The Political Economy of Postwar Europe* (Cambridge, MA, 1992)

Hopkins, Nicholas S. and Saad Eddin Ibrahim, eds, *Arab Society: Class, Gender, Power, and Development* (Cairo, 1997)

Ireland, Patrick, *Becoming Europe: Immigration, Integration, and the Welfare State* (Pittsburgh, PA, 2004)

Jacoby, Tamar, ed., *Reinventing the Melting Pot: The New Immigrants and What it Means to be American* (New York, 2004)

Jennings, Francis, *The Invasion of America: Indians, Colonialism, and the Cant of Conquest* (Chapel Hill, NC, 1975)

Jensen, Joan M., *Passage from India: Asian Indian Immigrants in North America* (New Haven, CT, 1988)

Jordan, Bill and Franck Duvell, *Migration: The Boundaries of Equality and Justice* (Cambridge, 2003)

Kimmerling, Baruch and Joel S. Migdal, *The Palestinian People: A History* (Cambridge, 2003)

King, Russell, ed., *Mass Migration in Europe: The Legacy and the Future* (London, 1993)

Koslowski, Rey, *Migrants and Citizens: Demographic Change in the European State System* (Ithaca, NY, 2004)

Lan, Pei-Chia, *Global Cinderellas: Migrant Domestics and Newly Rich Employers in Taiwan* (Durham, NC, 2006)

Lapidus, Ira M., *A History of Islamic Societies* (Cambridge, 2002)

Leonard, Thomas M., *Castro and the Cuban Revolution* (Westport, CT, 1999)

Levine, Robert M., *The History of Brazil* (Westport, CT, 1999)

Lewis, Bernard, *What Went Wrong? The Clash Between Islam and Modernity in the Middle East* (New York, 2002)

Lischer, Sarah Kenyon, *Dangerous Sanctuaries: Refugee Camps, Civil War, and the Dilemmas of Humanitarian Aid* (Ithaca, NY, 2005)

Long, David E., *The Kingdom of Saudi Arabia* (Gainesville, FL, 1997)

Longva, Anh Nga, *Walls Built on Sand: Migration, Exclusion, and Society in Kuwait* (Boulder, CO, 1997)

McKeown, A., 'Global Migration, 1846–1940', in *Journal of World History*, 15 (2004), pp. 155–89.

McLeod, W.H., *The Sikhs: History, Religion, and Society* (New York, 1989)

McNeill, William, *Plagues and Peoples* (New York, 1998)

Ma, Laurence J. C. and Carolyn Cartier, eds, *The Chinese Diaspora: Space, Place, Mobility, and Identity* (Lanham, MD, 2003)

Maimbo, Samuel Munzele and Dilip Ratha, eds, *Remittances: Development Impact and Future Prospects.* (Washington, DC, 2005)

Martin, Philip, Susan Martin and Patrick Weil, *Managing Migration: The Promise of Cooperation* (Lanham, MD, 2006)

Massey, Douglas S. et al., *Worlds in Motion: Understanding International Migration at the End of the Millennium* (Oxford, 1998)

Mehdi, Abbas, 'Globalization, Migration and the Arab World', in *Arab Migration in a Globalized World* (Geneva, 2004)

Meredith, Martin, *The Fate of Africa: From the Hopes of Freedom to the Heart of Despair* (New York, 2005)

Meyer, Michael C. and William H. Beezley, eds, *The Oxford History of Mexico* (New York, 2000)

Moch, Leslie Page, *Moving Europeans: Migration in Western Europe since 1650* (Bloomington, IN, 2003)

Morgan, Kenneth O., *Britain since 1945: The People's Peace* (Oxford, 2001)

Murphy, Brian, *The Other Australia: Experiences of Migration* (Cambridge, 1992)

Navarro, Sharon Ann and Armando Xavier Mejia, eds, *Latino Americans and Political Participation* (Santa Barbara, CA, 2004)

Nugent, Paul, *Africa Since Independence: A Comparative History* (Houndmills, 2004)

Nugent, Walter T. K., *Crossings: The Great Transatlantic Migration, 1870–1914* (Bloomington, IN, 1992)

Ogata, Sadako, *The Turbulent Decade: Confronting the Refugee Crisis of the 1990s* (New York, 2005)

Ogden, Philip E. and Paul E. White, eds, *Migrants in Modern France* (Boston, MA, 1989)

Ostergaard-Nielsen, Eva, ed., *International Migration and Sending Countries* (Houndmills, 2003)

Ovendale, Ritchie, *The Origins of the Arab-Israeli Wars*, 3rd edn (New York, 1999)

Pagden, Anthony, *Peoples and Empires* (New York, 2003)

Pan, Lynn, ed., *The Encyclopedia of the Chinese Overseas* (Cambridge, MA, 1999)

Panayi, Panikos, ed., *The Impact of Immigration: A Documentary History of the Effects and Experiences of Immigrants in Britain since 1945* (Manchester, 1999)

—, *An Ethnic History of Europe since 1945* (Harlow, 2000)

Papademetriou, Demetrios G. and Philip L. Martin, eds, *The Unsettled Relationship: Labor Migration and Economic Development* (New York, 1991)

Parreñas, Rhacel Salazar, *Servants of Globalization: Women, Migration and Domestic Work* (Stanford, CA, 2001)

—, *Children of Global Migration: Transnational Families and Gendered Woes* (Stanford, CA, 2005)

Perez, Jr, Louis A., *Cuba: Between Reform and Revolution* (New York, 2006)

Peteet, Julie, *Landscape of Hope and Despair: Palestinian Refugee Camps* (Philadephia, PA, 2005)

Rabil, Robert G., *Embattled Neighbors: Syria, Israel, and Lebanon* (Boulder, CO, 2003)

Rakodi, Carole, ed., *The Urban Challenge in Africa: Growth and Management of Its Large Cities* (Tokyo, 1997)

Rasanayagam, Angelo, *Afghanistan: A Modern History* (London, 2003)

Reynolds, David, *One World Divisible* (New York, 2000)

Rock, David, *Argentina, 1516–1987: From Spanish Colonization to Alfonsín* (Berkeley, CA, 1987)

Rutledge, Paul James, *The Vietnamese Experience in America* (Bloomington, IN, 1992)

SarDesai, D. R., *Vietnam: Past and Present*, 3rd edn (Boulder, CO, 1998)

Schaebler, Birgit and Leif Stenberg, eds, *Globalization and the Muslim World* (Syracuse, NY, 2004)

Schlesinger, Jr, Arthur, *The Disuniting of America: Reflections on a Multi-Cultural Society* (New York, 1992)

Schulze, Reinhard, *A Modern History of the Islamic World* (New York, 2000)

Shaw, Alison, *A Pakistani Community in Britain* (Oxford, 1988)

Sherry, Virginia N., *Saudi Arabia: Bad Dreams, Exploitation and Abuse of Migrant Workers in Saudi Arabia* (New York, 2004)

Shillington, Kevin, ed., *Encyclopedia of African History*, 3 vols (New York, 2005)

Shore, Zachary, *Breeding Bin Ladens: America, Islam, and the Future of Europe* (Baltimore, MD, 2006)

Shukla, Sandhya, *India Abroad: Diasporic Cultures of Postwar America and England* (Princeton, NJ, 2003)

Silverstein, Paul A., *Algeria in France: Transpolitics, Race, and Nation* (Bloomington, IN, 2004)

Simone, AbdouMaliq, *For the City Yet to Come: Changing African Life in Four Cities* (Durham, NC, 2004)

Sirageldin, Ismail and Eqbal Al-Rahmani, eds, *Research in Human Capital and Development: Population and Development Transformations in the Arab World* (Greenwich, CT, 1996)

Skeldon, Ronald, *Migrational Development: A Global Perspective* (London, 1997)

Skidmore, Thomas E. and Peter H. Smith, *Modern Latin America*, 6th edn (New York, 2005)

Skidmore, Thomas, *Brazil: Five Centuries of Change* (Oxford, 1999)

Sowell, Thomas, *Migrations and Culture* (New York, 1996)

Stalker, Peter, *The No-Nonsense Guide to International Migration* (London, 2001)

—, *Workers without Frontiers: The Impact of Globalization on International Migration* (Boulder, CO, 2000)

Stern, Robert, *Changing India: Bourgeois Revolution on the Subcontinent*, 2nd edn (Cambridge, 2003)

Talbot, Ian, *Pakistan: A Modern History* (New York, 1998)

Tatla, Darshan Singh, *The Sikh Diaspora: The Search for Statehood* (Seattle, WA, 1999)

Tessler, Mark, ed., *Area Studies and Social Science: Strategies for Understanding Middle East Politics* (Bloomington, IN, 1999)

Tinker, Hugh, *A New System of Slavery: The Export of Indian Labour Overseas, 1830–1920* (Oxford, 1974)

Tirman, John, ed., *The Maze of Fear: Security and Migration after 9/11* (New York, 2004)

Toro-Morn, Maura I. and Marixsa Alicea, eds, *Migration and Immigration: A Global View* (Westport, CT, 2004)

Tranter, N.L., *Population and Society, 1750–1940* (London, 1985)

Tschirgi, Dan, ed., *The Arab World Today* (Boulder, CO, 1994)

Vo, Nghai M., *The Vietnamese Boat People, 1954 and 1975–1992* (Jefferson, NC, 2006)

Wang, Gungwu, *The Chinese Overseas: From Earthbound China to the Quest for Autonomy* (Cambridge, MA, 2000)

—, ed., *Global History and Migrations* (Boulder, CO, 1997)

Watts, Sheldon J., *Epidemics and History: Disease, Power and Imperialism* (New Haven, 1998)

Weiner, Myron, *The Global Migration Crisis: Challenge to States and Human Rights* (New York, 1995)

White, Stacey, Andreas Danevad and Oliver Watts, eds, *Internally Displaced People: A Global Survey* (London, 2002)

Wiesner, Louis A., *Victims and Survivors: Displaced Persons and Other War Victims in Vietnam, 1954–1975* (Westport, CT, 1988)

Winn, Peter, *Americas: The Changing Face of Latin America and the Caribbean* (Berkeley, CA, 1999)

Wood, Alan T., *Asian Democracy in World History* (New York, 2004)

Wynbrandt, James, *A Brief History of Saudi Arabia* (New York, 2004)

Yoshida, Chisato and Alan D. Woodland, *The Economics of Illegal Immigration* (Houndmills, 2005)

Zegeye, Abebe and Shubi Ishemo, eds, *Forced Labour and Migration: Patterns of Movement in Africa* (London, 1989)

Zimmerman, Klaus F., ed., *European Migration* (Oxford, 2005)

Zolberg, Aristide R., *A Nation by Design: Immigration Policy in the Fashioning of America* (Cambridge, MA, 2006)

Zuniga, Victor and Rubin Hernandez-Leon, eds, *New Destinations: Mexican Immigration to the United States* (New York, 2005)

Acknowledgements

Much of what follows is based on the work of specialist scholars in the field of migration studies. Now in its fifth year, the Migration Policy Institute, an independent research organization in Washington, DC, hosts an especially useful and informative home page. In particular, I have relied heavily on the work of leading scholars who have published through the Institute's online journal, *Migration Information Source*. Valuable time to work on this project was provided by my home institution, the University of North Carolina at Asheville. My librarian colleagues have been especially helpful (and patient) with me over the years. Special thanks to Bryan Sinclair, Leith Tate, Helen Wykle, Helen Dezendorf and Anita White-Carter, all of Ramsey Library at UNC Asheville. I am fortunate to work in a community where academic administrators are encouraged to maintain their scholarly interests. My former Provost, Mark Padilla, supported my work with the precious gift of time over the past two years. As with earlier projects, Nancy Costello and Robert Burke offered support at important junctures, while Margaret Costello provided timely editorial suggestions on each chapter.

Index